More Constitutional Dimensions of Contract Law

Luca Siliquini-Cinelli • Andrew Hutchison
Editors

More Constitutional Dimensions of Contract Law

A Comparative Perspective

 Springer

Editors
Luca Siliquini-Cinelli
School of Law
University of Dundee
Dundee, UK

Andrew Hutchison
Faculty of Law
University of Cape Town
Cape Town, South Africa

ISBN 978-3-030-15106-5   ISBN 978-3-030-15107-2   (eBook)
https://doi.org/10.1007/978-3-030-15107-2

This Springer imprint is published by the registered company Springer Nature Switzerland AG.
The registered company address is: Gewerbestrasse 11, 6330 Cham, Switzerland

Acknowledgements

Our thanks are owed to the contributors of this volume for participating in this project and for their kind cooperation, as well as to Anke Seyfried, Julia Bieler and Springer's editorial team for their assistance and professionalism.

Dundee, UK   Luca Siliquini-Cinelli
Cape Town, South Africa   Andrew Hutchison
February 2019

Contents

Contributors

Gunther Hernán Gonzales Barrón Professor of Civil Law at the Universities Antonio Ruiz de Montoya, San Ignacio de Loyola, Lima, Peru

Member of the Water Administrative Court, Lima, Peru

National of San Marcos, Lima, Peru

Lucas Abreu Barroso Professor of Civil Law, Universidade Federal do Espírito Santo, Vitória, Brazil

Professor of Civil Law, Universidade Vila Velha, Vila Velha, Brazil

Head of the Research Group "Civil Law in Legal Post-modernity", Vitória, Brazil

Marcos Catalan Professor of Consumer Law, Universidade La Salle, Canoas, Brasil

Professor of Civil Law, Unisinos, São Leopoldo, Brazil

Head of the Research Group "Legal Social Theories", Canoas, Brazil

Elia Cerrato García Lecturer, Centro Universitario de Estudios Financieros (CUNEF), Madrid, Spain

Jaakko Husa Professor of Law and Globalisation, Faculty of Law, University of Helsinki, Helsinki, Finland

Juha Karhu Professor of Contract and Tort Law, Faculty of Law, University of Lapland, Rovaniemi, Finland

Hiroyuki Kihara Professor, Faculty of Law, Asia University, Taichung City, Taiwan

Salvatore Mancuso Honorary Professor of African law, Xiangtan University, Xiangtan, China

Visiting Professor of Comparative African law, University Paris 1 Panthéon-Sorbonne, Paris, France

David Ramos Muñoz Assistant Professor, Universidad Carlos III de Madrid, Madrid, Spain

Ngozi Odiaka Lecturer, College of Law, Afe Babalola University, Ado-Ekiti, Nigeria

Ada Ordor Associate Professor and Director, Centre for Comparative Law in Africa, Faculty of Law, University of Cape Town, Cape Town, South Africa

Comparative Constitutional Contract Law: A Question of Legal Culture

Luca Siliquini-Cinelli and Andrew Hutchison

Abstract This introductory chapter sets out the book's purpose and outlines the contributions which compose it. It connects the constitutionalisation of Contract law theme to questions of legal culture, thereby showing why this increasingly relevant topic in the theory and practice of Contract law ought to be approached contextually. In so doing, it further links this book's content to the first volume of this two-book set: The Constitutional Dimension of Contract Law. A Comparative Perspective (published by Springer in 2017).

1 Beyond the Ordinary Comparative Law Scholarship

This volume brings to completion a project that commenced in 2015. We were then working on a paper with the aim of addressing the extent to which, within the area of specific performance, the development of the law of contract is being influenced by constitutional values and Fundamental rights issues in South Africa, the UK, and Australia.[1] Given the lack of Contract, Constitutional, and Comparative law literature on the constitutional dimension of Contract law, we decided to broaden the purview of inquiry and ask leading scholars, as well as emerging researchers in the law of contract to explore the relationship between contract(s), constitutional principles, and Human rights in their own jurisdictions. That theoretical effort led to the publication, in 2017, of the first volume of this two-book collection of essays.[2] The list of the legal systems covered included England (François du Bois), France (Jean-Baptiste Seube), Belgium

---

[1] Siliquini-Cinelli and Hutchison (2016).
[2] Siliquini-Cinelli and Hutchison (2017).

L. Siliquini-Cinelli (✉)
School of Law, University of Dundee, Dundee, UK
e-mail: l.siliquinicinelli@dundee.ac.uk

A. Hutchison
Department of Commercial Law, University of Cape Town, Cape Town, South Africa
e-mail: Andrew.Hutchison@uct.ac.za

(Annekatrien Lenaerts), Italy (Pier Giuseppe Monateri), South Africa (Andrew Hutchison), Australia (Philip H. Clarke), Germany (Béatrice Schütte), Portugal (Elsa Dias Oliveira), and Canada (Nicolas Lambert). Two further chapters were dedicated to European Union law (Joasia Luzak) and to expounding some philosophical reflections on the contemporary development of the notions of *pactum* and good faith in the public and private dimensions, particularly in the Common law jurisdictions (Siliquini-Cinelli).

Further, the present volume extends the comparative analysis to other jurisdictions in Europe (Finland and Nordic countries in comparative perspective, Spain), Asia (Japan), Africa (Somalia and Nigeria), and Latin America (Brazil and Peru). Hence, this book's title, which serves to highlight the continuity with the first volume, while at the same time emphasising the importance of having these legal systems covered in a single, English-written Constitutional Contract law book for the first time. However, as the project's aims and methodologies of inquiry have been extensively outlined in the first volume, they will not be re-stated here. As with the first volume, contributors have been asked to choose a topic and delve into it from a 'law in action', and thus experiential, rather than 'law in book', point of view.

Surely, there is a growing elaboration of general Contract law theories.[3] Yet, opting for a contextual approach to embark upon a comparative analysis of the kind suggested here is inevitable if we are to uncover the inner dynamics through which Public (i.e. Constitutional) and Private (i.e. Contract) law operate, interact, and (at times) inform each other whilst also enhancing our understanding of law's nature, functioning, and transformative potential at the macro, meso, and micro levels. This theoretical effort will, in turn, assist scholars and practitioners in conceptualising and operationalising the working logic(s) of those hard and soft regulatory mechanisms and normative transplants that characterise the uncertain legal architecture of our time and challenge the 'public/private' dialect. The contemporary development of Chinese Private (and in particular, Contract) law is a good example of this. "With the enactment of the Chinese Civil Code," James Gordley writes,

> systems of private law modelled on those of the West will govern nearly the entire world. Western legal systems, moreover, are much both alike. Both 'common law' systems such as those of England and the United States and 'civil law' systems such as those of France, Italy, and Germany have similar doctrinal structure based on similar legal concepts. They divide private law into certain large fields such as property, tort, and contract, and analyze these fields in a similar way ... The organization of the law and its larger concepts are alike even if particular rules are not. Accordingly, though answers may differ, the problem of whether a boy is liable for injuring a playfellow or a seller is liable for defects in his merchandise is analyzed in much the same way in Hamburg, Montpelier, Manchester and Tucson, or for that matter in New Delhi, Tel Aviv, Tokyo and Jakarta.[4]

As mentioned in the Introduction of the first volume, however, the need for the suggested comparative analysis is also because of the uncertain future which attends national constitutions in our post-national age, characterised by increasing regulatory density, complexity, and uncertainty. Thus, the necessity to determine whether

---

[3]Critically, see Bix (2017).
[4]Gordley (1991), p. 1.

constitutions still matter in the current pluralist regulative landscape, and if so, why, how and to what extent. This, in turn, might shed new light on the much-discussed topic of what is Private law able to do for justice.[5] On the one hand, indeed, in terms of *juris genesis* and development, constitutions appear to be in line with the dynamics that characterise current pluralist regulative phenomena. More particularly, scholars have recently come to stress that constitutions are themselves the result of transnational drafting processes. Thus, Gregory Shaffer has noted that constitutions "are transnational legal orders in so far as they reflect similar structures and norms that transcend and diffuse across nation-states."[6] On the other hand, though, and as pointed out by Alberto Febbrajo and Giancarlo Corsi, it appears that "constitutions have lost their strategic roles, and even among the public there is a more widespread perception of the profound social distance between the constitution and everyday life – with complex effects on the politically-based democratic order itself."[7] In addition, as Alexander Somek writes, "the core values of constitutionalism no longer seem to be firmly in place."[8] This explains why scholars have been spending a considerable amount of effort in trying to determine what repercussions, if any, current post-national developments are having on the 'public/private' (law) dichotomy and forms of government and governance. A debate which is rendered even more complicated by the profound challenges that global and supra-national processes of institutionalisation and protection of basic rights and expectations face and the corresponding rise (or return?) of nationalisms both within and outside the West.

Importantly, to the trend described by Febbrajo and Corsi one must add the challenges that both theorists and practitioners face in working with vague constitutional texts and bills of rights which require them to rely on secondary sources and practices—a feature which inevitably leads to self-reflective political and legal developments. "In the form they take today," Corsi further notes

> values and fundamental rights are formulated to be substantially generic or even aspecific. In the case . . . of the classical constitutional values of equality and freedom, it is easy to see where the difference lies compared to previous eras: it is impossible to state who is equal to whom and who is free from what, because that would introduce discrimination that would be incompatible with the fundamental law's general nature. These values' universalism thus seems to oblige to be semantically empty. How they should be specified in concrete terms is left up to ordinary law, to the legislator, to the courts, to procedures and to the organisation criteria of decision-making, which can change with ordinary proceedings and so be receptive to the changes that are constantly taking place in society.[9]

It should be noted that these challenges are also faced by those private, and particularly, contract lawyers who work at the intersection between the Public and Private law dimensions in the West. What renders their job increasingly difficult is,

---

[5]Recently, see Michelon (2018). Cf. Weinrib (2012).

[6]Shaffer (2017), p. 1. More broadly, see Thornhill (2012), p. 411: "The formation of a distinct transnational legal apparatus can in fact in many cases be interpreted as a *structural precondition* of stable national state institutions." (Emphasis in original).

[7]Febbrajo and Corsi (2016), p. 1.

[8]Somek (2014), p. 98.

[9]Corsi (2016), p. 14.

first, what Gunther Teubner has described as the "hybridisation of contract"—i.e. the phenomenon according to which

> contract is no longer the consensual exchange relationship between two legal subjects to which the judge grants legal force as long as the *nudum pactum* can at least be endowed with a *causa*. In the dynamics of social fragmentation, in which one and the same contract appears as the simultaneous expression of different and divergent rationalities, the old two-person relationship of the contract has metamorphosed into a polycontextural relationship, which, though consensual, is impersonal. And the binding force of the contract disappears "in between" the contextures. Now, what are the consequences of this fragmentation?
>
> Today's individual contract typically breaks down into several operations within different contexts: (1) an economic transaction that, recursively intermeshed in accordance with the intrinsic logic of the economy, changes the market situation; (2) a productive act that, in accordance with the intrinsic logic of the relevant social context (e.g., technology, medicine, media, science, art, and other social areas where goods and services are produced), changes the productive situation; and (3) a legal act that, recursively intermeshed with other legal acts in accordance with the intrinsic logic of the law, changes the legal situation. The outcome of the prevailing extreme social differentiation is the real (not just analytical) splitting of the one contract into three acts, a legal act, an economic transaction, and a productive act, and the enabling of their simultaneity (*"uno actu"*). The single contract is fragmented into a multiplicity of different operations, each occurring in a different mutually-closed discourse. It is at once transaction, production, and obligation — but it is at the same time a fourth thing, the "between," the interdiscursive relation of the various performative acts.[10]

In addition to (or as part of) this general trend, one may witness, in the Common law tradition, the move away from the focus on certainty and predictability of Contract law rules, principles, and doctrines which characterised the classical period of the law of contract in the nineteenth century. Surely, if compared to other Private law branches, such as Tort law, Contract law may be said to be rather static.[11] However, over the past two centuries there have been major changes in both the theory and practice of the law of contract which have also affected, and continue to affect, its relationship with the Public law sphere. Among these, of peculiar importance are the movement towards generalised principles (i.e. good faith, co-operation and fairness), equitable doctrines, and discretionary powers that aim to achieve 'just' outcomes; the emergence and spread of extra-legal (i.e. moral, relational, feminist, economic, critical, etc.) theories of contract(s); the statutory initiatives against abusive practices arising from the inequality of bargaining powers; and the growing use of information technologies.[12] Similar developments, with some notable

---

[10]Teubner (2006), pp. 51–53.

[11]A statement we make with the due caution given some important, if not drastic, changes which have occurred in some jurisdictions, such as in the United Kingdom, over the past few years. Cf., for instance, *Patel v Mirza* [2016] UKSC 42.

[12]Among others, see Macneil (1978, 1987); Fried (1981); Adams and Brownsword (1987); Drahos and Parker (1990); Collins (1999); Goldwasser and Ciro (2002); Campbell et al. (2003); Mulcahy (2005); Kovač (2011); Hogg (2011); Seddon et al. (2012), ch 28; Mitchell (2013); Keyes and Wilson (2014); Katz (2014); Brownsword et al. (2017). All of this has led Morgan (2013), p. 89, to call for a minimalist approach to contract law which, among other things, "[does not] serve any "external" goals of regulatory policy (i.e. other than providing a framework for commercial contracts) – such as the promotion of social justice and European solidarity. Nor should contract law concern itself with distributive justice or regulation of fairness."

exceptions,[13] might also be noticed in the Civil law tradition—a phenomenon which prompts the question as to whether this might also occur in such Civil law-oriented jurisdictions as China and Japan.

It should be obvious that these changes combine—along with many more regarding the capabilities of state-based constructs of recognition, legitimation, and control—to pose a wider interrogative on the capabilities of the modern legal infrastructure under current processes of globalisation and transnationalism of trade. In her influential new monograph—which also explores such topics as the choice of the right law of contract, the complexity of commercial and consumer contracts, and strengths and flaws of 'build-to-performance' and (standardised) 'build-to-print' contracts—Gillian K. Hadfield rightly observes that today's "pace of change is making it more urgent than ever to rethink the rules of our economic and social relationships."[14] This is because of the fact that, as Hadfield goes on:

> [o]ur mechanisms for creating and implementing law—or what I call more generally our *legal infrastructure*, the almost invisible platform of rules and practices on which we build everything else in our economy—is not up to the task. Our existing systems for developing the rules and legal practices we need to manage the galloping progress of the global digital economy are drowning in cost and complexity.[15]

Thus, Hadfield further affirms a littler later, "law needs to be something understood and designed by economists, policymakers, entrepreneurs, business leaders, and ordinary people, not just lawyers."[16] That this also applies to Constitutional law, and thus, to Human rights policies seems difficult, if not impossible, to dispute given their structural relationship with modern, state-based fundamental values and democratic processes of participation and validation. The need for Contract law to be sufficiently understandable and predictable *ex ante* are key considerations in the development of a system on which an economy depends. In this sense, the potential for the certainty of classical Contract law to become clouded by the opaque standards of Human rights law is a factor sometimes used to argue against the constitutionalisation of Contract law. How to incorporate the constitutional dimension of Contract law in a given legal system, along with the appropriate balancing of Human rights inspired fairness and commercial certainty, is an important question for each jurisdiction to consider. Above all, these are questions of domestic legal culture, to be assessed in the context of a given jurisdiction and juridical (rather than merely legal) mentality.[17]

Indeed, what should be clear by now is that our contextual approach reveals comparative questions of a socio-legal nature. By describing what Contract law

---

[13] Such as those regarding the approach to, and use of, good faith, which has always been a cornerstone of Civil law systems.

[14] Hadfield (2017), p. 2.

[15] Hadfield (2017), p. 3.

[16] Hadfield (2017), p. 20.

[17] This also explains the difference in writing and argumentative styles which characterises the essays presented here.

means to those who use it and the context in which such operation occurs, we necessitate a consideration of the role of legal culture. Legal culture has been defined by Karl Klare as follows:

> By legal culture, I mean professional sensibilities, habits of mind, and intellectual reflexes: What are the characteristic rhetorical strategies deployed by participants in a given legal setting? What is their repertoire of recurring argumentative moves? What counts as a persuasive legal argument? What types of arguments, possibly valid in other discursive contexts (e.g., in political philosophy), are deemed outside the professional discourse of lawyers? What enduring political and ethical commitments influence professional discourse? What understandings of and assumptions about politics, social life and justice? What "inarticulate premises, [are] culturally and historically ingrained" in the professional discourse and outlook?[18]

As one might expect, the role of culture is an important element of Comparative law/legal studies inquiry, and has been long-debated in the relative literature.[19] The chapters in this book are written by insiders of the various legal systems described: the Comparative law element of this work thus consists largely in the juxtaposition of these separate accounts where the authors all operated under a similar mandate. It is our intention that each author's approach and choice of focal topic, should in itself reflect legal culture.[20]

Importantly, as 'culture' is a contested terrain in (comparative) legal scholarship, we do not intend here to open the Pandora's Box of the relativism versus universalism debate which has long characterised the international Human rights discourse.[21] This is not to deny, however, our interest in questions such as what the concept of duties, as captured in Article 29 of the African Charter of Human and Peoples Rights, could mean for Contract law.[22] Questions as to what pluralism of laws, cultures, and values might reveal about Gordley's claim above (that most world systems of Contract law are converging on the Western model) when unpacked 'in action' are undoubtedly fascinating issues for future study. Legal anthropologist Merry argues as follows:

> Human rights is obviously a Western liberal legalist construction, but in the post-colonial world, it is no longer owned by the West. As indigenous groups seek to define a space for themselves in the modern world, they seize and redefine law as the basis for their claims to justice. . . . Like the English spoken in Africa, the colonial law imposed by the West is developing its own cadences and vocabulary. It is becoming a vernacular law rather than transnational imperial law.[23]

---

[18]Klare (1998), pp. 166–167 (footnotes omitted).

[19]Among others, see Kahn-Freund (1974); Friedman (1997); Watson (1993); Nelken (1995, 1997); Legrand (1997, 2003 2017); Nelken and Feest (2001); Husa (2015).

[20]An interesting description of a comparative legal cultures methodological approach can be found in Steinmetz (2000).

[21]Key arguments here are made by: Wa Mutua (1995); Ibhawoh (2000); Nussbaum (2000). In Comparative law literature, see Samuel (2014), p. 130.

[22]For a preliminary analysis along these lines, but in a South African context, see Hutchison (2017).

[23]Merry (1996), p. 68.

The comparative study of contracting culture is a vital aspect of understanding how Human rights are or are not incorporated in the Contract law of each jurisdiction covered in both this and the previous volume. This implicates further questions of a social (some would say scientific) nature, such as those relating to national history and politics, or to the economic standing of a particular country in focus. As mentioned, one of the main contributions of this book is the compilation of first-hand accounts (in English) of many contracting cultures which remain off the beaten track for conventional Comparative law works. It also provides additional evidence for a comparative assessment of whether the general trend in world legal systems is towards a more nuanced concept of Human rights informed contracting, in line with more general developments in Human rights law from the twentieth century onwards.

2 Arguments: Outline of Book Chapters

In the next chapter, Jaakko Husa and Juha Karhu offer an insightful account of the constitutionalisation of Contract law in Finland and other Nordic countries. The premises of Husa and Karhu's analysis is that the interrogative regarding the long-established relationship between Constitutional and Contract law in Finland is a difficult one to solve because of the Finnish law's and legal culture's proximity to the Swedish legal system and the profound differences between the Nordic constitutional traditions. After having provided an account of the Finnish constitutional landscape and principle of parliamentary sovereignty, the analysis moves on to exploring how the Finnish Constitution indirectly protects freedom of action in private relations, as well as property and related contract relations. This is in addition to the implementation of Fundamental rights via parliamentary legislation and adjustment of unfair contracts provisions (Section 36 of the Finnish Contracts Act). As Husa and Karhu show, this approach is structurally related to how economic self-determination is conceived—i.e. freedom of trade and possession and protection of property rights. An important step was taken with the 1995 reform, which was inspired by the European Convention on Human Rights (although its scope is wider) and which the authors explore in detail. After that the discussion covers such delicate and much relevant topics as constitutional review and case law. The latter in particular offers an invaluable opportunity to critically examine the Supreme Court's approach to the subject. The chapter's third section deals instead with the Contract law component of the analysis, and shows how the latter is culturally embedded. In particular, the section develops around three key-principles: freedom of contract, reliance principle, and the principle of fairness. Then the authors explore three kinds of illustrations that shed further light on constitutional dimension of Finnish Contract law. The first one concerns the a priori constitutionality control; the second one reopens one of the Supreme Court cases that was touched on earlier on in the analysis; the third issue concerns what happens when a priori and a posteriori views collide with one another. Husa and Karhu's overall conclusion from their detailed examination is that while it cannot be argued that there is a distinct area of law in the Finnish legal system that can be called 'Constitutional Contract law', there certainly is a clear overlapping between the Constitutional and Contract law dimensions. Surely, as the authors note, Finland is not alone in this as other European countries too have been increasingly witnessing the positivisation of Fundamental rights within the Private sphere.

In the following chapter, David Ramos Muñoz and Elia Cerrato Garcia explore the constitutionalisation of Contract law in Spain. In particular, the authors ask 'what correct tool should be applied by ordinary courts and Fundamental right courts in those cases where there is not only a friction between private interests and Fundamental rights, but also the original consent is revoked, and there is a multi-party relationship?'. In answering this important interrogative, the authors start from the position that both Contract law and Fundamental rights law are about party autonomy, which is conferred on another by consent. However, they further note that because of the nature of Fundamental rights, consent in this context should not be irrevocable as in Contract law. The authors centre their discussion on a particular case involving professional posed photographs of a nude female model, who had contractually conferred her consent to publish the images on the photographer. The photographer in turn assigned his rights to the photos to Playboy magazine. When the model later tried to revoke her consent through the courts, the Spanish Constitutional Court in a decision reported in 1994 upheld the rights of Playboy magazine as being contractually conferred and hence irrevocable. This case study in turn informs a broader inquiry into the potential conflict between contractual rights and Fundamental rights, where there is a third party assignee involved. The authors argue that Fundamental rights should be treated differently to contractual rights, because of the concept of dignity inherent therein. Indeed, they argue that the model's case against Playboy was incorrectly decided. The complicating factor here of course is that the presence of a remote third party makes it more difficult for Fundamental rights to trump contractual rights, which the authors argue is a remedy more readily available between immediate parties, in the process setting out the relevant law and legal theory. The authors end with a check list of factors which may guide future courts when dealing with such clashes, particularly where there are third party rights at play.

In his contribution, Hiroyuki Kihara discusses the constitutional dimension of Contract law in Japan in general terms, as well as from the perspective of such topics as public policy regulations and good morals. Kihara's analysis commences with a useful historical contextualisation of the development of Japan's Constitution(s) and Contract law system(s) from the period of the Tokugawa shogunate (dating 1603–1868) to date. The analysis then moves on to outlining the Human rights provisions in the current (1946) Constitution as set out in its Chapter 3 (Articles 10–40). This paves the way for the discussion which follows, in which it is shown that the indirect application (*Kansetsu-Tekeiyo-Setsu*) of Fundamental rights is the preferred route by both the majority of Constitutional law scholars and the courts. However, Kihara notes, given the rigid separation between the Public and Private law spheres in Japan, most Contract law scholars are not interested in the way

Fundamental rights and values are implemented (or whether they are at all). Rather, it is generally thought that the Constitution and the Civil Code (enacted in 1898 during the Meiji Period and comprehensively reformed recently only, with a new Code coming into force in 2020) function in parallel and, at times, overlap. In contrast to their constitutional colleagues, Contract law scholars tend not to acknowledge the Constitution's priority over the Civil Code. In this sense, the case study of Article 90 of the Civil Code—one of the key-provisions for regulating unfair contract terms and concerning public policy and good morals and whose scope of application has significantly extended over the past years—proves to be extremely useful to operationalise the constitutionalisation of Japanese contract law. As one might expect, this ultimately is a matter of judicial discretion. Further, case law analysis reveals that some types of public policy or good morals violations are closely linked to the protection offered by Articles 13 and 18 of the Constitution (concerning the rights to life, liberty, and the pursuit of happiness; and slave restraint and hard labour respectively), as well as to Article 90 of the Civil Code and Article 5 of the Labour Standards Act. Interestingly, Kihara's analysis also shows that while the Contract law regime is in line with Article 14 of the Constitution on general equality rights, the same cannot be said in regards to Article 24, which concerns equality rights for marriage and family life as not all cases of mistress are void under Article 90 of the Civil Code. Finally, while there can be no doubt that some types of violation are unconstitutional, both the courts and a majority of academics who support the indirect application theory tend to solve issues without reference to the Constitution.

Salvatore Mancuso's chapter on Somalia traces the evolution of the legal system in this country from decolonisation through to the present day. The opening section presents a legal history of Somalia and its Constitutional law beginning with independence in 1960 and the original constitution of the same year, which was closely modelled on the Italian version. Mancuso mentions the resultant culture clashes between this legal transplant and the contemporary African society, as well as the feature of legal pluralism which characterises this jurisdiction. He pays particular attention to Shariah law in this regard, as well as local customary norms. This is followed by discussion of the succeeding constitutions of 1979 and 1990. These are the legal milestones amidst the country's history of a bloodless coup in 1969, a following period of socialist rule under President Siad Barre, and then the collapse of Somalia into a failed state in the 1990s with the toppling of Barre in 1991. Thereafter, the chapter turns to the Civil law of Somalia, particularly its Contract law. The Somali Civil Code of 1973 is modelled primarily on the Egyptian version, which draws strongly on French law. Finally, with reference to the present, there is a brief discussion of the current (preliminary) Somali Constitution of 2012. Mancuso concludes by noting that one of the core challenges of law in Somalia is how best to regulate in an environment of legal pluralism, particularly with regard to the question of how to marry Shariah precepts with Civil and Customary law. His closing message is to argue for a modernisation of the law of contract through the enactment of a future revised Somali Civil Code.

With regard to Nigeria, Ada Ordor and Ngozi Odiaka note that the separate divisions of the law remain largely compartmentalised and that there is no recognised field of inquiry into constitutional contract law. Indeed, Nigerian contract law remains largely fixed in the English Common law mould, with the law as it stood in England on 1 January 1900 still being the official source of Nigerian contract law. The authors note, however, that this position has been ameliorated by the Nigerian courts, which have interpreted the English law to better suit the Nigerian context, as well as to fill gaps and to modernise it. From a Constitutional law perspective, Ordor and Odiaka describe the transition from colonial era constitutions, beginning in 1922, to the first independent constitution of 1960. The latest version of a founding document for this post-colonial state is the 1999 Constitution. This document contains a Bill of Rights, although socio-economic interests are not included among the justiciable constitutional rights. The authors do note, however, that civil society groups tend to militate around socio-economic issues and pressure the government in other ways to act in this regard. With regard to substantive legal discussion, the authors have chosen to focus on three key areas which evidence a mutation of the received law of contract under public interest-type pressure. These areas are first, public sector employment contracts, where judicial precedent has caused a shift in contract law policy away from employment at the 'whim of the Crown' to a more accountable system, based on the published rules and procedures. Secondly, in consumer law, statute law has encroached on the traditional freedom of contract by imposing duties on suppliers, as well as new methods of consumer dispute resolution, and there has also been a move towards a regime of products liability. Finally, the authors place emphasis on legal pluralism and the role which customary law plays in the Nigerian system of contracting, discussing, in particular, customary land tenure, financing arrangements secured according to customary means, and contracts which affect customary succession law. The authors conclude by noting that while the concept of a constitutional influence on contract law is novel in the literature on Nigerian law, the sources which they rely on for their argument are all entrenched legal precedents.

In their chapter, Lucas Abreu Barroso and Marcos Catalan focus on the particularly relevant topic of how disabled people's Fundamental rights are recognised and protected in a market society like Brazil. As the authors show, this is a complicated area of law in which the Constitutional and Contract law regimes have conflicted for decades. In the 1916 Civil Code, for instance, disability was considered as affecting the subject to the extent of rendering her incapable of performing any valid act. Things did not improve with the 1988 Constitution, which despite its alleged pluralist essence, did not achieve any result regarding the protection of the rights of people with mental or physical disabilities. Then, in 2015, the Statute on Persons with Disabilities was enacted to ensure and promote, on equal terms, the exercise of the rights and freedoms of disabled people, as well as to guarantee their effective social inclusion. However, Barroso and Catalan explain, the new law was immediately challenged on constitutional grounds. In particular, a direct action of unconstitutionality was brought about before the Federal Supreme Court to challenge § 1 of its Article 28, according to which private institutions cannot seek payment of additional fees or tuitions. The Court rejected the injunction on several grounds, including the legal impossibility of having distinct educational systems, one public and inclusive and another private and exclusive. This is, it should be noted, first and foremost a matter of socio-political and legal culture, as the Court itself makes clear in its judgment. Through a meaningful analysis of the disabled people's place in market (i.e. consumeristic) societies, which also considers such matters as consumer vulnerability and policy considerations, the authors praise the Court's take on the issue at hand which, they write, 'has impeded a clear social backlash and affront to quality education' and social inclusiveness.

In the chapter on Peru, Gunther Hernan Gonzales Barron tackles the fundamental issue of freedom of contract. His approach is largely abstract, starting from first principles with humans in their primitive state, through the later development of vocational specialisation and the generation of a surplus, to the modern market economy. He notes the centrality of contract to economic exchange and thus trade, as well as the necessity of the related ideas of freedom and sanctity of contract. Barron tempers this market orthodoxy, however, with an account of the rise of constitutionalism in the twentieth century, as well as the Human Rights movement. He argues that from a Contract law point of view, this is given effect in Civil law systems through the general clauses in a country's Civil Code, particularly those on good faith and related norms. On the subject of codified law, he remarks that the conflicts and complexities of law in a postmodern world lead some to question the continuing relevance of codified law and positivist legal science. With regard to Contract law in particular, Barron notes that positivist norms of freedom of contract in the individualist mode need to be tempered in the age of Human Rights by reciprocity and concern for the other party to the contract. Moving on to Peruvian law itself, Barron notes that that country's constitution enshrines a market economy, but in the social model. There is respect for private property and freedom of contract, but at the same time there is concern for constitutional values of freedom and justice, as well as the social and democratic rule of law. While the author notes that contracting is a social act, he argues that contracting is intended to be a memorial of exchange, rather than an intimate act. Barron's overall position is that this measure of objectivity should reflect the supremacy of freedom and sanctity of contract in Peru, the former of which is in fact included as a binding constitutional principle.

References

Adams JN, Brownsword R (1987) The ideologies of contract. Leg Stud 7(2):205–223

Bix BH (2017) The promise and problems of universal, general theories of contract law. Ratio Juris 30(4):391–402

Brownsword R, van Gestel RAJ, Micklitz H-W (eds) (2017) Contract and regulation: a handbook on new methods of law making in private law. Edward Elgar, Cheltenham

Campbell D, Collins H, Wightman J (eds) (2003) Implicit dimensions of contract. Discrete, relational and network contracts. Hart, Oxford

Collins H (1999) Regulating contracts. OUP, Oxford

Corsi G (2016) On paradoxes in constitutions. In: Febbrajo A, Corsi G (eds) Sociology of constitutions. A paradoxical perspective. Routledge, London, pp 11–28

Drahos P, Parker S (1990) Critical contract law in Australia. J Contract Law 3(1):30–49

Febbrajo A, Corsi G (2016) Introduction. In: Febbrajo A, Corsi G (eds) Sociology of constitutions. A paradoxical perspective. Routledge, London, pp 1–7

Fried C (1981) Contract as promise: a theory of contractual obligation. Harvard University Press, Cambridge

Friedman LM (1997) Law and society: an introduction. Englewood Cliffs, Prentice-Hall

Goldwasser V, Ciro T (2002) Standards of behaviour in commercial contracting. Aust Bus Law Rev 30(5):369–394

Gordley J (1991) The philosophical foundations of modern contract doctrine. OUP, Oxford

Hadfield GK (2017) Rules for a flat world. Why humans invented law and how to reinvent it for a complex global economy. OUP, New York

Hogg M (2011) Promises and contract law. Comparative perspectives. CUP, Cambridge

Husa J (2015) A new introduction to comparative law. Hart, Oxford

Hutchison A (2017) Decolonising South African contract law: an argument for synthesis. In: Siliquini-Cinelli L, Hutchison A (eds) The constitutional dimension of contract law. A comparative perspective. Springer, Dordrecht, pp 151–184

Ibhawoh B (2000) Between culture and constitution: evaluating the cultural legitimacy of human rights in the African state. Hum Rights Q 22(3):838–860

Kahn-Freund O (1974) On the uses and misuses of comparative law. Mod Law Rev 37(1):1–27

Katz AW (2014) Economic foundations of contract law. In: Klass G, Letsas G, Saprai P (eds) Philosophical foundations of contract law. OUP, Oxford, pp 171–192

Keyes M, Wilson T (eds) (2014) Codifying contract law. International and consumer law perspectives. Routledge, London

Klare KE (1998) Legal culture and transformative constitutionalism. S Afr J Hum Rights 14 (1):146–188

Kovač M (2011) Comparative contract law and economics. Edward Elgar, Cheltenham

Legrand P (1997) The impossibility of 'legal transplants'. Maastricht J Eur Comp Law 4:111–124

Legrand P (2003) The same and the different. In: Legrand P, Munday R (eds) Comparative legal studies: traditions and transitions. CUP, Cambridge, pp 240–311

Legrand P (2017) Jameses at play. Am J Comp Law 65(1):1–132

Macneil IR (1978) Contracts: adjustment of long-term economic relations under classical, neoclassical, and relational contract law. Northwest Univ Law Rev 72:854–905

Macneil IR (1987) Relational contract theory as sociology: a reply to professors Lindenberg and de Vos. J Inst Theor Econ 143(2):272–290

Merry SE (1996) Legal vernacularization and Ka Ho'okolokolonui Kanala Maoli, the people's international tribunal, Hawai'i 1993. Polit Leg Anthropol Rev 19:67–82

Michelon C (2018) What has private law ever done for justice? Edinburgh Law Rev 22(3):329–346

Mitchell C (2013) Contract law and contract practice: bridging the gap between legal reasoning and commercial expectation. Hart, Oxford

Morgan J (2013) Contract law minimalism: a formalist restatement of commercial contract law. CUP, Cambridge

Mulcahy L (2005) The limitations of love and altruism – feminist perspectives on contract law. In: Mulcahy L, Wheeler S (eds) Feminist perspectives on contract law. Glasshouse Press, London, pp 1–20

Nelken D (1995) Disclosing/invoking legal culture: an introduction. Soc Leg Stud 4(4):435–452

Nelken D (ed) (1997) Comparing legal cultures. Routledge, London

Nelken D, Feest J (eds) (2001) Adapting legal cultures. Hart, Oxford

Nussbaum M (2000) Women and human development. CUP, New York

Samuel G (2014) An introduction to comparative law theory and method. Hart, Oxford

Seddon N, Bigwood R, Ellinghaus M (2012) Chesire & Fifoot law of contract, 10th Australia edn. Butterworths LexisNexis, Chatswood

Shaffer GC (2017) Introduction: transnational elements of constitution-making. UC Irvine J Int Transnational Comp Law 2(1):1–4

Siliquini-Cinelli L, Hutchison A (2016) Constitutionalism, good faith and the doctrine of specific performance: rights, duties and equitable discretion. S Afr Law J 133(1):73–101

Siliquini-Cinelli L, Hutchison A (eds) (2017) The constitutional dimension of contract law. A comparative perspective. Springer, Dordrecht

Somek A (2014) The cosmopolitan constitution. In: Maduro M, Tuori K, Sankari S (eds) Transnational law. Rethinking European law and legal thinking. CUP, Cambridge, pp 97–121

Steinmetz W (2000) Introduction: towards a comparative history of legal cultures, 1759–1950. In: Steinmetz W (ed) Private law and social inequality in the industrial age: comparing legal cultures in Britain, France, Germany and the United States. OUP, Oxford, pp 1–41

Teubner G (2006) In the blind spot: the hybridization of contracting. Theor Inquiries in Law 8 (1):51–71

Thornhill C (2012) National sovereignty and the constitution of transnational law: a sociological approach to a classical antinomy. Transnational Leg Theory 3(4):394–460

Wa Mutua M (1995) The Banjul Charter and the African cultural fingerprint: an evaluation of the language of duties. Virginia J Int Law 35:339–380

Watson A (1993) Legal transplants: an approach to comparative law, 2nd edn. The University of Georgia Press, Athens

Weinrib EJ (2012) The idea of private law, 2nd edn. OUP, Oxford

The Constitutionalisation of Contract Law in Finland

Jaakko Husa and Juha Karhu

Abstract This chapter discusses the constitutionalisation of Contract law in Finland and makes frequent comparative references to the other Nordic systems. It aims to describe how Constitutional law has gradually started to influence Contract law. Moreover, the analysis seeks to predict some key future developments concerning Constitutional Contract law in Finland. This chapter illustrates how relevant constitutional actors consider these two areas of law and how these actors may sometimes collide because of key doctrines and the constitutional structure. It is concluded that references to Constitutional and Human rights law are not going to *replace* traditional Contract law argumentation. In most cases, nevertheless, Constitutional and Human rights law offer a useful means to clarify and modify the arguments used in traditional Contract law reasoning. The authors expect growing significance and legal relevance of the relationship between Constitutional law and Contract law.

1 Introduction

How are Constitutional law and Contract law related in Finland? This question cannot be answered in a straightforward manner. The Finnish legal system is, generally speaking, based on the Nordic and Continental European traditions.[1] In practice, Finnish law and legal culture are, especially in key areas of Private law such as Contract law, Tort law and Company law, close to the Swedish system. In fact,

---

[1] See Husa (2011a).

J. Husa (✉)
Faculty of Law, University of Helsinki, Helsinki, Finland
e-mail: jaakko.husa@helsinki.fi

J. Karhu
Faculty of Law, University of Lapland, Rovaniemi, Finland
e-mail: juha.karhu@ulapland.fi

© Springer Nature Switzerland AG 2019
L. Siliquini-Cinelli, A. Hutchison (eds.), *More Constitutional Dimensions of Contract Law*, https://doi.org/10.1007/978-3-030-15107-2_2

15

Nordic Contract laws were shaped and drafted in close legislative co-operation.[2] However, there are significant differences in Nordic constitutional traditions, and when dealing with Constitutional Contract law there are even less similarities as national Nordic constitutional characteristics differ in many respects, despite many essential similarities.[3]

This chapter deals with Finnish Contract Constitutional law-related themes and questions. Where appropriate, comparative remarks and comments especially in relation to the other Nordic systems will be made. Additionally, the discussion seeks to predict some key future developments concerning Constitutional Contract law in Finland. The remainder of the chapter is organised as follows: after the introduction, Sect. 2 deals with the constitutional landscape. Section 3 discusses the fundamentals of Contract law and explains the key content and ideas of Finnish Contract law. Section 4 illustrates how relevant constitutional actors consider Constitutional law and Contract law and how they may sometimes collide because of the key doctrines and the constitutional structure. The final part draws together the main themes and findings along with giving a critical discussion.

2 Constitutional Landscape

2.1 The Finnish Constitution

The Constitution of Finland is technically enshrined in a single Act: the Constitution of Finland Act that entered into force in 2000.[4] Before the present Constitution Act, there were four separate Acts—following the Swedish tradition—which were the Form of Government Act (1919), the Procedure of Parliament Act (1922), the Ministerial Responsibility Act (1922) and the Act on the High Court of Impeachment (1922). The Constitution Act provides the catalogue of Constitutional rights and provisions on the principles of the exercise of public power by the government, its organisation and the relationships between the highest organs of the state. In 2012, the Constitution Act was amended. These amendments clarified the division of powers between the president of the republic and the government.

Finland is a parliamentary democracy with certain semi-presidential elements, i.e. it has a president as the head of state, equipped with powers enumerated in the Constitution Act. On a day-to-day basis, the Finnish system functions as a parliamentary system, and the President plays a minor role in non-foreign relations related politics (which include also most EU policies). Generally, we may say that Finnish

---

[2]See for an example Andersen and Runesson (2015) and Lando (2016). However, from today's point of view we may also see problems with the Scandinavian Contract Act. See the critical discussion by Ramberg (2007).

[3]See, e.g. Suksi (2014).

[4]This section is based on Husa (2011b).

governance normally works in a way that seeks consensus rather than partisan solutions backed by a temporary majority. In other words, Finnish constitutional culture strives towards consensus.[5] This produces a certain rigidity: the Constitution, both in a legal and political sense, changes relatively slowly.

The Finnish system is based on core principles according to which power is vested in the people, who are represented by deputies assembled in parliament. Crucially, legislative power is exercised by parliament, whereas the president of the republic plays a minor role. According to the Constitution Act, the top level of governance is in the Council of State (i.e. the government), which is headed by the Prime Minister and a requisite number of other ministers. Following the principle of a parliamentary system, the government and its individual members must have the confidence of the parliamentary majority. Another key point is that judicial power is vested in independent courts of law, which at the highest level are the Supreme Court and the Supreme Administrative Court.[6] Of these top courts, the Supreme Court plays an important role in the birth and evolution of constitutionally relevant Contract law.

2.2   Contract and Constitution

The Constitution provides the catalogue of constitutional rights and provisions covering the main principles of the exercise of public power by the Government, the Government's organisation and the relationships between the highest institutions (executive, legislative and judicial branches) of the state. In 2012, the Constitution was amended, but these amendments did not concern Constitutional rights. Besides Constitutional rights; Human rights—particularly the European Convention on Human Rights (ratified in 1990) and the case law of the European Court of Human Rights—are relevant for Constitutional Contract law.

In the Finnish Constitution there is no section that deals expressly with contracts, contracting or freedom of contract, nor is there direct reference to the basic social or economic values in relation thereto. However, it is generally acknowledged that the Finnish Constitution *indirectly* provides legal protection of freedom of action in private law relations, and further that the protection of property encompasses the protection of (freely created) contractual relations (i.e. they are considered to constitute private property in a broad sense).

More concretely, the legal protection provided by the Constitutional right is constructed as two dimensions in legal reasoning. First, Fundamental rights are normally expected to be implemented through parliamentary legislation. Legislation providing contracts is composed of one general piece of legislation, the Finnish Contracts Act (FCA; originally from 1929) and several specific Acts in separate

---

[5]For a broader view, see Raunio (2004).
[6]About the institutional structure, see Husa (2011b), pp. 41–50; and Saraviita (2012), pp. 237–250.

areas of law (sales law, consumer law, insurance law, real estate law etc.). Secondly, and from a content perspective, the FCA, like its Nordic counterparts, contains a general norm, entrenched in 1983, that enables the adjustment of unfair contracts. Section 36 is a provision that permits the general evaluation of the fairness of all contacts and their terms. It is considered a part of the '*ordre public*' of the Finnish Contract law system. Therefore, the application of foreign Contract law is barred if it does not recognise the adjustability of unfair contracts.

Because of the open list of circumstances that can be considered when considering alleged unfairness, the Finnish Contract law system is open to Human and/or Constitutional rights dimensions as part of legal argumentation and judicial decision-making. For example, the argument based on the Constitutional right of access to justice has been used to block the application of arbitration clauses in a business contract where the proceedings would not have been effective. This could be because of the other party's lack of means to pay the required down payments for the arbitration court's expenses and fees. As such, the arbitration proceedings would not have been started at all and proceedings in a general court of law would have still been legally blocked. Thus, Section 36 is a kind of general entrance gate to test and include constitutional aspects in Contract law reasoning.

In a broader view, the constitutional dimension of Contract law is connected to the right of economic self-determination that is, in Finland, related not only to the freedom of trade and profession but also broadly to the protection of property. To simplify a great deal, constitutionally protected property rights affect the legal validity of contracts. Essentially, the right to property contains a *bundle* of such rights that have economic value, i.e. all parties' legitimate expectations of fair economic benefit from the contact are protected. In practice, this means that enjoying the constitutional right to property requires protection of the freedom of contract, which means that there is a freedom for individuals or legal entities to enter into contracts and decide the contents of their contractual relations without the interference of the state or unwarranted legislative restrictions. Typically, the economic value of constitutional property right comes from the fact that an individual or legal entity can make an agreement with the economic value being based on its own plans and calculations. In other words, even if the freedom of contract is not constitutionally protected as such, it indirectly enjoys constitutional protection. Already before the reform of Fundamental rights in 1995, existing contractual relations were constitutionally protected when they are normal and reasonable use of property. Thus, Contract law has a factual constitutional dimension based on what can be arguably characterised as Constitutional Customary law.

Moreover, we can see that the idea of freedom of contract is in many ways an underlying dimension in the system of constitutional rights: there are economically relevant constitutional rights that can be deployed mainly or sometimes even only by means of making legally binding agreements between parties. For example, the right to choose one's profession and employment or place of stay normally requires contracts that enable these choices. In relation to access to justice, the freedom of contract is an important part of the rule of law principle that protects also the rights of a claimant. To put it differently, the rights and duties of all parties belong to the constitutionally protected right to property. However, as a constitutional right, the right to property cannot be conceived only by itself and in isolation, but it must be a part of the system of constitutional and Human rights that are deployed.[7]

After the constitutional rights reform in 1995 references in legal practice to constitutional and Human rights have increased significantly. These rights are applied a posteriori by the courts and other judicial and supervisory bodies and no longer exclusively by the Constitutional Committee a priori.[8] After 1995, there has been clear development towards a heightened role for Constitutional law and Human rights law in the area of Contract law. Characteristically, contract law has been one of the 'testing grounds' for the whole area of Civil law to replace the sole value of freedom by Human and Constitutional rights.[9] These constitutionally relevant innovations foreshadow a change in the basic legal concepts, as well as in the principles. Further, instead of abstract concepts of legal subject and legal relation, open and contextual concepts of the interest of the parties and risk positions may be used as a basis for legal analyses and judicial argumentation. Furthermore, traditional systematic doctrines like the abuse of rights, good faith and unfairness could receive concrete content, and even the role of 'ordre public intern', by reference to Human and Constitutional rights.

In addition, the constitutionalisation of Finnish Private law in general and Contract law in particular might also have a reverse effect: the privatisation of the public power. This tendency is fuelled by the private outsourcing of many welfare state functions, especially in the areas of health care and basic social aid. Concretely, these situations are hybridised, consisting of elements originating from both private and public law realms. Constitutional rights have a key constructive role in the understanding of the interrelations of these often-conflicting elements.

2.2.1 Constitutional Rights

Although it is not a simple task to pinpoint how Constitutional law and Contract law became partially intertwined, the rise of constitutional rights is intimately connected to the process. Contract law and Constitutional law have been inter-connected in the Finnish system for a long time. This has occurred mostly through the wide interpretation of the constitutional protection of property already under the old constitutional norms from 1919, which themselves were based on even older Swedish norms as described in greater detail below. But when we are dealing with the contemporary conception of constitutional rights, we need to emphasise the role and significance of the comprehensive reform that came into force in August 1995. The ECHR functioned as a key inspiration for this process. The present Constitution Act contains, comparatively speaking, a comprehensive list of constitutional rights. It houses

---

[7]Länsineva (2002).
[8]Cf. Länsineva (2012), pp. 117–119.
[9]See Pöyhönen (Karhu) (2003).

classical civil and political rights but also more modern economic, social and cultural rights.

To a certain extent, the Finnish catalogue of constitutional rights goes beyond the scope of the ECHR. For instance, the catalogue contains specific provisions regarding environmental rights, including everyone's responsibility for the environment. Additionally, other Human rights instruments may have bearing on Contract law.[10] In general, we may claim that the Finnish constitutional culture has transformed into being far more rights-oriented than was previously the case, and this development has taken place contemporaneously with the heightened profile of constitutional judicial review.[11] The transformation of Nordic legal culture has, however, not been an easy process, but it remains a fact that rights are now more important within the Nordic legal cultural sphere than ever before.[12]

Crucially, it would be inaccurate to point out only one or two constitutional rights and argue for their being the exclusive basis of Constitutional Contract law in Finland. In fact, there are many occasions when different constitutional rights dimensions are interlinked and overlapping. From a business perspective, contractual rights are often linked with freedom of profession and other market related rights. Nonetheless, we can still highlight the special significance of Section 15 of the Constitution Act which concerns the protection of property.

The Constitution Act's Section 15 is sparse in its wording. It does not provide much precise information about the content of the constitutional protection of property.[13] In essence, the provision states, in a somewhat laconic way, that the property of everyone is protected and that a provision concerning expropriation must be laid out in a Parliamentary Act. Section 15 also restricts the constitutionally-permissible scope of expropriation legislation by stating that such a tool must be used exclusively for public needs and against full compensation. Although the constitutional right to property has deep historical roots in the Finnish system, it was codified only as late as 1919 in the Form of Government Act. Yet, if we consider the interpretation practice of the Constitutional Committee, we may note that this right has been frequently applied over the years of independent Finland (1918-), and quite often as a restriction to economic and social reforms (protection of existing economic relations).

After the reforms of 1995, the practice of the Constitutional Committee has been expanding in the sense that the protection of property is still conceived in a relatively broad manner, but also more prominently as forming part of the whole system of

---

[10]Importantly, The Council of Europe's revised European Social Charter has been in force since 2002. And, the EU Charter of Fundamental Rights also contains a wide range of ESC rights that may have relevance in the context of contract law. Furthermore, there are other important conventions such as the European Convention on Social Security and many International Labour Organization (ILO) conventions and recommendations.

[11]See for a broader discussion Lavapuro et al. (2011).

[12]See Husa (2011c).

[13]Section 15 provides that, 'Provisions on the expropriation of property, for public needs and against full compensation, are laid down by an Act.'

Constitutional and Human rights. For instance, today, there is room for group rights, which may further restrict the scope of the broadly understood right to use one's property in relation to constitutional environmental limitations.[14] In fact, property rights are no longer—if they ever were—absolute rights, although the constitutional right to property still holds a strong position in the constitutional system. Furthermore, it seems that the Finnish protection of property rights is further-reaching than the ECHR's, especially regarding the question of how 'possession' is defined and understood.[15]

An indication of the strength of the right to property is given by the landmark case on constitutional judicial review decided in 2004 by the Supreme Court. It concerned the protection of private property. In short, the owner of a building was deprived of benefits from its premises because of a temporary prohibition by the relevant public authority ('interior of value' i.e. cultural environment protection). Later, the prohibition was cancelled, and the owner demanded compensation. However, the Parliamentary Act in question only provided for compensation in cases of permanent prohibition. The Supreme Court held (following a narrow split) that the provision in the Act was clearly contradictory with the Constitution Act's right to property.[16] This was the first case in which the Supreme Court overruled a provision in the Parliamentary Act based its giving rise to an unconstitutional outcome in a concrete case.

Now, this landmark case dealt with the protection of ownership of a building within the context of protection of the cultural environment. The analogy to contractual relations becomes apparent by viewing the latter as possible risk positions for further actions (such as when the housing company could rent the space for another purpose to that originally designated). A similar line of legal reasoning is established via the perspective of legitimate expectations. What is protected is not only (or mainly) a static position (as a negative protection against intrusions by outsiders) but also the freedom of action in the future based on the—to use a German expression—'Geschäftsgrundlage' adopted by the contract parties. This is also in line with the 'bundle of rights' idea behind the constitutional understanding of property.

This line of argument can be seen in the practice of the Constitutional Committee. Two examples highlight this: There are special housing company arrangements ('asumisoikeus') where the persons or families living in a flat are somewhere in between owners and tenants. They pay a certain threshold sum to the housing company when entering into the relationship on top of monthly rents. The housing company is, and remains, the owner of the flat. These threshold payments were the

---

[14]Section 20 on the responsibility for the environment provides that 'Nature and its biodiversity, the environment and the national heritage are the responsibility of everyone. The public authorities shall endeavour to guarantee for everyone the right to a healthy environment and for everyone the possibility to influence the decisions that concern their own living environment.'

[15]See Husa (2011b), pp. 186–187.

[16]KKO 2004:26. (KKO stands for 'Korkein oikeus' in English 'Supreme Court'.)

high priority subject-matter in a case where the relevant housing company was liquidated (which meant that the tenants would be paid back the threshold sums before other non-mortgage creditors of the housing company). When this priority position was lowered by a new law (to enable the housing companies to get credit more easily and cheaply), the legitimate expectations of the tenants had to be considered, even if these were not part of the rental contract (not written down or guaranteed in the contract between the tenants and the housing company). The reasoning went that the contractual arrangement formed part of a housing arrangement and, especially about long-term housing for families with limited resources, it related it to the Fundamental right of decent living conditions.[17] Here we can see that the constitutional dimension was meaningful for the interpretation of a contractual issue.

Secondly, several national support mechanisms were introduced for Finnish agriculture throughout the last century (*'tilatuki'*) that require constant alignment with the agricultural policies of the EU.[18] One of these mechanisms has been long-term agricultural loans with reduced interest rates. So, when the interest rates were raised in line with EU norms—and even where this unilateral raise had been enabled in the contract terms of the loans and necessitated by the EU—the Constitutional Committee gave significance to the legitimate expectations of the farmers. They required that no rapid changes were allowed in national agricultural policies if they would result in essential detrimental effects on these loans as long-term agricultural investments. Again, there was a link to other Fundamental rights besides the protection of property, and in this case the freedom to choose one's profession.

Crucially, as noted above, a contract enjoys constitutional status as a part of a broadly understood umbrella of protection of property provided by the Constitution Act and the accompanying interpretative practice by the Constitutional Committee and the Courts. This protection is always made visible when there are legislative proposals affecting the area of freedom of contract (either as relating to already existing contractual relations or to possibilities that belonged to the legitimate expectations of the involved parties in the normal course of things). In this sense it is safe to argue that Contract law has a constitutional dimension in Finland, i.e. there is something that can be labelled as Constitutional Contract law. To explain in more detail how these two fields became fused, we need first to explain how constitutionality review works in Finland.

2.2.2 Finnish System of Constitutionality Review

As already mentioned above, there is no constitutional court in Finland, but the ordinary courts are allowed and obligated to engage in judicial review of all

---

[17]PeVL 45/2002 [PeVL stands for *'perustuslakivaliokunnan lausunto'*, i.e. Statement of the Constitutional Committee].

[18]PeVL 25/2005.

legislation—albeit only to a certain limited extent. This became possible after the total reform of the Constitution Act in 2000. The idea of constitutionality, however, is not upheld exclusively by *judicial* review; in addition to courts, other public authorities are obliged to interpret legislation in such a manner that adheres to the Constitution and respects Human rights. According to the Constitution Act (Article 106), the courts must give preference to the Constitution when they decide a case if the application of a parliamentary Act would manifestly conflict (in Finnish '*ilmeinen ristiriita*') with the Constitution Act. There are a handful of cases, starting as the one mentioned above from 2004, in which courts have applied Article 106. But in the overall picture, judicial review by the courts plays a minor role when it comes to guarding the constitutionality of parliamentary Acts.[19] Lately, there have been signs of the incrementally growing constitutional role of the judiciary, despite its often being considered secondary and supplementary to that of the Constitutional Committee.[20] If the role of judiciary becomes stronger, it makes sense to speculate that constitutional dimensions of Contract law will also become more significant and pronounced.

In practice, the constitutionality of standard parliamentary Acts' provisions are normally examined in advance, i.e. before the legislation comes into force. Review takes place mainly in parliament's influential Constitutional Law Committee (*Perustuslakivaliokunta*). The function of this parliamentary bound control is to prevent, in advance, legislation which conflicts with the Constitution from being enacted in the ordinary legislative procedure. From the constitutional point of view, the Committee's key function is to issue statements on bills sent to it for consideration, as well as on the constitutionality of other legislative matters and their bearing on international Human rights. Although the Committee's members are ordinary members of the Parliament, the Committee calls experts (based on constitutional convention) to give evidence, and the Committee itself operates in a non-party political manner when giving its reports to the Parliament. These reports are official statements and the government, which seeks to amend the provisions that the Committee has found to be unconstitutional before bills are passed, respects them. If the unconstitutionality is significant, this will mean in practice that the bill is withdrawn and the government must reconsider how to proceed. This is because, in a multiparty-system, government are unlikely to have the required qualified majority to change the Constitution Act.

Therefore, Constitutional Contract law related issues might surface in the work of the Constitutional Committee in the Finnish Parliament when this Committee pre-reviews legislative Bills put forward by government which are thought to be potentially constitutionally problematic. The Committee tries to strike a balance between the protection of (the economic value of) existing contracts and other constitutional rights or important social goals pursued by the Bill. Commonly, the reasoning adopted by the Committee may be characterised as laying emphasis on the

---

[19] See Husa (2011b), pp. 186–187.
[20] See Ojanen (2009).

legitimate expectations of the contracting parties towards the fundaments of their contract (reminiscent as already mentioned above to the German doctrine of the *Geschäftsgrundlage*) whilst at the same time disregarding whether these expectations are based on legislation providing the framework for the contract in question or on specific contract clauses. Thus, contractual relations can obtain protection against new statutory law in the courts if the application of the legislation is regarded as manifestly violating these relations. Depending on the circumstances, the level of this constitutional protection can vary from issue to issue; hence, this leaves room for judicial interpretation in which constitutional arguments may play a role. For example, in situations where framework legislation is later amended because of rising environmental concerns, the question of constitutional protection becomes an issue: how much should compensation amount to for private companies that rely on the possibility of realising their long-term investment plans? On the one hand, the sovereignty of parliament should not be restricted in essential political issues, but on the other hand, existing arrangements made with reasonable reliance on the continuity and persistence of the policy lines adopted by the government and public authorities should be protected.

From a comparative point of view the fact that the Constitutional Committee functions in a non-political, quasi-judicial manner (e.g. statements are based on the evidence given by Constitutional law experts, the Committee follows its own 'precedents' and there is no political party discipline) is particularly significant. All this results in a unique system of control over the constitutionality of legislation, in which abstract ex ante, and concrete case-bound ex post facto review mechanisms are combined. Importantly, the significance of the '*Perustuslakivaliokunta*' is reflected in the whole legal system, and its statements hold a special status as a source of law as de facto precedents.[21] Only with slight exaggeration, one may characterise the weight of these statements as de facto 'constitutional precedents'. Concretely this means that if the court later considers the same question of constitutionality as does the Constitutional Committee in its statement, the court should not, as a rule, regard the conflict between the Constitution and the legislative provision as manifest.

2.2.3 Case Law

As was explained above, the Finnish system of constitutionality supervision is a two-tier one. The Constitutional Committee in parliament makes an a priori evaluation of proposed legislation in relation to the Constitution and Fundamental rights. Courts then have the opportunity and mandate to oversee the possible tension between the application of parliamentary legislation and Fundamental rights in concrete cases. Accordingly, it is to be expected that there is a room for tension

---

[21]See Husa (2011b), pp. 78–88.

between these tiers. These tensions are clearly visible in the 1959 a Supreme Court case that concerned contract and alleged unconstitutionality.[22]

In that case, a waterpower company proposed a regulation to the ministry regarding the flow of water in the Iijoki river. The government approved the proposal, and the company proceeded to build five plants in the river, only for the river to become protected by special legislation in 1987.[23] The company then received compensation (provided for in the 1987 protective legislation) for the investments it had made based on the 1959 arrangement. However, the statutory compensation did not include lost profits. The company thus sued the state of Finland for breach of contract. At its heart, this case is an example of a judgment in which Contract law and Constitutional law arguments are combined into something we might describe as a genuine Constitutional Contract law.

The company relied on several grounds, one of which was the unconstitutionality of the 1987 legislation for a violation of the right to the protection of its property. One of the counter-arguments made by the state was that parliament is sovereign and therefore free to make new laws without being constrained by contractual arrangements made based on old laws. Furthermore, the company argued that the Constitutional Committee had reviewed the 1987 legislation and had indeed considered it to be in alignment with Fundamental rights. The Supreme Court noted the first-tier of a priori supervision of the parliament itself. Nevertheless, Article 106 of the Constitution also contains a duty to give priority to the Constitution if there is an obvious conflict between the application of the parliamentary legislation and the Constitution. Even if lost profit is one of the protected rights in the bundle of rights constituting ownership, the Supreme Court did not see the discrepancy as obvious (manifest)—with reference to the opinion of the Constitutional Committee. Simply put, the company lost the case based on constitutional arguments.

In another case, the Supreme Court had to evaluate the validity of an arbitration clause in a business contract.[24] One of the parties did not have the resources for the arbitration proceedings, and the other did not offer to pay the whole costs. According to Finnish law, the arbitrators had the right to obtain compensation for their expenses and a fee, and the common practice was that a down payment by the parties was required to cover these before the proceedings would start.[25] The arbitration clause as such was considered valid in the business contract at hand. However, the outcome would have been unreasonable to the party without any resources. The perspective for evaluating this unreasonableness was that of access to justice. This point was specifically mentioned by the Appeal Court in its reasoning. The constitutional dimension of this case was that the party without resources would have been

---

[22]KKO 2006:71. The environmental dimensions of cases like this are dealt with in Sect. 4.2.

[23]The Act on the Protection of Rapids (35/1987). The main function of the Act is to protect Finland's most precious waterways from construction.

[24]KKO 2003:60.

[25]Arbitration Act (967/1992) Section 46 (3) 'The arbitrators have the right to demand an advance on the compensation or a security therefor.'

deprived of the constitutional right to have their case heard by a legally competent court.[26]

3 Contract Law's Landscape

All law is related to the society and culture in question. Finnish Contract law is no exception to this. Accordingly, it has several important roots nourishing the more concrete legal outlooks that have been created through legal norms and Contract law legislation. These social and cultural background features are the formative context of Finnish Contract law. Key expressions of this formative context are the Contract law principles—freedom of contract, the principle of trust and reliance, and 'the third principle', which takes various forms as a reaction to adjusting Contract law norms to fit the changing reality. As a result, we may describe Finland's contract law as Nordic in its nature.[27]

It is of course already a choice to describe any Contract law system by reference to its leading principles. The principles-based description leads to an analysis that emphasises the aims and goals of legislation, the possible wider systematic impacts of norms (the formal application area of which is restricted to certain specific contracts), the precedents by supreme courts and, most importantly in relation to Nordic Contract law, consequential and practical arguments in concrete cases ('*reella överväganden in casu*').[28]

There is one simple reason for justifying the choice of this path of principles: Nordic countries, including Finland, do not have a comprehensive Civil Code or even a comprehensive code of Contract law. The Finnish Contracts Act (FCA, originally of 1929)—is the most relevant general piece of Contract law legislation, which follows in all relevant respects similar Nordic codes, such as that of Sweden (the *Avtalslagen*), as well as Norway, and Denmark. This FCA—provides regulation only for contract formation, invalidity of contracts and certain types of authorisation, but it says nothing, for example, in regard to the interpretation of contracts or consequences of contractual breaches.[29] Even if the text of that code and its clauses have not been modified (besides one essential amendment on the adjustment of unfair contracts), the application of the clauses has changed, and will change, essentially, over its lifespan of 100 years.

---

[26]Constitution Act Section 21 (1) Protection under the law: 'Everyone has the right to have his or her case dealt with appropriately and without undue delay by a legally competent court of law or other authority, as well as to have a decision pertaining to his or her rights or obligations reviewed by a court of law or other independent organ for the administration of justice.'

[27]For a general description, see Bernitz (2007) ('flexible, not so doctrinaire approach of Scandinavian law', p. 29). See also Husa (2011a).

[28]See, e.g. Niemi-Kiesiläinen (2007).

[29]The Contract Act (228/1929) [Contains several later amendments].

The emphasis on aims and goals, and through them, the legal principles of Finnish Contract law, does not give a simple answer to all basic questions about a Contract law system. So even if no genuine line of thought privileged by 'the Founding Fathers' of modern Nordic Contract laws exists, the FCA clearly sets limits on the possibilities of framing problems as Contract law questions.[30] This is true also when analysing the relations between Contract law and Constitutional law, as exemplified in the case examples in the previous Sect. 2.

3.1   The Principle of Freedom of Contract

The FCA does not contain a separate clause providing for the protection of freedom of contract. However, freedom of contract and private autonomy of contracting parties are implied, and strongly supposed, in several clauses in the FCA. For example, the clauses on invalidity of contracts contain direct references to flaws in the formation of the will of the contracting party (physical coercion, mental coercion, mistake in expressing one's will etc.).[31] Even on a systematic level, the clauses providing for the formation of contract through offer and acceptance are non-mandatory, i.e. they are optional and reflect the starting point where the contracting parties are free to decide on the procedure of contract formation, as well as on the content of the contract.

The discussion of freedom of contract regarding Finnish Contract law normally breaks this freedom down into its key elements. One of these, the choice to make a contract, or not, is clearly visible in the systematic idea that forcing anyone to make contracts needs specific justification. These exceptions include, for example, marketing promises that are individual enough to create legitimate expectations by the other party or the need to protect the basic economic means of consumers in a market society, like the possibility to open a bank account or to have internet access. The freedom to choose one's contracting party, another of these key elements, has again become limited not only because of mandatory contracting for social reasons (social solidarity) but also for Competition law norms (to protect the appropriate functioning of the market mechanism by limiting the effects of dominant market positions). But then again, it is the need for these specific justifications, and specific legislation enabling the restrictions in the basic freedom, that actually justifies the freedom itself as a starting point.

---

[30]There are two recent excellent general presentations of Nordic contract law systems. The book published in 2015 titled *The Nordic Contracts Act* contains essays in celebration of the 100th anniversary of those laws. *Restatement of Nordic Contract Law* from 2016 is a systematic overview relating to various sections of the laws.

[31]See FCA Chapter 3: Invalidity and Adjustment of Contracts (as amended in 1982).

Obviously, the most important of these elements is the freedom to choose the terms of the contract: contractual autonomy *sensu stricto*. It is compactly visible in the accepted rule of contract interpretation '*falsa demonstratio non nocet*', which means that when interpreting the contract, the specific meaning meant by the contracting parties should be adopted even if it is contrary to the normal use of the terms. However, from a systematic point of view the most significant feature of Nordic Contract law is that it embraces general norms (*Generalklausel*) to enable the adjustment of a contract because of the unfairness of its content. The famous Section 36—a Finnish version of the BGB's famous §242—is addressed later in a more comprehensive manner.

Now, Finnish Contract law contains key elements compatible with and supporting the freedom of contract principle. More concretely, this freedom is embedded and supposed in the clauses of the FCA that protect the significance of the free will of the contracting parties to form contracts. The definition of 'contract' extracted from these norms would be consensus of wills or a meeting of minds. However, it is precisely this definition that is challenged by those who would, instead of a straightforward freedom of contract, rather see reliance as the leading principle. Today Finnish Contract law contains, besides arguments based on freedom of contract, strong bases for arguments relating to reliance and legitimate expectations that are created by the mutual co-operation under the contract.

Notably, although the Constitution Act does not expressly provide for freedom of contract, this is deemed to have an undisputed constitutional basis on the praxis of the Constitutional Committee of the Parliament. Crucially, all possible limitations of the freedom of contract must be evaluated according to the established doctrine on restricting constitutional rights with the means of ordinary legislation.[32]

3.2 Reliance Principle

Several sections of the FCA contain famous 'second sub-paragraphs'. These sub-paragraphs protect the legitimate expectations of a contracting party in good faith.[33] More concretely, they are situations where it is obvious that no meeting of minds has taken place, but a contract is still seen to be made. The party who made the offer should have realised that the party who received the offer believed a meeting of minds had taken place, and the omission to correct this opinion results in a contract with the content of the legitimate expectations by the receiving party.

---

[32]See Husa (2011b), pp. 198–199.

[33]Good faith clauses, Section 11(2), Section 19, Section 28(2), Section 32(82), Section 33, Section 34, Section 35 and Section 39. A typical example is Section 39: 'If, according to this Act, the validity of a contract or other transaction depends on the fact that the person to whom the transaction was directed neither knew nor should have known of a circumstance or that he/she otherwise was in good faith, regard shall be had to what he/she knew or should have known when he/she learned of the transaction.'

Moreover, these 'second subparagraphs' in the clauses that regulate offer and acceptance get systematic support from a key clause of the invalidity of contracts, that of '*Treu und Glaube*', or good faith and fair dealing in contractual arrangements.[34] This invalidity is caused by one party behaving contrary to good faith and fair dealing. An example of this is misusing the other party's lack of rational judgment caused by old age or evident misunderstanding of the key characteristics of the situation at hand. Thus, the reliance principle has rather strong institutional support in several clauses in the FCA.

However, it is important to recognise the difference of the tension between freedom and reliance in Finnish Contract law in the twentieth and twenty-first centuries and the German nineteenth century quarrels between will theory and reliance theory. This is so even if the German scholarship provided material for the Nordic scholars and legislators for discussion. In the classical German debate, it was actually more about the ways to construct the will that was constitutive of the contract.[35] There was a disagreement in the discussion in regard to how much this construction should respect only the real state of mind of the party expressing her will and how much (if at all) the construction could be made on the conception of the expressed will as understood by the receiving party. In the Nordic twentieth century context, the necessity to find a will was substituted by a more radical idea that the concept of contract itself could be directly based on the reliance. In Finnish and Nordic debates, the reliance principle has been linked to the interests of the exchange, that is the market. It would not be efficient to require economic actors to find out the real state of mind of a possible contracting party if the information exchanged between the contracting parties matches the normal market behaviour leading to contracts. Keeping this in mind, and the important role given to contextual and consequential arguments, the background of the Nordic scholars supporting the reliance principle should be seen as more similar to the German twentieth century '*Wertungs- und Interessenjurisprudenz*' than to the older classical nineteenth century '*Vertrauenstheorie*'. In this century, an even stronger leaning towards normal and typical is evidenced for example in the case dealing with parking on private land where pure actions in a social practice (parking a car) were considered enough to constitute a valid contract without any reference to the state of mind of the person parking the car.[36]

The Supreme Court summarised this Finnish way of understanding the various possibilities of contract formation in a leading precedent in 2010.[37] There, the Supreme Court clearly stated that, under Finnish law, contracts could still be formed

---

[34]FCA 36(1): 'If a contract term is unfair or its application would lead to an unfair result, the term may be adjusted or set aside. In determining what is unfair, regard shall be had to the entire contents of the contract, the positions of the parties, the circumstances prevailing at and after the conclusion of the contract, and to other factors.'

[35]See Tolonen (1973).

[36]KKO 2010:23.

[37]KKO 2010:23.

and evaluated by an offer-and-acceptance model. However, contracts can and are made by just participating in a social behavioural practice, which gives rise to rights and duties for the participants. In this latter model, it is not necessary to try to find a separate offer and its final acceptance, but the contract is attached to the overall evaluation of the situation. The concrete circumstances in that case were parking a car in a restricted area that was only marked by specific signs warning of monetary fines if these restrictions were not followed. The Supreme Court considered the relations between the person parking the car and the owner of the land to be contractual. This case contains, however, also serious constitutional issues, which we will discuss later in Sect. 4.3.

3.3   The Principle of Fairness

Besides principles finding their justifications in the value of freedom or the aim to enhance functioning markets through the reliance principle, there is the principle of fairness and its paradigm expression in the general clause that enables adjustment of unfair contracts, i.e. Section 36 of the FCA. It states that if a contract or a contractual clause is unfair, or if its application would lead to unfairness, the clause or the contract can be adjusted. When considering if a contract or a clause of is unfair the following factors must be taken into consideration: the circumstances leading to the contract, the whole content of the contract, the position of the contracting parties, later changes in circumstances, and other relevant considerations.

As is obvious from the text of Section 36, there are no general restrictions in the application of this section. Therefore, it also applies to contracts between business parties and not only consumer contracts or contracts between private persons. The court or arbitrator is given full freedom in the adjustment, from just declaring the clause null and void, to re-writing the clause and/or other parts of the contract, to even declaring the whole contract null and void. An adjustment is possible even if the party making a claim for it would have been aware of the unfairness when the contract was made. Consequently, it is generally considered that the possibility to adjust all contracts is part of the 'ordre public' of the Finnish Contract law system.

Section 36 already highlighted its characteristic of an 'ordre public' nature during the legislative procedure of the early 1980s. The Constitutional Committee was faced with the problem of retroactivity.[38] In its short opinion it was bluntly stated that unfair contractual relations do not enjoy the (normal) protection of property. This seems to apply both to contracts, which are overall and totally unfair, and to those parts of otherwise valid contracts that are (or would lead to the contract being) unfair. Section 36 could be given retroactive effects because there was no violation of protection of property in unfair contractual relations.

---

[38]PeVL 3/1982.

The principle of fairness finds several normative institutional backgrounds and support in the Finnish Contract law discussions.[39] Obviously one way is to connect it directly to Section 36 of the FCA and to the possibility of adjustment of contracts. The principle of fairness could also be seen to have a role in other general areas like contractual interpretation (avoiding interpretative outcomes which would be unfair). Secondly, the principle of fairness can be related to norms that give protection to the weaker parties in contractual relations. Contracting parties' resources are sometimes unequally divided in as much as one of the parties end up with an unfair advantage during the bargaining process (inequality of bargaining power). Even if equality before the law normally refers only to the vertical relation between the public authority and the citizen, a horizontal dimension of equality can also be detected in the principle of fairness. The principle of fairness could, then, be anchored also in the mandatory legislation protecting weaker parties; for example, in the specific norms providing for a kind of 'social force majeure' to private persons if their debts are overdue because of unexpected events like sickness, unemployment, divorce or similar events. In situations of 'social force majeure', there is often a link to many Fundamental rights in the enabling dimension.

Thirdly, the principle of fairness can be seen as an elaboration or extension of good faith and fair dealing. The principle of fairness would then have its emphasis not only in the negotiation phase but throughout the whole life span of the contractual relation. As such, in this wide scope of application it resembles the German Civil Code's Section 242 on 'Treu und Glaube'. Fourthly, as one of the most recent topical discussions in Nordic Contract law, the principle of fairness can be seen as partly overlapping with the principle of loyalty between the contracting parties.[40] Loyalty duties embrace various information obligations and other co-operation measures that enable the smooth execution of the contract. Most significantly, loyalty may require that a contracting party must refrain from pushing its own interests to the full if there would be another line of action that better matches the interests of the other party (for example avoiding a significant unilateral loss suffered by the other party).

Besides legal principles, the general part of Finnish Contract law contains several parts closely relating to constitutional issues. For example, the rules of invalidity because of a lack of genuine consent (because of coercion, duress and undue influence) can be seen to protect the Fundamental right of freedom in the conclusion of contracts. Moreover, the requirement of the age of maturity (presently, 18 years) is related to the right of children to be treated accordingly to their age and maturity that is provided in the constitution. The requirement in the specific provisions of the FCA which states that restrictions to professional activities should not be unreasonable is related to the freedom to choose one's profession and earn a livelihood according to

---

[39]See Pöyhönen (Karhu) (1988).
[40]See Andersen and Runesson (2015).

one's own choice. This right is also directly connected to the Constitution Act's right to work and the freedom to engage in commercial activity.[41]

Mandatory contracting is a paradigmatic example of the interest of basic social values breaking classical doctrines of Contract law. It is done often to protect and enable access rights. One type of access rights deals with access to basic services like communication in an information society and financial services like bank accounts and basic insurances. Here the service provider has only very limited possibilities to deny the service for private individuals wanting to conclude a contract. Such services are necessarily needed to enjoy many of the Fundamental rights, giving the justification to set the business party under an obligation to conclude the contract. A second type of access rights are needed to secure access to the contract itself. A paradigm example here is the limits of the effectiveness of an arbitration clause. First, under Finnish law arbitration clauses are not valid in consumers' contracts.[42] The reason here is to guarantee an easy and affordable possibility for dispute resolution. Secondly, an arbitration clause may not be effective even in a contract between two business parties in special circumstances. As described earlier, the Supreme Court held that an arbitration clause in a contract over financial services would lead to unfairness and allowed a party to sue in a normal court despite an arbitration clause.[43]

Finally, Corporate Social Responsibility (CSR) is a topical test case. In Finnish Contract law, debates on the subject have been raised, but not with great enthusiasm. The main counter-argument is simply to argue that it is enough for businesses to comply with valid legislation—anything more would be unwarranted from a legal point of view even if there could be affordable social or charity reasons to do so. This is because valid legislation embeds and gives regard to Fundamental and Human rights to a sufficient degree. Moreover, from a doctrinal point of view, the Contract law argument in support of CSR needs to refer to the horizontal effects of Fundamental and Human rights. In the preparatory works for the Finnish Constitution, the idea of horizontal effects of Fundamental rights was seen as possible but not 'mainstream'.[44] Moreover, traditionally in Finland the idea was that Fundamental rights are 're-written' or transformed in parliamentary legislation, and therefore there is no need, or indeed no possibility, to apply these rights directly. However, with the Constitution Act of 2000 the competence of retroactive control was given to courts in cases of manifest discrepancy between parliamentary legislation and Fundamental rights. The possibility of an even wider competency directly to apply fundamental rights is related to the doctrine of division of public powers. Tendencies that make

---

[41]Constitution Act Section 18(1): 'Everyone has the right, as provided by an Act, to earn his or her livelihood by the employment, occupation or commercial activity of his or her choice. . .'.

[42]Consumer Protection Act 38(1978) 12 1d (1)—Handling of disputes (amended in 1997): 'A term in a contract concluded before a dispute arises, under which a dispute between a business and a consumer shall be settled in arbitration, shall not be binding on the consumer.'

[43]KKO 2003:60.

[44]HE 309/1993 (HE stands for 'Hallituksen esitys' in English 'Government's bill'.)

these issues global set pressures in these respects to at least allow arguments relating to the CSR when deciding contractual disputes as kinds of global consequential arguments ('*globala reella hänsyn*').

4 Illustrations

This section contains three kinds of illustrations that shed light on the Finnish Constitutional Contract law. The first one addresses the issue from the point of view of a priori constitutionality control. The second one reopens a Supreme Court case that was already shortly dealt with above. The third issue deals with a situation in which a priori and a posteriori views collide with one another.

4.1 A Priori: Constitutional Law Committee

Contract law related questions are not the commonplace for the Constitutional Law Committee. However, from time to time there are constitutional issues that arise from the government's legislative bills that also have significant Contract law dimensions. A telling example is the government's Bill relating to the right-of-occupancy-dwelling that concerned the constitutional right to property.[45] Needless to say, Constitutional Contract law issues are dealt with typically in context of the right to property questions. The Constitutional Committee provided its statement at the request of the parliament's Environment Committee, which typically deals with matters relating to housing, planning and construction but also to environmental protection and nature conservation.[46] The interpretation assumed by the Constitutional Law Committee has later been followed in other similar type of issues.[47]

According to the Constitutional Law Committee the constitutional protection of legitimate expectations is connected to contracts in such a manner that the parties to a contract must have a constitutional right to trust the constancy and stability of relevant parliamentary legislation. Underlying this there is a constitutional idea according to which legal certainty has a significant weight in the legal order, i.e. the legal system should be predictable and reliable and thus enable planning and reasoned decisions as normal courses of action. However, this does not mean that pieces of parliamentary legislation should remain unchangeable but rather that the will of the legislator cannot be exercised completely freely. Alternatively, the legislator must consider the constitutional safeguard for legitimate expectations as a part of the broadly understood constitutional protected right to property. In short, the

---

[45]HE 100/2002.
[46]PeVL 45/2002.
[47]PeVL 4/2008 and PeVL 41/2013.

Constitutional Law Committee has interpreted the right to property as containing an idea according to which the position of contracting parties cannot be unreasonably weakened by means of ordinary parliamentary Acts. Moreover, as emphasised by the Constitutional law Committee, when the legitimate expectations are based on a legislative Act—as is the case in this example—it is of particular importance that the constitutional protection of legitimate expectations occurs as an extension of property rights and thus reflects the 'pre-1995' ideas of the protection of normal, usual and reasonable use of property.[48]

4.2   A Posteriori: Courts

As described above, the a priori control of constitutionality, including compliance with Fundamental and Human rights, is done during the legislative process in Parliament. When there is a statement by the Constitutional Committee on these matters, it is held in high regard in the a posteriori control by the courts. A paradigmatic case here is the first matter heard by the Supreme Court in which Section 106 was used. The facts have been described already above—they concerned a demand for compensation for a temporary restriction order during the preliminary assessment of a culturally significant environment (an old pharmacy). The assessment did not lead to an actual order of protection. The housing company owning the premises sued the Finnish state for the loss of rental income caused by the temporary restriction order. The state rejected this stance by claiming that the legislation did not contain such a compensation—it argued that compensation was explicitly denied by the parliament. However, the Constitutional Committee had, in its opinion, stated that such a possibility should be included in the legislation to avoid a conflict with the fundamental right of protection of property.[49] The Supreme Court used this statement as a core argument in its reasoning to set aside the Parliamentary legislation and thereby enable the housing company to make a claim for damages.

Another area of examples is connected to environmental protection. This case—which formed part of a series of cases—concerned the legislation dedicated to protecting Finland's rapids.[50] The legislation is special because it contains specific reference to the rapids meant to be placed under protection; it is not a general norm of protection to be applied by the environmental authorities and courts. The constitutionality of the act has therefore been challenged in the courts. The cases have been brought by waterpower companies claiming damages arising from long-term investments made on the premise of future building possibilities. In these types of cases the Constitutional Committee had evaluated the specific compensation system

---

[48]PeVL 45/2002 4–5.
[49]Report of the Constitutional Committee PeVM 10/1998.
[50]See besides KKO 2006:71, KKO 1991:171, KKO 2000:28 and KKO 2000:97.

established in these special legislations and had considered it to be in line with protection of ownership.[51] The facts of these cases involved complex circumstances where the Finnish state had acted by favouring the building plans in other roles than the legislative role.

However, one of the main preliminary questions was if the parliamentary legislation could be questioned over its constitutionality even when the Constitutional Committee had given its acceptance. The Supreme Court answered this preliminary question affirmatively, although the outcomes in the cases have varied. Moreover, the courts have emphasised the full-scale use of the possibilities of using harmonious interpretation of Fundamental rights as the primary methodology instead of overruling the legislation.

4.3 Collision of Interpretations

Three auxiliary lines of reasoning legally soften the possibility of the courts overriding Parliamentary legislation. First, as just mentioned, courts should primarily exhaust all possibilities of legal interpretation. Secondly, the discrepancy between legislation and fundamental rights must be manifest. Thirdly, the opinions of the Constitutional Committee should be given a key role in the reasoning, which means concretely that they should be followed if there are no exceptional circumstances. However, these softening methods are not always enough to block a collision in systematic interpretations. A paradigmatic case here is the Private Parking Supervision situation. It has been dealt with both by the Constitutional Committee and the Supreme Court with clashing outcomes.

The background of the situation is the development of privately-managed parking zones with outsourced supervision methods. Usually this supervision is executed by private companies specialised in parking services. The core of the legal issue has been the fines included in the supervision in situations where the parking conditions have not been followed (payment, parking time or resident parking permits). These fines were challenged by a private person with a variety of arguments, including a claim that parking fines involve the use of public power to an essential extent and could therefore not be executed by private companies. The Supreme Court constructed the situation as a contractual one, as described earlier. Yet, even if the basis for the fines was contractual, it was not enough for their validity. The Supreme Court had to evaluate whether there really was an essential use of public power. In short, the answer it gave was negative.[52]

---

[51] KKO 2004:26.

[52] KKO 2010:23. The amount of the fine in question was 40 € which was the normal level of private fines at that time and which was on par with fines ordered by public parking supervision in similar situations.

During the same period, the Constitutional Committee had a similar issue to decide. There was an effort to solve the tense situation of this Private Parking Supervision through legislation by enabling such supervision only under specified conditions. The core question was about these conditions—and actually whether the supervision powers could include giving fines at all. Despite the name given to the monetary payment for wrongful parking, the Constitutional Committee saw it involving the use of public power.[53] Thus, the Constitution did not allow such power to be transferred to private bodies, and so the private companies were instead required to take the position of municipal parking assistants as a practical solution in the circumstances.

The solution of allowing only municipal parking assistants (and of course in extreme cases the police) to issue fines for private parking violations did not earn the Supreme Court's approval. It is possible here to combine arguments bound to new forms of contract-making with arguments relating to the power of ownership. The parking spaces are part of the land covered by the ownership rules, which enable a wide variety of different uses. It is the variety of these uses that often form a large part of the essential value of the property. To require the service by public authorities in important issues of functionality (such as a parking lot) would at the same time mean a restriction in the ownership. This special requirement could be avoided if issuing the fines were not seen as involving the essential exercise of a public power. The Supreme Court specifically noted that the private person receiving the fine could always invoke normal court procedures to dispute it and thus secure legal protection for their rights and interests. Notwithstanding, this issue is still unresolved and shows how difficult these kinds of collisions are to solve if the Parliament is unable to pass a new piece of legislation that would solve the conflict statutorily.[54]

5 Discussion

Can we argue that there is a distinct area of law labelled 'Constitutional Contract law' in Finland? The answer to this question, from a legal systematic point of view, is probably a negative one. However, as we have shown in this chapter, these two areas of law have many noteworthy contact points; specifically, there are many Contract law issues that have constitutional dimensions. Accordingly, we may rather safely argue that these two areas of law tend to overlap. In particular, we can see that contract law issues are related to Fundamental rights. But the discourse goes deeper than rights, as the case of private parking lots shows: it illustrates that a question may be tackled differently depending on if it is conceived from the point of view of Constitutional law or from the point of view of Contract law. In the future, the

---

[53]Statement 57/2010 of the Constitutional Committee.

[54]See the Statement of the Constitutional Committee (PeVL 23/2013), which finds a constitutional problem with the Government's bill and, thus, effectively stops the bill on constitutional grounds.

relationship between these two areas of law may become more intertwined than is the case today. This is because of the constitutionalisation of Private law[55]; a development that has to do with a general trend of more frequent recourse to Fundamental rights in debates on various Private law issues.[56] Finland, however, is not alone in this. All over Europe we have witnessed a spectacular rise in the recourse to Fundamental rights in debates on civil liability. This is part of a pervasive process of constitutionalisation, of Private law in general and Tort law in particular.

When considering the constitutionalisation of Finnish Contract law, three different paths can be detected. First, opening up to arguments relating to constitutions and especially Fundamental and Human rights. A good example here is the changing role of norms protecting the weaker parties in contractual relations. Previously, the reasoning in the application of these norms focused on the specificity thereof, which created closed situations separated from one another. Now, a more general line of thinking is seen when linking this protection to the underlying values protected as fundamental rights (work, housing, health etc.). Liberty and freedom need to be supplemented by other social values as basic principles in Contract law. These supplementary values need also to become part of the conceptual structure of Contract law, and they need, for example, to stress in the understanding of freedom, the *positive* freedom, instead of the purely negative one. Once Human and Fundamental rights obtain a more prominent and manifest place as the foundation of the Finnish legal system, their role and significance will be reflected throughout the various fields of law, including Contract law. There are old and new meeting points between traditional Contract law issues and themes and constitutional issues and themes; with old points being re-interpreted and new points adding to the vocabulary of Contract law debates on a case-by-case basis. Essentially, Finnish Constitutional Contract law is taking shape only gradually, layer by layer.

Secondly, the Constitution is receiving a stronger role in the systematic fabric of Contract law. It is commonplace that several other fields of law are explicitly linked to Constitutional rights. For example, Environmental law is fuelled by the Fundamental right of the environment in setting out responsibility to the environment and nature for all actors in its ecological, cultural, and diversity dimensions. Likewise, Criminal law gets its starting point in the constitutional provision of legality in the '*nulla poena sine lege*' provision. Labour law is linked to the special protection of occupations and Competition law to the freedom of trade and profession. Also, Contract law has its deep level legal background in the provision providing for the protection of property, as described earlier on in this chapter. Being constitutionally-

---

[55] According to Smits (2006), p. 10: 'The constitutionalisation of private law can be described as the increasing influence of fundamental rights in relationships between private parties, fundamental rights being those rights that were originally developed to govern the relationships between the State and its citizens'.

[56] It should be mentioned, however, that when this topic is discussed in the private law academic literature the mainstream attitude is rather restrictive, see for example Helin (2012). Even if the possibility of constitutional arguments is allowed, such an argumentation is seen to have only a limited area of relevance. Our prediction is, notwithstanding, that this situation is changing.

founded does not only suggest a formal link to the Constitution but also a requirement for openness towards the whole system of Fundamental rights. Concretely, this
means that the interaction and overall functioning of Fundamental rights make up
one element in the framework for an overall legal evaluation of the issues at hand.
However, contrary to what some critics have been suggesting,[57] references to
Fundamental rights are not going to replace more traditional Contract law reasoning.
In an overwhelming number of situations, this perspective will only—but importantly—offer a further point to clarify and modify the arguments used in the Contract
law reasoning.

Thirdly, the catalogue of Fundamental rights in the Finnish Constitution is quite
extensive and comprehensive. Moreover, through memberships of the ECHR and
the EU the charter of Fundamental rights also finds application. The number of
Fundamental rights relevant in single cases is bound to become numerous, leading to
the necessity of weighing and balancing them. This balancing act is not foreign to
more traditional private law argumentation, but it was seen more as being a special
case rather than normal and natural. In more recent legislation in the Contract law
area it is typical that sections of law include provisions requiring an overall evaluation of the situation at hand. Paradigmatic in this respect is Section 36 of the FCA.
There seems to be room to develop Contract law argumentation not only when
applying Section 36 but also more generally to learn from the experiences of the
weighing and balancing of Fundamental and Human rights.[58] One concrete topic
already taken up by the Finnish discussion is the abuse of rights. It has been
suggested that as on a general level also contractual rights could be misused and
that this argumentation is exceptionally compelling when there is a link to Fundamental rights. A concrete example here is the misuse of a dominant market position
(through contracts)—which is of course null and void because of competition law
rules—but that could also be invalidated through Contract law arguments.[59]

One final aspect for the future on the constitutionalisation of Contract law should
not be forgotten. Whatever globalisation means and will mean for law and legal
cultures, we need more dialogue and common grounds for mutual understanding.
Because Fundamental and Human rights and constitutions by their nature invoke a
general challenge for all legal systems, they could also—without an idea of a definite
and absolute content—become interlinking bridges in these kinds of discussions.
Differences and similarities between various Contract law systems could be better
understood, not so much in formal-technical issues (do already unilateral promises
bind or only mutual contracts), but rather in background value systems (what are the
other values and how are they included besides the freedom of contract in the
system?). To conclude, the background issues are the very points where we can

---

[57]See Helin (2012), pp. 25–27.

[58]This seems to be one aspect of an ongoing research for a PhD thesis by Mr. Joonas Norr from the
University of Turku, where he deals with the additional value of constitutional rights-based
argumentation in Contract law.

[59]See Pöyhönen (Karhu) (2003).

expect to see a growing significance and legal relevance of the relationship between Constitutional law and Contract law.

References

Andersen BM, Runesson E (2015) An overview of Nordic contract law. The Nordic Contracts Act. In: Essays in celebration of its one hundredth anniversary. Djøf Forlag, Copenhagen, pp 15–41

Bernitz U (2007) What is Scandinavian Law. Scandinavian Stud Law 50:14–29

Helin M (2012) Perusoikeuksilla argumentoinnista [About making arguments on fundamental rights]. Juhlajulkaisu Jarmo Tuomisto, pp 11–30

Husa J (2011a) The stories we tell ourselves – about Nordic law in specific. Isaidat Law Rev, 1. https://ssrn.com/abstract=2176029 or https://doi.org/10.2139/ssrn.2176029

Husa J (2011b) The constitution of Finland – a contextual analysis. Hart, Oxford

Husa J (2011c) Nordic constitutionalism and European human rights – Mixing oil and water? Scandinavian Stud Law 55:101–124

Lando O (2016) A short survey of the laws of the Nordic countries – the laws in general and contract law in particular. In: Lando O et al (eds) Restatement of Nordic contract law. Djøf Forlag, Copenhagen, pp 13–45

Länsineva P (2002) Perusoikeudet ja varallisuussuhteet [Fundamental rights and property relations]

Länsineva P (2012) Fundamental principles of the constitution of Finland. In: Nuotio K, Melander S, Huomo-Kettunen M (eds) Introduction to Finnish law and legal culture. Oikeustieteellinen tiedekuntapp, Helsinki, pp 111–125

Lavapuro J, Ojanen T, Scheinin M (2011) Rights-based constitutionalism in Finland and the development of pluralist constitutional review. Int J Constitutional Law 9(4):505–531

Niemi-Kiesiläinen J (2007) Comparing Finland and Sweden: the structure of legal argument. In: Husa J, Nuotio K, Pihlajamäki H (eds) Nordic law – between tradition and dynamism. Intersentia, Cambridge, pp 89–108

Ojanen T (2009) From constitutional periphery toward the center – transformations of judicial review in Finland. Nordic J Hum Rights 27:194–207

Pöyhönen (Karhu) J (1988) Sopimusoikeuden järjestelmä ja sopimusten sovittelu [The system of contract law and contract arbitration]

Pöyhönen (Karhu) J (2003) Uusi varallisuusoikeus [A new theory of property rights]

Ramberg C (2007) The hidden secrets of Scandinavian contract law. Scandinavian Stud Law 50:249–256

Raunio T (2004) The changing Finnish democracy. Scandinavian Polit Stud 27:133–152

Saraviita I (2012) Constitutional law in Finland. Kluwer Law International, Alphen aan den Rijn

Smits J (2006) Constitutionalisation of private law: a sceptical view. In: Barkhuysen T, Siewert Lindenbergh S (eds) Constitutionalisation of private law. Brill, Leiden, pp 9–22

Suksi M (2014) Markers of constitutional identity. Retfaerd 37:66–91

Tolonen J (1973) Om begreppet rättshandling inom det traditionella rättssystemets ram [The concept of transaction in the framework of the traditional legal system]. Tidskrift utgiven av Juridiska Föreningen i Finland 108:340–364

The Fundamental Right to Image, Contract and Third Parties in Spain: A Roadmap for Pluralist Private Relations?

David Ramos Muñoz and Elia Cerrato García

Abstract Fundamental rights and Private law can collide in private-to-private relationships (horizontal situations) where the rights of two or more parties are compromised. In contractual cases, both Private law and Fundamental rights courts tend to solve their respective conflicts between private interests or Fundamental rights using the same tool: party autonomy, which is exercised through consent. Consent is also key to regulate the exercise of both private rights and Fundamental rights. However, Fundamental rights do not behave in the same way private rights do, so unlike contracts concerning private rights where the consent is enforceable and irrevocable, in contracts that waive Fundamental rights, consent needs to remain revocable. This chapter draws the following question: what correct tool should be applied by ordinary courts and Fundamental right courts in those cases where there is not only a friction between private interests and Fundamental rights, but also the original consent is revoked, and there is a multi-party relationship? The decision by the Spanish Constitutional Court 117/1994, where the Fundamental right to image and reputation is at stake and multiple parties are involved, provides useful insights in this regard. In our view, in pursuit of the correct solution in such a complex case the basic elements of personality rights had not been taken into consideration. For that reason, we propose a different approach than that followed by the Court, where (1) the Private law logic where Fundamental rights can be inserted should be applied, because of the fact that it could helped Courts examine the original agreement between the parties, and analyse the actual

David Ramos Muñoz is a member of Proyecto DER2016-78572-P, Infraestructuras e instituciones de Derecho Privado, nacional e internacional, en mercados en red: entre la regulación y la competencia. Solución arbitral de conflictos, funded by the Spanish Ministry of Economy and Competitiveness.

D. R. Muñoz
Universidad Carlos III de Madrid, Madrid, Spain
e-mail: dramos@der-pr.uc3m.es

E. C. García (✉)
Colegio Universitario de Estudios Financieros (CUNEF), Madrid, Spain
e-mail: elia.cerrato@cunef.edu

position of a third-party assignee from a different perspective; (2) the importance of ascertaining whether there is a clash between two private interests, or a clash between a Fundamental right and a third-party's contractual right; and (3) in cases where there are interferences with Fundamental rights, the third party's good faith status should not prevail over the holder's Fundamental right to image and reputation.

1 Introduction

The comedian Jon Stewart once said that 'religion has given people hope in a world torn apart by religion'. In Western, and increasingly secular, countries, Fundamental rights enjoy the moral standing historically reserved for religion, and although they do not threaten to tear society apart (indeed, they are arguably one of the most significant forces of peace in human history[1]), oftentimes they may be difficult to deploy in concrete cases. This is at least the case where Fundamental rights come accompanied by a cacophony of conflicting appeals to 'dignity'.

This is particularly the case in situations involving Private law. Unlike vertical relationships where Fundamental rights act as a barrier to interference by the State, in relationships between individuals, especially those where criminal law is absent, considerations of government interference may often be secondary, and the collision will take place *between* Fundamental rights of different individuals. In those cases, Fundamental rights cannot, *prima facie*, promise a 'superior' protection, since the gain in one person's rights comes at the expense of the rights of another person (thus, 'superior for whom' would be the question), nor a more predictable solution. Yet, in our view, the confluence of Fundamental rights with Private law can offer useful insights for both. To do that, we choose what is one of the most evanescent rights (the right to one's own image and reputation) and one of the most cumbersome situations (plurilateral relations; in particular where the right in question is transferred to third parties), as it was analysed in the Spanish Constitutional Court (also 'Tribunal Constitucional' or 'TC') decision 117/1994.

The remainder of this chapter is organised in three parts. Section 2 provides some general criteria to analyse Fundamental rights in Private law settings—we illustrate how these criteria apply in the case of a person's right to image and reputation, and we discuss the factual setting of the decision 117/1994. Section 3 provides a critical analysis of the decision's express and implied arguments. Section 4 concludes.

---

[1]Pinker (2011), pp. 378–382.

2 Fundamental Rights and Private Law: Basic Underpinnings and the Right to Image and Reputation

In this section, we first offer a general approach to the relationship between Fundamental rights and Private law (Sect. 2.1) Then, we discuss those general aspects in the specific case of the rights to one's image and reputation (Sect. 2.2) Finally, we present the TC decision 117/1994 (Sect. 2.3).

2.1 Fundamental Rights and Private Law: A Roadmap

One of the very first difficulties when analysing the interplay between Fundamental rights and Private law is getting rid of the term *'against'*, which seems to hover around the relationship. One can conclude that Fundamental rights do not conflict with Private law as a matter of principle: both focus on the individual holder of the rights, and both organise around notions of freedom and dignity.[2]

Furthermore, the approach followed when dealing with horizontal, or private-to-private situations, is different from that of vertical, government-to-private situations. Unlike the latter, where only one party may have Fundamental rights, whose scope and intensity may result in their trumping public policy, in private-to-private settings the rights of at least two parties are compromised, i.e. the gain in one's right comes partly at the expense of a sacrifice of the rights of another.[3] This prompts a change in tone, and not just in content: a decision is more difficult to be hailed as a 'triumph' of privacy or honour, when that comes at the price of freedom of expression, or another right. That is no bad thing, since temperance in expression is a useful ally when situations are increasingly complex and sophisticated.

Once the private-to-private setting for Fundamental rights is defined for what it is—as a clash between Fundamental rights—which overlaps with a collision between private interests—the nature of the problem becomes clear. Fundamental rights do not conflict with private rights. Rather, the solution to the clash between Fundamental rights given by Constitutional law may differ from the solution given by Private law to the collision between private interests. For example, non-discrimination may prevail over freedom of association, despite Private law's granting to an association the right to not admit a certain member.

Yet, worse than that is the risk that the *methodology* itself differs significantly. In non-contractual cases, which are typical examples of this, Private law would tend to solve the case by determining whether the aggrieved party has a 'right' to damages compensation, by examining issues such as the damage itself, causation and fault. In short, the right would be a 'conclusive' reason that would settle the dispute.[4]

---

[2]Ramos (2017), pp. 1051–1053.
[3]Collins (2012), pp. 25–32.
[4]Raz (1975); Dworkin (1986), pp. 153–167.

Conversely, a Fundamental rights court would tend to weigh, or 'balance' the rights (e.g. freedom of expression against privacy or reputation) against each other, to see which has a superior weight considering the circumstances. It could thus be said that the rights would be 'prima facie' reasons, in need of *ex post* adjustment.[5] This divergence is bound to cause methodological friction, as shown by the fact that in honour/privacy v. freedom of expression cases the constitutional argument and methodology have, for all purposes, displaced Private law tools, without, we may say, a clear gain in certainty and predictability. As to fairness, the jury is still out on the issue.

This methodological friction, however, is significantly reduced in *contractual* cases, since the basic tool to address the conflict between private interests is the same as the tool to solve the conflict between Fundamental rights, and it is none other than party autonomy, exercised through consent. This should not be a shock: free will is a cornerstone of both Private law and Fundamental rights, where notions of dignity are associated to the free development of one's personality.[6] Thus, it is not surprising that party autonomy, in addition to its substantive dimension, which explains a large part of the content of Fundamental rights and Private law rights, should also have a methodological dimension, as a mechanism to settle disputes between diverging rights and interests.[7]

What, then, remain causes for friction? If we follow the above logic, they should be either 'inside' the appraisal of consent, or 'outside' it. The typical examples of the first instance are cases where consent is appraised differently or has different binding force. Consent is appraised differently in cases where Fundamental rights courts require a 'clear and unequivocal' consent,[8] and look with suspicion, more suspicion than ordinary courts do, at cases where consent was given in a situation of unequal bargaining power (especially where the government or its institutions was on the other side[9]). Consent has different binding force since, in Fundamental rights cases,

---

[5]See the classical case of Lüth, BVerfGE 7, 198; 1 BvR 400/51 of 15 January 1958, where the issue of the horizontal effect of fundamental rights, but also the conflict between them, was more prominently raised.

[6]Ramos (2017), pp. 1051–1055, and the sources cited therein.

[7]Ibid pp. 1055–1060.

[8]Applications 10588/83, 10589/83, and 10590/83 Barberá, Messegué and Jabardo v. Spain, 6 Dec. 1988, ECLI:CE:ECHR:1994:0613JUD001058883; Application 11662/85 Oberschlink v. Austria, 23 May 1991, ECLI:CE:ECHR:1991:0523JUD001166285; Application 12151/86 FCB v. Italy, 28 August 1991, ECLI:CE:ECHR:1991:0828JUD001215186; Application 18954/91 Zana v. Turkey, 25 November 1997, ECLI:CE: ECHR:1997:1125JUD001895491; Application 1603/06 Suda v. Czech Republic, 28 October 2010, ECLI:CE:ECHR:2010:1028JUD000160306.

[9]Application 57325/00 D.H. and others v. Czech Republic, 13 November 2007, ECLI:CE: ECHR:2007:1113JUD005732500 at 203 (where the ECtHR rejected the validity of consent by Roma parents to put their children in schools conceived for the mentally handicapped children). See, in contrast, see Applications 6903/75 Deweer v. Belgium, 27 March 1980; 31737/96 Osmo Suovaniemi v. Finland 23 February 1999, ECLI:CE:ECHR:1999:0223JUD000031737; or STC 136/2010, of 2 December, Fundamento Jurídico (FJ) 2, all of which examined (and validated) consent for arbitration clauses.

the general rule is that consent is always revocable, while in Private law consent, at least when part of a binding contract, is, as a general rule, irrevocable.[10]

Friction 'outside' consent itself arises in cases where Fundamental rights and/or Private law protect 'goods' or interests, outside free will. For Fundamental rights, this would be the case of dignity, this time understood not as the free development of one's personality, but as a notion of 'minimum self', which may not be traded away,[11] or equality and non-discrimination, especially when it has an impact beyond the individual, such as in in cases where it is systematic.[12] For Private law, this would be the case of the protection of a 'reasonable reliance' on the consenting party's promise, and the implied duties that normally attach to that reliance. For example, in normal Private law contracts, a party expects the other party to go through with her promise and may expect a series of obligations that may not have been expressly consented upon, e.g. for the obligations to be executed with 'care', or in 'good faith', or for the performance of those obligations to fit within certain implied criteria of 'conformity'.[13] In employment contracts an employer may expect the employee to follow her directives.[14] In either case, counterparty and employer will expect to have remedies in case of non-performance, which, in case of ordinary Private law agreements (not including employment contracts), may include specific performance of the other party's obligations.[15]

This gives rise to a taxonomy of problems—the majority of which are not difficult to identify—but that are often confused because of the lack of systematic analysis. Cases where an employer is curtailed in her directing power by the employee's Fundamental rights, or where a counterparty does not have the opportunity specifically to enforce contractual obligations are less vexing for Private law's edifice as cases where consent is deemed irrevocable by Private law and revocable by the law of Fundamental rights, which, in turn, are less disruptive than cases where contracting freedom is curtailed by principles such as dignity or non-discrimination. 'Vexing' or 'disruptive' are not used in a negative moral sense, but merely as an indication of the impact that each kind of decision may have in the internal consistency of Private law, and the level of adjustment that may be required as a result. An adjustment of a contract's 'implied obligations', such as

---

[10]On physical integrity, see Art. 5 para. 3 Oviedo Convention on Human Rights and Biomedicine. On privacy, see Art. 2 (3) Organic Act 1/82 on the Right of Honor.

[11]Ramos (2017), p. 1054. See also the distinction between dignity as 'constraint' and dignity as 'empowerment'. See Brownsword (2003).

[12]See e.g. Application 57325/00 D.H. and others v. Czech Republic, 13 November 2007, ECLI:CE: ECHR:2007:1113JUD005732500 (systematic discrimination by a State).

[13]See, e.g. Art. 35 (2) of the Vienna Convention on Contracts for the International Sale of Goods.

[14]SSTC 204/1997, of 25 November, and 1/1998, of 12 January, or 192/2003, of 27 October all of which discuss the worker's fundamental rights in the context of his/her duties arising from good faith, loyalty, and compliance with employer's instructions.

[15]See, e.g. Section 241 of the German Civil Code, or Arts. 1096, 1098 and 1124 of the Spanish Civil Code.

those arising from good faith or a party's 'reasonable' or 'legitimate' expectations can be adjusted without much difficulty. These concepts are open-textured on purpose: changes in what has not been expressly agreed, but a party can nonetheless *legitimately* expect from a contract, is the way Private law can adapt to socioeconomic reality, not a genuine source of friction, least of all a friction between Fundamental rights and party autonomy. This is because the duties and obligations do not stem from an express agreement but rather from the parties' expectations protected by the law. A similar argument can be made about contract remedies, where Fundamental rights do not curtail the obligations consented upon by a party, but the means that the State puts at the disposal of the non-breaching party to enforce those obligations, and which are, themselves, subject to limits based on open-textured concepts. Consider how damages must be 'foreseeable'[16] and specific performance cannot impose 'unreasonable' costs.[17]

Cases where consent is genuinely appraised differently are more disruptive, since there is, in principle, no open-textured concept, such as 'good faith' or 'reasonableness', which may absorb the new input from Fundamental rights and adapt Private law in consequence. Unsurprisingly, disruption (again, not meant in a negative sense) by Fundamental rights courts is less frequent in these contexts. Cases where a party's consent was deemed valid by ordinary courts, and invalid by Fundamental rights courts, are relatively rare, and mostly concentrated in instances where the government was another party,[18] which means that they were not Private law cases. Conversely, while Fundamental rights courts may frequently stress the need for 'clear and unequivocal' consent in agreements that waive Fundamental rights, like arbitration clauses do with the right of access to justice, they tend to render those clauses valid with the same frequency.[19] There are no doubt some famous 'disruptive' examples, like the *Bürgschaft* case, where the German Constitutional Court re-appraised consent and party autonomy in light of the 'social State' clause of the Constitution.[20] Yet, we tend to think that this, and similar cases, are examples of the so-called 'availability heuristic', where the likelihood of an event is appraised by the ease with which an example comes to mind, and not its actual probability. The *Bürgschaft* case is famous precisely because it was a rare, unexpected, occurrence; a ripple, rather than a tide, in Fundamental rights case law.

---

[16]See, e.g. Art. 74 of the 1980 Vienna Convention on Contracts for the International Sale of Goods.

[17]See, e.g. Arts. 46 (2) and (3) of the 1980 Vienna Convention on Contracts for the International Sale of Goods, or Art. 7.2.2. of the UNIDROIT Principles on International Commercial Contracts.

[18]Application 57325/00 D.H. and others v. Czech Republic, 13 November 2007, ECLI:CE: ECHR:2007:1113JUD005732500; Application 30078/00 Konstantin Markin v. Russia, 22 March 2012, ECLI:CE: ECHR:2012:0322JUD003007800.

[19]Applications 6903/75 Deweer v. Belgium, 27 March 1980; 31737/96 Osmo Suovaniemi v. Finland 23 February 1999, ECLI:CE:ECHR:1999:0223JUD000031737; or STC 136/2010, of 2 December, FJ 2.

[20]BVerfG 19 October 1993, BVerfGE 89, p. 214 (Bürgschaft).

Finally, arguably the most disruptive instances may be those where a Fundamental rights court effectively limits a party's freedom of contract because of a superior interest that 'trumps' it. Since it is the most disruptive hypothesis, it is subject to quite strict conditions; those generally reserved for cases of non-discrimination and deployed in situations where the aggrieved party had not consented, or her consent was dubious at best. Typical situations are those where the discrimination transcended beyond the discriminating and aggrieved parties, because the former was an establishment open to the public,[21] or because the discrimination was systematic or blatantly obvious[22]; or, conversely, where it was so hidden that the party being discriminated was not aware, and could thus not challenge it, let alone consent to it.

2.2 Fundamental Rights and Private Law: The Right to Image and Reputation

Spanish and European case law involving Fundamental rights and Private law show sobriety and restraint. Fundamental rights courts are not a threat to Private law's integrity. If anything, they tend to protect the core of party autonomy by ensuring that consent is clear and unequivocal, as well as revocable, while Private law's focus is less on the consenting party's free will, and more geared to her counterparty's expectations.

Thus, since Fundamental rights have some lessons to offer to Private law, the question is whether the opposite may be true: whether some instance could be found where Private law's reasoning could help add some analytical rigour to the law governing Fundamental rights. We believe there is, and we have chosen to use the right to image and reputation, in cases where multiple parties are involved, as an example.

First, we need some brief introduction. The right to reputation is a Fundamental right enshrined in the Spanish Constitution, which also characterises it as a personality right,[23] a category of rights considered as the most closely connected with a

---

[21]See e.g. Art. 59 (1) (d) of Royal Decree 2816/1982, applicable to all establishments open to the public, Art. 21 (d) of the Act 4/1995 of the Basque Country, on Public Spectacles, or Art. 24 of Act 17/1997 of the Region of Madrid, on the same subject. In contrast, see decision by the Spanish Constitutional Court STC 73/1985, of 14 June, where the Court held that refusing to grant access to a casino to a person based on his potential to cause trouble was not discriminatory.

[22]Ramos (2017), pp. 1080–1081.

[23]The right to reputation laid down in Art. 18 of the Spanish Constitution of 1978, along with the rights to honour and privacy. In this regard, the right to reputation is also recognised as a subjective right, that is a situation of power granted by the legal system to any person, who will be able to make her own decisions and defend herself from any illegitimate interference. Thus, when an illegitimate infringement of the fundamental right has been established, Art. 9.3 of the Organic Act 1/1982 provides, that harm will be presumed, and that compensation will include moral damages.

human being's dignity. This right allows any person to protect her own image from moral damages caused by an unauthorised use of her image.[24]

Party autonomy is part of these rights' critical core. The Spanish Constitution and the Organic Act 1/1982 for the civil protection of Rights to Honour, Privacy and Own Image (hereinafter: Organic Act 1/1982) protect personality rights from any illegitimate interference, but contemplate the possibility where interferences are allowed by the right.[25]

Thus, through the exercise of consent, which is an expression of the party autonomy principle, it is possible to negotiate and sign contracts for the commercial use of one's image.[26] When a person's image is made 'marketable', it may be subject to one or more transfers. Thus, in cases where the holder voluntarily consented to limit his/her personality rights by assigning the commercial use of his/her image to a beneficiary, the exercise of the faculty of revocation of consent may conflict with another person's rights or freedoms also enshrined in the contract and in the Constitution, such as the freedom of enterprise or freedom of expression. Indeed, the Organic Act 1/1982 establishes that any person can revoke her consent at any time, with no justified reason, but she must *compensate those damages* caused to the other party, including those arising from that party's legitimate expectations.

This equation becomes even more complicated when we incorporate third parties, which, typically, occurs when the initial beneficiary of the right to exploit or use a party's image (hereinafter: beneficiary or first assignee) transfers those rights to a third party (hereinafter: second assignee). The question in such case is what are the limits for the exploitation and commercial use by the second assignee of the holder's image? What is the bearing of the holder's consent, and revocation, in the contract between the first assignee and second assignee? Should the solution be in a constitutional 'balance' of the rights at stake, or in the conceptual edifice of Private law?

---

[24]See STC 81/2001, of 26 March, where the TC rules that the right to reputation is

> susceptible to special legal basis insofar as it is the subject of a fundamental right that attributes to its holder the power to determine the graphic information generated by their physical features personal and, in its negative dimension, to prevent the capture, reproduction and publication of their image.

[25]The Spanish Constitution protects the right to avoid any interference with the personality rights with the aim to protect the person's dignity. STC 139/2001, of 18 June, FJ 5: the right to reputation permits that individuals can decide what aspects of their personality want to preserve from dissemination so that individuals can ensure a private develop their own personality outside of external interferences. Art. 2.3 of the Organic Act 1/1982 singles out the inexistence of illegitimate interference when it is expressly authorised by law or when the holder of the right has granted express consent for the interference.

[26]Currently, the possibility of exploiting one's image rights is beyond doubt. See e.g. Palacios and Placer (2014), p. 3.

2.3 The Right to Image and Reputation, Private Law Agreements, and Multi-Party Situations: The Spanish Constitutional Court Decision 117/1994

Section 2.1 showed that, in contract cases, a relevant part of the interplay between Fundamental rights and Private law is 'inside' consent—the appraisal—and the binding nature of consent, or 'outside' it—the protection of the legitimate expectations of the parties other than the holder of the right. Section 2.2 showed that the rights to image and reputation initially fit that picture and open the door to complex situations involving third-party assignees.

This is the main topic of discussion of this article, which focuses on the decision by the Spanish Constitutional Court (*Tribunal Constitucional*, or, hereinafter: TC) 117/1994. In that case a constitutional appeal (*recurso de amparo*) was filed before the TC by Ana Obregón, a Spanish actress and celebrity. She had signed an agreement with a Spanish magazine (first assignee) to have her nude pictures taken, and those pictures, together with the rights to exploit them, were, in turn, assigned to Playboy magazine, which was the second assignee. Miss Obregón revoked her consent and requested the withdrawal of all materials containing the pictures. Ordinary courts (up to the Supreme Court) had held that her revocation of consent was valid but not effective pursuant to Art. 2.3 of the Organic Act 1/1982 against the Playboy magazine because of the severe damages that the latter would have suffered if it had lost the right to publish the pictures.[27] The plaintiff argued that this decision undermined her rights to image and reputation.

In a controversial decision the Spanish Constitutional Court focused on the exercise and enforceability of consent, holding that ordinary courts offered a reasonable interpretation of the law when they held that the publication of the pictures by the second assignee had been set in motion when the process was initiated, which means that, at the time when the right holder wanted to exercise her right to revocation, the publication could be considered a past event, and consent was not enforceable.[28]

In our view, the decision will not go down in history as the Court's finest hour. The decision has been criticised for misunderstanding what the rights of image and reputation are about, especially in the case of women, and for failing to differentiate the right to image and the right to honour.[29] We will explore some of these aspects in

---

[27]The actress and a photographer ('beneficiary') had initially signed a non-remunerated agreement in January 1985. According to such agreement, the actress granted to the beneficiary the full right to distribute worldwide, for journalistic purposes, certain nude pictures that have previously been selected and approved by her. Subsequently, the actress revoked her consent right after the beneficiary had transferred the pictures to Playboy magazine, but before Playboy magazine released the pictures. In return, the beneficiary received the amount of 1,000,000 pesetas. Finally, the nude pictures were published together with some captions, which motivated the appeal filed by the holder.

[28]STC 117/1994, of 25 April, FJ 7-9.

[29]Baines and Rubio-Marín (2010), pp. 274–275.

Sect. 3. Yet, even if the Court may have made a mistake, it is a mistake that has become precedent, so instead of crying over spilt milk, we will try to use the avenues that the Court left unexplored. These mostly require a better interweaving between Fundamental rights and Private law. This, in our view, could help accommodate a more updated understanding of the rights at stake, especially in what concerns multiparty relationships.

3   A Discussion and Critique of the Court's Arguments

In this section we provide a critique of the Court's reasoning. We begin by addressing the arguments that the Court itself discussed (Sect. 3.1) and then move to the arguments that the Court did not openly discuss but were really at stake (Sect. 3.2).

3.1   What the Court Said: Personality Rights' Moral and Patrimonial Dimensions, Timing of Revocation and Overreach of Assignees

The possibility of transferring the right to image, or just some specific aspects related to that right has been discussed by the Spanish case law and scholarly writings. Some scholars support that, although the right to reputation is a Fundamental right, it is capable of being waived or transferred.[30] Others argue that its status as a Fundamental right renders it inalienable and unwaivable and, by extension, non-transferable.[31] Yet, this seems at odds with reality, which shows that, when a person permits an interference with her image rights (personality right), such person is actually exercising an 'act of disposal' (*acto de disposición*) over her own personality right. To try and circumvent the objections arising from the intrinsic moral value of the right itself, it could be argued that the right to reputation has a dual nature: on one side, the patrimonial aspect of the right may be the subject of private

---

[30]In the decision by the TS (hereinafter: STS) 1212/2007 the Court understood that the players transferred the right to exploitation on the litigious images to the claimant, so they were not entitled to claim the improper commercial use of those images, but their claim fell outside of the scope of their right. See e.g. Salvador (1990), pp. 380–382.

[31]The ruling in STS 281/2001, ECLI: ES:TS:2001:2325, FJ 1 held that 'the right to privacy and own image were unwaiveable rights, but they were subject to certain conditions'; in STS 400/2001, ECLI: ES:TS:2001:3256, FJ 2, the TS ruled that 'inalienability entails the unavailability of these rights, by the holder thereof, although the holder has the faculty to dispose on certain aspects of the recognised right;' the TS's holding in STS 1120/2008, ECLI: ES:TS:2008:5992, FJ 2, established that 'the law provides the holder with the right to dispose of their rights in certain cases by authorising the dissemination of one's image for the purposes the holder deems appropriate'.

agreements when the holder so consents; on the other side, the fundamental dimension of the right is non-transferable.

The first or third views seem to prevail in practice. The Spanish Constitution seeks to safeguard the autonomy of the protection of a person's own image, including its use for business purposes.[32] Yet, the mere fact that such uses are contemplated by the specific protective laws means that individuals can choose to limit the constitutional protection offered by the Spanish Constitution,[33] including the permission to reproduce and exploit pictures of a person's physical features. The party autonomy principle helps to overcome the apparent 'contradiction' between the inalienability of personality rights and the holder's willingness to waive his personality rights. Consent is an expression of party autonomy, which is a core principle in Private law and Fundamental rights,[34] and an expression of the person's right to self-determination[35] and the control of external manifestations of her own personality. This can be done with economic purposes. Regardless of whether one holds the view that Fundamental rights can, themselves be subject to consent and waiver, or whether they have a dual nature, where some of the right's

---

[32]Art. 18 of the Spanish Constitution provides that 'the right to honour, to personal and family privacy and to the own image are guaranteed'. The civil protection of a person's image rights comprises a list of acts that are considered illegitimate infringements of this right, such as, pursuant to Art. 7.5 of the Organic Act 1/1982, 'the taking, reproduction, or publication, by photography, film, or any other process, of a person's image captured in places or moments of her private life or outside of those settings. . .,' and under Art. 7.6 of the Organic Act 'the use of the name, voice, or picture of a person for purposes of advertising, business, or of a similar nature'. See e.g. STC 81/2001, of 26 March, where the TC rules that the right to reputation is the right to avoid that others different from the holder can reproduce the crucial element of one's image right without the specific authorisation. Consequently, the capture, reproduction, or publication of any person's image will be considered as a violation of the fundamental right to reputation.

[33]See e.g. Palacios and Placer (2014), p. 46, where the authors argue that the right to reputation does not have an absolute character given the limitations foreseen in Art. 8 of the Organic Act 1/1982 of 5 May for the civil protection of Honour, Privacy and Own Image. Other Spanish scholars asserts that personality rights protect the person and her personality by granting absolute subjective rights which are established in Art. 1.1 of the Organic Act 1/1982. According to the latter line of though, on the one hand, Arts. 9.1 and 9.3 of the Organic Act 1/1982 provides the individual with the possibility of claiming remedies to recover the injured subjective right and, on the other hand, Arts. 1.3, 2.2 and 2.3 determine the scope and, more importantly, the limits to party autonomy. See e.g. Vendrell (2014), Chap. I, p. 4.

[34]Some scholars argue that despite one person can permit that a third party publish or use her image, the holder of the right to reputation will be the assignor of the exploitation rights. In short, only partial assignments are permitted. See e.g. Vendrell (2014), Chap. II, pp. 36ff.

[35]This principle 'cuts out across very different fundamental rights,' see Ramos (2017), pp. 1051–1053. In addition, some scholars argue that private autonomy is a fundamental right that derives from the right to liberty (Art. 5 ECHR), and others from the right to property (Art. 1 First Protocol to the ECHR). Under Spanish legal system, party autonomy is recognised as a general principle applicable to private relationship pursuant to Art. 1255 of the Spanish Civil Code of 1989 (hereinafter: Civil Code), but also is connected to human dignity and the free development of the personality, fundamental rights set out in Art. 10 of the Spanish Constitution.

prerogatives can be subject to such consent, the TC, in its 117/1994 decision, clearly held that:

> ...it is clear that, by authorisation of the holder, the image can become an autonomous patrimonial value subject to the economic traffic and this situation leads to confusion about whether the enforceability of the revocation is limited to the scope of the contract or whether it derives from the personality right... but it must be affirmed that in such cases the consent may also be revoked, because the personality right prevails over other rights created by contractual assignments.[36]

The TC accepted the existence of a patrimonial aspect which is inherent to the personality right, so rather than dividing the right to reputation into an extra-patrimonial right (or privacy right) and a patrimonial right,[37] one can say that the TC recognised the right to reputation as an autonomous right, with a dual nature.[38] Unlike other jurisdictions, the Spanish legal system seems not to recognise an autonomous right of publicity, but rather to include the possibility to control the commercial use of one's identity as part of the personality right,[39] although the moral component of the right cannot be transferred.[40]

Yet, if the right to image and reputation is a single right, then it will be difficult to dissociate its extra-patrimonial and patrimonial aspects, and thus one aspect is affected by the other. Thus, one question remains: whether the right holder may have recourse to the special procedure set out in the Organic Act 1/1982 if, say, the

---

[36]STC 117/1994, of 25 April, FJ 3. The TC considered that both the patrimonial aspect of the right to reputation and the constitutional aspect fall under Art. 18 of the Spanish Constitution.

[37]Unlike Spanish legal system, the approach governing the French law is strongly dualistic; it is expressed through a clear separation of patrimonial and extra-patrimonial aspects of a person's image, rather than establishing an exclusive autonomous right to reputation comprising both dignity and patrimonial interests. The legal regime of the right to reputation under the Spanish law also differs from the American right of publicity, which is conceived as an independent right not linked to the right of privacy. The prior right protects the patrimonial dimension of one's person (i.e., publication of pictures) whilst the right of privacy is connected to the more personal aspects of a person (i.e., intimacy, privacy, dignity). See also Moskalenko (2015), pp. 113–120.

[38]STC 17/1994, of 17 February, where the TC declares that the protection of economic values, patrimonial or commercial, despite worthy of protection, falls out the scope of fundamental rights...through the holder's authorisation, one's image can turn into an autonomous patrimonial right which is incorporated into the economic traffic.

[39]This approach differs from the right of publicity, a right created in the United States (common law jurisdiction) whose scope, although varies widely between States, comprises the protection of unpermitted commercial uses of one's image. The term 'commercial' is defined narrowly, referring to promotion or advertising. See e.g. Barnett (1999), pp. 555–571; Vendrell (2014), Chap. I, pp. 37–39. See also Moskalenko (2015), pp. 113–120, where the author cites that according to North American jurisprudence and scholars 'the inherent right of every human being to control the commercial use of his or her identity' is called right of publicity. In other civil law traditions, personality rights are conceived as rights that 'concern the various aspects of the human personality' and seek to safeguard the 'dignity' aspect of a person's image, see e.g. Mak (2007), p. 57.

[40]See e.g. Vendrell (2014), Chap. I: The subjective right acquired through the assignment of one's right to reputation is a right to exploit the physical features of a person, but never the personality right; Igartua (1991), pp. 18–20.

assignee of commercial rights has overreached in its faculties causing damage to the right holder's right to reputation, or whether she would only have the possibility to rely on the Private law of contracts.[41]

In these situations, it is important to determine (1) whether there was an unauthorised use of someone's image for commercial use, exploitation or similar purposes; and (2) whether, in the presence of valid initial consent, there was an overreach of the faculties granted under the contract, or a subsequent revocation of consent.

On the first issue, it is generally understood that consent given through a contract or authorisation excludes illegitimate interference with the holder's image rights to the extent that such consent is binding. Specifically, the existence of consent through an agreement denotes the holder's will to dispose of his right commercially.[42] Yet, the existence of consent does not fully exclude the possibility of illegitimate interference. Accordingly, the consent given by any person related to an agreement for the commercial use of one's image can be revoked by the holder.[43] This may be justified by the fact that 'contractual' consent does not exclude the interest beneath (right to reputation) because the commercial use of one's image may affect the privacy and dignity of the holder.[44] More simply, Fundamental rights primarily protect party autonomy; this comprises not only the possibility to consent, but also to withdraw that consent. The assumption seems to be that the binding nature, or enforceability, of a promise consented to is less

---

[41] In STS 400/2001, ECLI: ES:TS:2001:3256, the holder assigned to a beneficiary some pictures in exchange for economic compensation. The beneficiary used the pictures overreaching the terms included in the assignment agreement. The TS ruled that the reproduction, transfer or disclosure of the pictures contravening the agreement did not undermine the holder's image, and thus constituted a case of breach of contract, a conclusion drawn from the holder's express consent. However, the existence of a contract would automatically not to lead to conclude that there is no violation of fundamental rights. It will depend on the activities consented by the holder.

[42] Clavería (1994), pp. 40–44, the author argues that, where there is contractual consent to permits illegitimate interferences with the holder's image rights, rather than the revocation of consent provided for in Art. 2.3 of the Organic Act 1/1982, the laws and rules that govern contracts must be applied so that, so in case of overreach the dispute shall be resolved in accordance with the rules of breach of contract. This line of reasoning posits that the commercial use of the right to reputation does not disrupt the 'moral dimension' of the right, since the values involved in a contract are different from those when there is a mere tolerance, so in case of overreach the dispute shall be resolved in accordance with the rules of breach of contract. The Spanish TS tends to link the existence of a contract for the commercial use of one's image to the application of the termination of contracts and remedies stated in the Civil Code. See also STS 830/2008, ECLI: ES:TS:2008:4866; STS 152/2009, ECLI: ES:TS:2009:613.

[43] Art. 2.3 of the Organic Act 1/1982. From a contractual perspective, the revocation of consent stated in the Organic Act 1/1982 may be understood as an exception to Art. 1256 of the Civil Code, which provides that: 'the validity and the fulfilment of the contracts cannot be left to the discretion of one of the contracting parties'.

[44] STS 266/2016, ECLI: ES:TS:2016:1779, FJ 9, where the TS rules that the revocation of consent not only impinges on the right to reputation as a patrimonial right, but also as a fundamental right.

grounded on party autonomy than on the protection of legitimate expectations of the other party. Thus, revocation of consent is a faculty established by the Organic Act, whose aim is to protect the party who chooses to recover control over her image rights, whilst the legitimate expectations of the holder's counterpart is protected by the holder's duty to pay damages arising from those legitimate expectations.[45]

The decision by the TC in 117/1994 focused on (1) whether consent was validly exercised, and if so (2) the efficacy of the revocation of consent.[46] On the first point, the TC held that 'contractual' consent does not exclude the possibility of revocation, which may be exercised at any time. In addition, the TC stressed that despite the consent given for the commercial use of one's image the right to reputation continues to be an autonomous right, which, as a personality right, prevails over other rights arising from assignment contracts.[47] On the second point, the TC's ruling was, however, more nuanced, since it stated that the revocation was not made effective given that the most important phases of the process for the publication of the pictures had been carried out at the time when the revocation was made. We will examine this second issue in the following section.

Consequently, the TC considered that the revocation of consent, although validly exercised, was not effective, since publication can be considered a 'process' with different stages, many of which had already taken place, which meant that the harmful 'act' in itself, had occurred, and the revocation arrived too late. It was not the last time that the Spanish courts mitigated the efficacy of a revocation when there were third parties involved, with some later decision by the Supreme Court (also

---

[45]Palacios and Placer (2014), p. 11. See e.g. Oliveira (2017), p. 264:

> [t]he right to personal development aims both at the protection of personality, since this free development of one's personality is an essential part of one's individuality, and also at the protection of freedom, in the sense that every human being should be able to decide how to act. Therefore, the right to personal development should also be protected within the relations between private persons; in order to guarantee that, the right to personal development is now also recognised as a personality right, which benefits from the protection and remedies stipulated in Civil law.

[46]STC 117/1994, of 25 April, FJ 4.

[47]Alternatively, both the moral and economic dimensions of the right of own image must be subject to Art. 18 of the Spanish Constitution. The validity of the revocation of consent in cases where the parties have signed a contract for the commercial use and exploitation of the holder's image right has been a controversial issue. On the one hand, some scholars advocate for the exclusion of the revocation of consent provided for in Art. 2.3 of the Organic Law when the parties signed a contract based on the idea that such contract should be subject to the rules of the Contract law. On the other hand, other scholars argue that the mere organisation of the holder-authoriser's interests and of the authorised by means of a contract cannot mean the automatic exclusion of the right to revocation of the consent in Art. 2.3 of the Organic Act 1/1982. A different matter may be ascertaining the specific legal nature that covers the exercise of this power when the consent is given in a long-term contract. See Santos (2004), pp. 2–10.

'Tribunal Supremo' or 'TS') holding that there was no illegitimate interference, although on different grounds.[48]

The reasoning by the courts (i.e. the TS and the TC which validated it) was somewhat baffling, for what exactly does it mean that publication is a 'process', which could be considered as 'practically concluded' when the revocation took place (considering that the magazines were not yet in circulation)? The reasoning would have made sense if the actress had consented the distribution of pictures by second assignees and revoked that consent *after* Playboy magazine had distributed pieces including the actress' pictures, because the harm would have already been done. However, since those acts had not yet been completed, the actress should have been able validly to revoke her consent and request that Playboy cease the marketing of the magazines.[49] Playboy magazine could then have claimed damages for the costs incurred and its legitimate expectations against the actress, but also against the photographer, in accordance with the terms and conditions of the contract. One wonders what the Courts' reasoning would entail in today's publishing business, where the 'process' between thinking and publishing (provided there is any thinking involved) can take seconds, minutes, hours, or days at the most.

The TC then compounded the above reasoning with a discussion of whether Playboy magazine had exceeded the scope of consent, a point where the decision stands even less the test of time. Adding insult to injury, the TC upheld the TS's reasoning, which held that when she consented, the celebrity *had to assume* that, given their nature, the photographs would 'without a shadow of a doubt', be published in magazines like the defendant's, 'and accompanied by comments like those denounced' by the plaintiff. Those comments, the Court held, were not in themselves 'defamatory', since, in the Court's view, 'despite their obvious crudeness and lack of elegance', they were not *offensive* to the plaintiff. Instead, 'within their style', they 'pretended to be a gross praise for the plaintiff's physical attributes.'[50]

Thus, to summarise the Court's view, 'she had it coming'. Apparently, once a woman decides to pose nude, she must necessarily expect her image to be distributed through any means, platform, and accompanied by any kind of comments. The sky, or male testosterone, seem to be the limit, with little that the woman can do about it. Thus, despite formally relying on consent and revocation, the decision (or at least this last part) did not see the issue in terms of party autonomy and self-determination, which would grant the right holder control over the process, but of honour and reputation, where the holder can merely choose to keep it or lose it. It is facile, to look at past decisions with the benefit of hindsight. But since those decisions can be binding precedents, it is important to at least point out where they got it wrong.

---

[48]STS 400/2001, ECLI: ES:TS:2001:3256, where a first assignee transferred the holder's image to a second assignee that published the pictures without the holder's consent. It is noteworthy that the second assignee was not responsible according to the TS on the grounds that, when the picture was published, it had already been disclosed previously and the holder had permitted such publication. Thus, when the second magazine published the picture, it had 'lost the connection with the holder.

[49]Vendrell (2014), Chap. II, p. 72.

[50]STC 117/1994, of 25 April, FJ 9.

3.2   What the Court Did Not Say: Multi-Party Relations, Private Law Logic and Fundamental Rights

The TC's view in its decision 117/1994 can be criticised for failing to grasp some basic elements of personality rights. However, an excessive focus on those short-comings risks overlooking other issues, which, at least in our view, were what was really at stake in the decision. This was the clash between the rights of privacy and self-image, and the (economic and expression) entitlements of third parties, who had acquired the commercial rights to exploit the pictures. In both the decisions by the TC and TS, two key elements were (1) the damages that could be suffered by Playboy in case the publication was stopped; and (2) the fact that Playboy was not the original signatory of the assignment contract, but rather a third party assignee, which had led the Supreme Court to apply the 'good faith third party' doctrine (*tercero de buena fe*).[51]

At first glance, one may consider anathema to apply doctrines conceived to facilitate the circulation of goods and rights with economic value to personality rights, with their morally absolute contents. But we argue that the application of at least the logic underpinning such doctrines can help to assess a trade-off between rights for which broader techniques, such as 'balancing' or 'proportionality' may be unsuited.

So how should one proceed to analyse the case using a Private law logic, where Fundamental rights can be inserted? In our view, one must first consider (1), the original agreement between the parties, and thereafter (2), the position of the third-party assignee.

(1) The agreement between the parties was 'original' in more than one sense of the word, because: (a) it was a non-remunerated agreement, subject to the condition that the photographer would disseminate the pictures for journalistic purposes; and (b) it failed further to define the terms of such dissemination. Let us examine these elements in turn.

   (a) The parties' (photographer and actress) undertaking, was not even characterised as a 'contract' but as an 'agreement',[52] due to the parties' supposedly aligned interests i.e. profit-based commercial distribution (pho-tographer and Playboy) and public relevance (actress). This also meant that there was no pre-agreed remuneration between the original parties, since the

---

[51] See STC 117/1994, of 25 April, narrative of the facts, para. 2, where the Court indicates that the court of first instance, the appellate court, and the Supreme Court had all three discussed the 'good faith third party' nature of Playboy magazine, and the substantial sums disbursed by it.

[52] Díez-Picazo (1996), p. 77, the author distinguishes contract and agreement depending on the interests of the parties; so, if the parties' interests are conflicting, there is a contract (i.e., a contract for the sale of a house); if the parties' interests share the same objective, there is an agreement (i.e., in STC 117/1994, of 25 April, the actress and the photographer wanted, at the time when the agreement was concluded, to promote the nude pictures of the actress to gain benefits).

actress was supposed to obtain a 'material benefit' from the international nature of Playboy's promotion. Under Spanish Private law, whether an agreement is onerous or gratuitous depends on the economic structure of the transaction, and whether the subject of the contract is given as a 'condition or consideration' for performance, or whether one of the parties procures from the other purely a profit or advantage.[53] In this sense, it is not obvious whether the agreement was a contract or an 'onerous donation'[54]: notwithstanding that there was no *animus donandi*, there was an 'obligation' to distribute the holder's pictures. The photographer did not pay a price for them, and could conclude new assignment contracts commercially to exploit the pictures and receive money in return.[55] Onerous donations are gratuitous agreements governed by contract rules where the value of the condition or charge imposed by the donor undershoots the value of the transferred good.[56]

When rights are not transferred in exchange for consideration, it is easier to effect a revocation. Art. 647 of the Civil Code provides that in a donation the donor can revoke her consent if the recipient fails to comply with any of the conditions imposed by the donor.[57] Such revocation determines the 'supervening inefficacy of the donation' (*ineficacia sobrevenida de la donación*), which entails restitution to the donor of the donated property (or the value it had at the time when the donation was made)—an obligation of restitution that encompasses third-parties acting in good faith.[58] The

---

[53]Díez-Picazo (1996), pp. 82–84. The objective theory argues that what is important to ascertain whether an agreement is onerous or gratuitous is the economic structure of the act, without considering the special interests of each party (animus donandi), which are legally irrelevant, and it will be also important detect if there are patrimonial advantages for both parties or only for one of them, although when those advantages could sometimes be indirect. The subjective theory is followed by French scholars. According to this theory, an agreement will be onerous only where there is a generosity intention. See e.g. Díez-Picazo (1996), p. 84.

[54]Arts. 619 and 622 of the Civil Code.

[55]Actually, he received the payment of 1,000,000 of pesetas in return when he transferred the pictures to Playboy magazine.

[56]Díez-Picazo (1996), pp. 80–84.

[57]Cañizares et al. (2014), p. 55 et. seq.; Díez Picazo and Gullón (2015), p. 83; Lasarte (2016), pp. 172–174; Gitrama (1962), pp. 301–375. The author argues that the revocation of consent was appropriate in those cases where third parties are entitled to interfere the personal sphere of the holder as a result of the mere tolerance of the holder. On the other hand, for 'contractual cases', the author accepts the revocation of consent in contracts where the parties did not agree on a specific duration and/or where the parties have agreed that the holder could revoke his consent.

[58]The ruling in STS 900/2007, ECLI: ES:TS:2007:5413, the donor revoked his donation of some plots to the Ministry of Defence (recipient) of Spain because the recipient had breached the 'conditions' imposed by the donor when the Ministry transferred the plots to a company for housing construction. The two critical aspects examined by the TS were the following: (1) the donor's will, and (2) the consequences of the revocation of the donation when the recipient does not satisfy the 'mode or condition' imposed by the donor. In relation to the first issue, the TS ruled in favour of the donor alleging that the donation was a modal (onerous) donation because the recipient accepted the

Supreme Court, in its ruling 900/2007, concluded that the revocation of a modal or onerous donation can be applied retrospectively (*ex tunc*), to restore each party's position to where it was before the donation was concluded. Through this ruling, the Court declared ineffective the agreement between the Ministry and the third party that had bought the plots,[59] and the plots were transferred back to the donor.[60]

It seems that respect of the donor's will is the cornerstone of the revocation of modal, or conditional, donations.[61] Thus, if the use or destination of the property donated is not related to the purpose of the donation and, by extension, the donor's will, the 'condition' imposed by the donor would be breached by the recipient.[62]

(b) In relation to this, and in second place, let us consider the terms under which the dissemination had to take place in the case subject to analysis. This would supposedly take place for broadly defined 'journalistic purposes', without a pre-specified contract period, or a definition of the terms and conditions under which the holder's pictures could be transferred to third parties for their commercial exploitation. Such vagueness is one of the typical conditions that justify a narrow reading of the agreement.[63] The commercial use of the contents should be limited to the minimum use that

---

destination imposed by the donor: the plot would be used as a military camp. The 'conditions' were unfulfilled by the Ministry since the plots were sold to a third party, regardless the Ministry's will to use the economic benefit received in return to achieve Ministry's interests. If the property donated is immoveable property, Art. 34 of Ley Hipotecaria will be applicable. In addition, the TS stressed that the argument alleged by recipient that the economic benefit received for the sale would be destined for the interests of the Ministry of Defence, must be rejected because the donation purpose (modo) was never intended for that destination, but for military use. See STS 900/2007, ECLI: ES: TS:2007:5413, FJ 3.

[59]Martínez de Aguirre Aldaz et al. (2016), pp. 467–471; Díez-Picazo (1995), pp. 449–469; Lasarte (2016), pp. 153–156.

[60]STS 900/2007, ECLI: ES:TS:2007:5413. The TS rules that the breach of the conditions by the recipient opens the door to terminate the contract and bring the immoveable property back to the donor, although the donated property had been acquired by a third person (i.e., *ex tunc* enforceability).

[61]Cañizares et al. (2014), pp. 55ff.

[62]Some scholars argue the revocation of consent provision avoids the possibility that the recipient could continue to enjoy the property donated by the donor after the former had breached the 'conditions' imposed by the donor (*enriquecimiento sin causa*). See e.g. in Cañizares et al. (2014), pp. 55 et. seq. The right to revoke the donation avoids the situation where the recipient has breached the condition required by the donor, but such recipient still enjoys the ownership of the property donated, what is namely unjust enrichment under the Spanish Civil law.

[63]Palacios and Placer (2014), p. 20. In those agreements where there is not a contract period included, the construction of consent should be narrow. In STS 266/2016, ECLI: ES:TS:2016:1779, the TS rules in a case where the assignment of a model's right to reputation was signed for one year with the possibility of renewal, that the faculty to exercise the revocation of consent 'at any time' necessarily excludes not only 'agreements in perpetuity', but also 'a period of subjection to the agreement', even if in the latter situation the holder must pay damages to the other contracting party.

derives from the circumstances of each case.[64] Thus, it is safe to conclude that, under the circumstances of the case, the agreement concluded between the parties was one where, given the vagueness of the agreement, consent should have been narrowly construed. More recent case law by the Spanish Supreme Court has held that an authorisation to permit the 'distribution' of one's picture does not entitle an absolute right in favour of the assignee to use the holder's right to any subsequent commercial purpose.[65]

(2) We now reach a critical point when we analyse the position of the third-party assignee. The nature of the relationship between the original assignor and assignee (or transferor and transferee) and its impact on the revocability of the assignment—or the scope of subsequent assignments—would lose importance if there were, superimposed to it, a rule that protected the third party, or second assignee, regardless of the initial arrangement. Civil courts, including the Supreme Court, seemed to insist on this point to protect the legitimate expectations of Playboy magazine. The question is: was this reasoning correct?

The courts' reasoning on the 'good faith third party' comes from the field of movable objects, where 'good faith' and 'just title' have traditionally been the two main requirements to protect the possession and ownership of a third party.[66] In case of personal rights and obligations the general rules are those on the assignment of receivables, and of debts or contracts, all of which contain stronger protective rules in favour of the debtor. Assignments of contracts or debts require the consent of the initial counterparty,[67] whereas assignments of receivables can be done without the debtor's consent, but the latter can exercise all the exceptions she had against the assignor.[68] The use of the logic of the transfer of movables in the context of personal rights and obligations is very limited, and its clearest example is the law of bills of exchange, cheques, notes, and other promises incorporated into a document with a specific form regulated by the law, whereby the limited protection of the initial

---

[64]STS 490/2002, ECLI: ES:TS:2002:2935 and STS 754/2008, ECLI: ES:TS:2008:4310, where the TS respectively held that the authorisation for the publication of a picture in a magazine does not entail subsequent publications by other magazines; and the consent to use a picture for the promotion of a product by a company does not include the permission to use the picture in a different promotion of a similar product by other company. In this vein, see e.g. Martínez (2011).

[65]STS 490/2002, ECLI: ES:TS:2002:2935. The TS held that despite the constitutional dimension of the right to reputation had not been undermined, authorisation gave to a magazine for the publication of pictures does not entail further authorisation to transfer the right to a third person. Accordingly, the consent to use a photo for a promotion does not include its use for the advertising campaign of a third-party.

[66]Art. 464 of the Civil Code. There are two different theories that defend the position of third parties acting in good faith: (1) when those parties possess 'proper title' (traditional theory), or (2) non-revocability principle should apply to the extent that the third party acted in good faith, except when the real owner has illegally been deprived of his property.

[67]See STS 37/2016, ECLI: ES:TS:2016:332, which, in case of doubt, classified the transaction as an assignment of contract.

[68]Pantaleón (1988), p. 1053.

debtor is justified by a protection of the economic traffic, by an 'exorbitant' regime of creditor protection, which operates as an exception to the general rules.[69]

Spanish Courts applied the logic of the 'good faith third party' in the understanding that the pictures were intellectual *property*, and thus property. However, the logic of facilitating the circulation of movables through the protection of third parties is that the emphasis on the thing dilutes the importance of the personal element, or the personal relationship between the original parties. This is only partly present in the case of intellectual property, whereby the 'moral right' allows the author of a work, among other things, to withdraw the work from economic traffic because of changes in her intellectual or moral convictions, provided she compensates the damages suffered to the holders of exploitation rights[70] (whoever they may be).

Considering the above, let us return to the circumstances of the case. The photographer who was the original assignee presumably transferred the possession of the pictures to Playboy magazine, but this did not automatically render the latter a 'good faith third party'. A transfer of possession of nude pictures is not equivalent to the transfer of a ton of bricks or bananas. The pictures were susceptible to have a strong impact in the subject's dignity,[71] an obvious and salient factor that no one can ignore, least of all a company whose business is to exploit rights over this kind of material for profit.

If Playboy magazine was not a 'good faith third party', it should have been expected to look at the circumstances under which the pictures were conveyed, or, in short, the conditions under which the rights of exploitation were transferred. Had they done so, they would have seen the original agreement, which contemplated 'the international distribution of some pictures for journalistic purposes'. Unlike the parties who signed the agreement, the relevant surrounding circumstances could not be considered for interpretative purposes. But saying that such a broadly drafted clause entitles the assignee to re-assign the rights of exploitation, without the need for authorisation or consultation with the holder of the right, is a stretch. Since a waiver of Fundamental rights requires a 'clear and unequivocal' consent,[72] there is, in our view, no way that a reasonable person could interpret this as a blank authorisation to distribute the pictures for any purpose, and for an indeterminate time.

---

[69]Paz-Ares (1995), pp. 81–106.

[70]Art. 14 6°, of the Spanish Intellectual Property Act.

[71]STC 14/2003, of 19 February, ascertains that the purpose of the right is to safeguard a personal space to freely decide the development of one's personality and, ultimately, a necessary environment to maintain a minimum quality of human life. This right is preserved by recognising the faculty of avoiding the illegitimate dissemination of one's physical aspect, since it constitutes the first element that shapes the privacy of any person. Thus, the fundamental value of human dignity is also preserved. In this vein, STC 72/2007; of 16 April.

[72]STS 266/2016, ECLI: ES:TS:2016:1779, FJ 9, 'the revocation of consent also affects the right to reputation as a fundamental right, that is, not exclusively in its purely patrimonial aspect or dimension, since the Organic Act 1/1982 grants an essential attribute'.

Some recent rulings by the Spanish Supreme Court show that the courts have refined their approach. In decision 266/2016,[73] an appeal was filed by a model who had signed an agreement for the commercial use of pictures and videos with erotic content by a 'second assignee' (*tercero de buena fe*) which had acquired the right to exploit the model's image. The model and a photographer signed a contract for the commercial use of her image with a one-year duration with the possibility of renewal, and a clause that allowed the assignee to continue using the assigned rights even after the contract was terminated, for any reason. The model terminated the contract and revoked her consent. The Supreme Court held that the clause that permitted the photographer to continue using the assigned rights after termination was null and void for being abusive, and that the revocation by the right holder of her consent was enforceable against the third party (second assignee), which bore secondary/subsidiary liability for the illegitimate interference, since it had been duly informed of the revocation.

Cases that offer a slightly contrasting perspective include the Supreme Court decision 754/2008[74] where the TS examined whether the damages suffered by a model, whose image was published by REVLON (second assignee) without the holder's express consent, were beyond the economic dimension of the right to reputation, undermining its *constitutional* dimension. Although the model was not involved in the negotiations between the photographer and REVLON, the damages caused by that situation had to be compensated. Yet, such compensation had to be made in accordance with terms of the contract and the corresponding provisions in the Civil Code, since the Court held that there was no illegitimate interference from a constitutional perspective.[75] In its 152/2009 decision, the Supreme Court held that there was no illegitimate interference with a football player's Fundamental right to image and reputation.[76] If this view by the TS turned also out to be the same view held by the Constitutional Court, third-party assignees of image exploitation rights

---

[73]See STS 1500/2016; ECLI: ES:TS:2016:1500.

[74]STS 754/2008, ECLI: ES:TS:2008:4310, an appeal was filed by a model alleging that a photographer had transferred the rights to exploit her image to REVLON, and this company had used her image without her consent. The TS focused on two points: (1) the consent given, and (2) the exploitation of the model's right by the REVLON.

[75]STS 754/2008, ECLI: ES:TS:2008:4310, the TS did not find that REVLON was responsible for the damages suffered by the model. In addition, the TS found that REVLON was not responsible given that, when REVLON acquired the pictures from the photographer, the express assignment seemed to be done by the owner of the pictures (the model), so that this situation created an appearance in which REVLON could trust.

[76]In similar terms STS 152/2009, ECLI: ES:TS:2009:613, where the Court's ruling established that the assignment of a football player's image to a company that published an advertisement that focused on the sport skills of the football player was not an illegitimate interference with the football player's fundamental right to reputation. In this vein, the assignee who makes an assignment that exceeds the powers assigned by contract, is convicted in accordance with Art. 1101 of the Civil Code, provided that the claimant proves the effective existence of the damage. It does not play, therefore, the provision of Art. 9.3 of the Organic Law 1/1982 in virtue of which the existence of the damage is presumed whenever the existence of the interference is proven.

can fail the test of 'good faith third parties' even in cases where their actions are not susceptible to impinge upon the Fundamental rights of the original holder. This reinforces our main argument: in cases of particularly sensitive content that is so susceptible to impinge upon a party's Fundamental rights, consent cannot be taken for granted, least of all as an open-ended blank check to do as one pleases with the content.

This helps to establish the points of connection between the logic of Private law and the logic of Fundamental rights, as well as their divergences. Consent is clearly the first common element to adjudicate over both the transfer of (economic) rights and the waiver of (fundamental) rights. Although despite the common importance of the holder's consent, a problem with this consent—for example, a lack of express authorisation for a second transfer of rights, or a revocation of consent—may result in a breach of private (contract) rights without there being a breach of Fundamental rights.

It is our view that a second commonality in the treatment of multi-party situations is that the position of third-party assignees depends partly, but not entirely, on the original consent. Alternatively, it also depends on how its position is characterised, the assumptions that the third party could make about the transfer of rights, and the behaviour of the holder of the right *vis-à-vis* the third party. This logic lay in the background of the Constitutional Court decision 117/1994, and in the express reasoning of the prior decision by the Supreme Court (as well as in later decisions by the latter Court). Such commonality should not blur the boundaries between private rights and Fundamental rights, which can still have defined contours. When Fundamental rights are involved this will typically result from a situation delicate enough as to exclude the presumption of good faith of the third party more often than when only private rights are involved. But since the management of one's public image is significantly more complex today than it has ever been, we cannot exclude the possibility that a certain use by a third party of the rights of image of a person constitutes an interference with those Fundamental rights without the third party being necessarily aware of that. In that case, a more evolved doctrine is necessary to consider the role of third-party assignees with more precision than the usual recourse to 'balancing and proportionality'. Far from diminishing the importance of Funda-mental rights we would acknowledge the nature and complexity of the real conflict.

4   Conclusions

Fundamental rights and Private law rights have important commonalities. Consent is key to explain the notion of 'autonomy' that lies at the core of both subsets of rights, and agreements based on consent are crucial to regulate the exercise of both private rights and Fundamental rights. Yet, Fundamental rights do not behave in the same way private ones do. Contracts that waive Fundamental rights are valid, but they are not enforceable like those concerning private rights, since consent needs to remain revocable.

This can be a source of friction in cases where (1) agreements have both a private dimension (economic rights of exploitation are transferred), and a Fundamental rights dimension (Fundamental rights are waived) since a single contract has varying degrees of enforceability; and (2) third parties are involved, since the protection of the third party may vary depending on whether the holder exercises a private right or a Fundamental right. If both sets of factors are present in a single case, this will likely be complex.

Such complexity, however, is compounded by the courts' reluctance to acknowledge that, in such cases, there is a genuine conflict of rights, and one whose profile needs a logic more sophisticated than a general appeal to the balancing of rights, or proportionality. In the decision by the Spanish Constitutional Court 117/1994, the case that serves as a basis for this work, this failure to acknowledge the real problem led to a decision that was flawed not only in its conclusions and assumptions, but also in its logic.

The ruling by the Spanish Constitutional Court was based on a distinction between 'validity' of the revocation of consent, and its 'effectiveness', but relied on the fact that the publishing process was already in motion—a weak argument— and the fact that, by broadly consenting initially to the distribution of the pictures, the actress had also consented to their distribution in any form, publication, and with any kind of written commentary. This was plainly wrong, since, when considering interferences with personality rights, as is the case with moral rights, it is context that matters.

The Courts would have done better to say that the case raised a conflict between the actress's right to image, and the magazine's freedoms of expression and to conduct business, in a case where the latter was a third party—an aspect that should have also been considered when weighing one right against the other. Despite this, we believe that the only correct conclusion was to hold that consent by the actress was too broadly formulated to meet the requirement of 'clear and unequivocal' that must inform a waiver of Fundamental rights, at least in what concerned the transfer of rights to third parties. We also contend that the magazine was not a 'good faith' third party, and nevertheless that this status was not key to the conclusion, other than to require that it was properly notified of the revocation.

Still, clarifying both elements should have helped the courts devise a roadmap to identify cases where the conclusion might have been different. It would have also helped to address the questions that are bound to arise once the basic aspects are clear, for example, when assessing the third party's 'good faith' status, should one adopt her perspective, the right holder's perspective, or a neutral perspective to determine the images/contents and use that are susceptible to injure the holder's Fundamental rights, and thereby require of the assignee a greater degree of diligence? What kind of inquiry is required of a third-party assignee, should the damages resulting from the assignee's expectations be limited to ensure that the right holder can effectively exercise her rights? Acknowledging the importance of consent, its revocation, and multi-party relationships in assessing conflicts of Fundamental rights, and their interplay with Private law rights can only improve the understanding of both.

The market for personal image is but one example where social interactions are becoming more complex. Part of that complexity lies in the fact that the use of rights is becoming more fluid, and more parties can interact between themselves. This makes it a priority to deal with the situations where those parties' interests collide, which, for those cases where Fundamental rights are involved, should be an even higher priority. Alas, the current approach is inadequate to deal with these problems, and, worse still, some precedents tend to sidestep the issue. We are taking a first step towards giving the issue the importance it deserves.

References

Baines B, Rubio-Marín R (2010) The gender of constitutional jurisprudence. CUP, New York

Barnett SR (1999) 'The Right to One's Own Image': publicity and privacy rights in the United States and Spain. Am J Comp Law 47(4):555–571

Brownsword R (2003) Freedom of contract, human rights and human dignity. In: Feldman D, Barak-Erez D (eds) Human rights in private haw. Hart, Oxford, pp 181–200

Cañizares L et al (2014) El contrato de Donación. Donaciones por razón de matrimonio. In: Yzquierdo M et al (coord.) Tomo II. Contratos de Finalidad Traslativa del Dominio (II) [(Civiles, Mercantiles, Públicos, Laborales e Internacionales, con sus implicaciones tributarias)]. Thomsons-Reuters, Madrid

Clavería LH (1994) Negocios jurídicos de disposición sobre los derechos al honor, intimidad y la propia imagen'. ADC 1994(3):40–44

Collins H (2012) On the (in)compatibility of human rights discourse and private law. LSE Soc Econ Work Pap 2012(2):25–32

Díez Picazo L, Gullón A (2015) Sistema de Derecho Civil, vol 2(2). Civitas, Madrid

Díez-Picazo L (1995) Fundamentos del Derecho Civil Patrimonial. Las Relaciones Jurídico-Reales. El Registro de la Propiedad. La Posesión, vol 3. Civitas, Madrid

Díez-Picazo L (1996) Fundamentos del Derecho Civil Patrimonial. Introducción a la Teoría del Contrato, vol 1. Civitas, Madrid

Dworkin R (1986) Rights as trumps. In: Waldron J (ed) Theories of rights. OUP, Oxford, pp 153–167

Gitrama M (1962) Imagen (Derecho a la propia). VV. AA. Nueva Enciclopedia Jurídica. Seix, Barcelona

Igartua F (1991) La apropiación comercial de la imagen y nombre ajenos. Tecnos, Madrid

Lasarte C (2016) Contratos. Principios de Derecho Civil III, 18th edn. Marcial Pons, Madrid

Mak C (2007) Fundamental rights in European contract law: a comparison of the impact of fundamental rights on contractual relationships in Germany, the Netherlands, Italy and England. Digital Academic Repository, Amsterdam

Martínez P (2011) Cesión inconsentida de la imagen para un uso comercial distinto del autorizado. Aranzadi civil-mercantil 1(5):85–124

Martínez de Aguirre Aldaz C et al (2016) Curso de Derecho Civil: Derecho de Obligaciones, vol 1. Teoría General de la Obligación y el Contrato, vol 2, 4th edn. Edisofer, Madrid

Moskalenko K (2015) The right of publicity in the USA, the EU, and Ukraine. Int Comp Jurisprud 1 (2):113–120

Oliveira ED (2017) Agreements on personality rights in the Portuguese system. In: Siliquini-Cinelli L, Hutchison A (eds) The constitutional dimension of contract law. Springer, Dordrecht, pp 249–269

Palacios MD, Placer FJ (2014) El Contrato de Cesión de Derechos de Imagen. In: Yzquierdo Tolsada M (ed) CONTRATOS- Tomo XII. Contratos sobre bienes inmateriales (I) [(Civiles,

Mercantiles, Públicos, Laborales e Internacionales, con sus implicaciones tributarias)]. Thomson Reuters, Madrid

Pantaleón F (1988) Cesión de créditos. ADC (4):1033–1132

Paz-Ares JC (1995) La desincorporación de los títulos-valor (el marco conceptual de las anotaciones en cuenta). El nuevo mercado de valores: seminario sobre el nuevo Derecho español y europeo del Mercado de Valores. Consejo General del Notariado, pp 81–106

Pinker S (2011) The better angels of our nature. Penguin Books, New York

Ramos D (2017) Do fundamental rights conflict with private law? Eur Rev Private Law 2017 (6):1051–1081

Raz J (1975) Practical reason and norms. Hutchinson & Co, London

Salvador P (1990) El Mercado de las Ideas. Centro de Estudios Políticos y Constitucionales, Madrid, pp 380–382

Santos JM (2004) Derecho a la propia imagen de artistas e intérpretes y explotación inconsentida de una obra audiovisual. Repertorio Arazandi del Tribunal Constitucional 2004(7):2–10

Vendrell C (2014) El mercado de los derechos de imagen. El consentimiento o autorización para la intromisión en los derechos de la personalidad y la transmisión de derechos de imagen. Thomson Reuters, Pamplona

Regulation of Contracts According to 'Public Policy or Good Morals' in Japan: Focusing on the Relationship Between the General Provision in the Civil Code and the Fundamental Rights in the Constitution

Hiroyuki Kihara

Abstract Article 90 of the Japanese Civil Code provides that, 'A juristic act with any purpose which is against public policy or good morals is void.' Contract is one of the components of these 'juristic acts'. Any contract or any term of a contract may thus be totally or partially void if it is deemed to be 'against public policy or good morals.' This provision is one of the main tools by which unfair contracts or unfair terms are regulated. However, it is inherently a general provision, the application of which is subject to judicial discretion. A lack of clarity hence remains in setting the scope and criteria for such application. In addition, public policy or good morals is considered to be an exceptional tool by which to intervene in the areas of private autonomy or freedom of contract to accomplish contractual justice. Some sort of justification or reasoning for its application is thus required, examples of which may include constitutional values such as Human rights.

This chapter examines the regulation of contracts according to public policy or good morals in Japan. First, the relationship between the Constitution and the Civil Code in Japan is discussed. The aim is to clarify the basic mechanism involved in the application of public policy or good morals, with consideration of the associated constitutional values. Second, justification for its application in relation to constitutional and other values is discussed with reference to existing academic opinions and relevant case law.

1 Introduction

This chapter addressing aspects of Japanese Contract law from the perspective of Constitutional law has two main aims. First, to analyse the impact of constitutional values on the Contract law dimension from a general point of view; and, second, to investigate how Constitutional law has affected a specific topic within Contract law.

H. Kihara (✉)
Faculty of Law, Asia University, Tokyo, Japan
e-mail: hykihara@asia-u.ac.jp

In general, the first half of this chapter describes the relationship between the Constitution and the Civil Code in Japan. Japan belongs to the Civil law or continental law system, and Contract law is included in the Civil Code, which was enacted in 1898. However, the current Constitution was enacted in 1946. This section thus provides a brief history of the enactment of these two laws, including their respective structures and characteristics. The priority relationship between these laws will also be discussed; specifically, whether the Civil Code and the Constitution are of equal stature, or whether the Civil Code is subordinate to the Constitution. The purpose of this section is to provide readers with the basic knowledge necessary for understanding Japanese law. This section is also an important precursor to the specific issue addressed in the second half of this paper, as it is impossible to examine any specific topic or issue without an understanding of the framework of the national legal system.

The specific issue addressed in the second half of this chapter is entitled, 'Regulation of Contracts by Public Policy or Good Morals in Japan'. Article 90 of the Japanese Civil Code provides that, 'A juristic act with any purpose which is against public policy or good morals is void.' Contract is one of the components of these 'juristic acts'. Any contract or any term of a contract may thus be totally or partially void if it is deemed to be 'against public policy or good morals.' This provision is one of the main tools used to regulate unfair contracts or unfair terms. However, it is inherently a general provision, and hence subject to judicial discretion in its application. A lack of clarity thus remains regarding the scope and criteria by which it is applied. In addition, public policy or good morals are considered an exceptional tool by which to intervene in the area of private autonomy or freedom of contract to accomplish contractual justice. Some sort of justification or reasoning for its application is therefore required, an example of which includes constitutional values such as Human rights. The justification of applying public policy or good morals in relation to constitutional and other values is discussed in this section with reference to existing academic opinions and related case law.

Finally, by way of conclusion, this chapter examines the question of how the Constitution has influenced Contract law in Japan. A summary will be given of a general issue concerning the relationship between the Constitution and the Civil Code (Contract law), and a specific issue relating to public policy or good morals.

2   General Issue: The Constitution and the Civil Code in Japan

This section outlines the history,[1] structure and characteristics of the Constitution and the Civil Code. The relationship between these two bodies of law will also be examined.

2.1   Historical Overview

From 1603 to 1868, the Tokugawa shogunate reigned over one quarter of Japan as a unified government, subduing the feudal lords in the other parts of the country. During this 260-year reign, known as the 'Edo Period', a seclusion policy was adopted. The country was almost completely isolated, with overseas travel forbidden and trading with other countries limited to China and the Netherlands at the Port of Nagasaki. However, in 1853, Commodore Matthew Perry and the 'Black Ship' of the U.S. Navy arrived in Japan, pressuring the Tokugawa shogunate to open its ports to trade. Eventually, the Tokugawa shogunate accepted their proposal and concluded commercial treaties with the United States, England, France, Russia and the Netherlands. These political pressures led to the reversion of sovereign power from the Tokugawa shogunate to the Emperor in 1867, marking the end of the Edo Period.

Emperor Meiji moved from Kyoto to Tokyo, which became the new capital of Japan and remains so until this day. The Meiji government was established in 1868. Emperor Meiji was installed as the ruling power, a position he held until his death in 1912. The years 1868–1912 is known as the 'Meiji Period', during which the new government attempted to abolish the treaties concluded between the Tokugawa shogunate and Western countries, which were unfair to Japan in terms of tariffs and extraterritoriality jurisdiction. Under these treaties, Japan had no autonomy to determine the rate of tax on imported goods, and no right to arrest and try foreigners committing crimes in Japan. To regain independence from the Western countries and to conclude new and more equal treaties, the Government sought to establish modern legal systems and to enact the Constitution, the Civil Code, the Penal Code and other important codes and statutes. The Constitution of the Empire of Japan, enacted in 1889 (hereinafter, 'the 1889 Constitution'), was modelled after the Prussian Constitution in Germany. Similarly, the Civil Code, enacted in 1898, was strongly influenced by both German and French law.[2]

Simultaneously, the Government implemented modernization measures to close the gap between Japan and the Western countries, both economically and militarily. After victories in the First Sino-Japanese War (1894–1895) and the Russo-Japanese

---

[1]For details, see Oda (2009), pp. 14–25; Matsui (2011), pp. 4–18.
[2]Oda (2009), pp. 113–117.

War (1904–1905), Japan gained control of Taiwan, Korea, and the southern half of Sakhalin. Thereafter, the country was recognized as a major global power.

The years 1912–1926 under Emperor Taisho is known as the 'Taisho Period'. When World War I broke out in 1914, Japan joined the Allied forces and expanded its territories in the East. The 'Showa Period' under Emperor Showa began in 1926. To overcome the serious social impact of the 1929 Great Depression, Japan embarked on its expansionist foreign policy. In 1931, it occupied Manchuria and built the puppet state of Manchukuo. Japan continued to invade other parts of China, leading to the outbreak of the Second Sino-Japanese War in 1937 that foreshadowed World War II in Asia, which began on a large scale when Japan attacked Pearl Harbor in 1941 and the U.S. retaliated. Japan fought against the Allied Powers in Asia, invading Southeast Asian countries with the aim of building a 'Great East Asia Co-Prosperity Sphere.' However, in 1945, following its unconditional surrender to the Allied Powers, Japan lost all territories acquired after 1894.

Following the end of World War II, Japan was occupied by the Allied Powers until 1952. The basic policy of the Supreme Commander for the Allied Powers (SCAP) was to demilitarize and democratize Japan. As a part of this occupation, the current Constitution, modelled after the United States Constitution, was enacted in 1946 (hereinafter, 'the 1946 Constitution') as an amendment to the 1889 Constitution. Power was allocated to the people, with the Emperor retained only as 'the symbol of the State and of the unity of the people', without any political power (Article 1). As part of the same democratization process, family law under the Civil Code was also subject to significant revisions. In 1951, Japan signed the San Francisco Peace Treaty with 48 nations, ending the state of war that still existed between them. The treaty came into effect in 1952, marking the end of SCAP occupation and allowing Japan to regain its independence. In 1956, Japan resumed its place in the world community by becoming a member of the United Nations. By 1964, Japan was admitted to the OECD, confirming its status as an advanced country attained because of its rapid growth since independence. The 'Showa Period', which oversaw the country's highest levels of post-war economic growth, ended with the death of Emperor Showa in 1989. This was followed by the 'Heisei Period', which has endured until the present day. However, Emperor Heisei has already announced his abdication, with the new era set to begin in 2019.

2.2   The Structure of the Constitution

2.2.1   Structure and Characteristics

The 1946 Constitution is composed of the following 11 chapters and 103 articles: The Emperor (Chp.1, Arts.1–8), Renunciation of War (Chp.2, Art.9), Rights and Duties of the People (Chp.3, Arts.10–40), The Diet (Chp.4, Arts.41–64), The Cabinet (Chp.5, Arts.65–75), Judiciary (Chp.6, Arts.76–82), Finance (Chp.7, Arts.83–91), Local Self-Government (Chp.8, Arts.92–95), Amendments (Chp.9,

Art.96), Supreme Law (Chp.10, Arts.97–99), and Supplementary Provisions (Chp.11, Arts.100–103).

The 1889 Constitution was based on the sovereignty and power of the Emperor. While true that there were some provisions for the separation of powers, parliamentary democracy, and the protection of certain individual Human rights, these were significantly limited. Human rights, for instance, were granted by the Emperor to his 'subjects', and only protected within the confines of statutes.[3] When a statute to restrict such Human rights was enacted, the judiciary hence did not have any power to review the constitutionality therein.

Many of these difficulties were resolved by the enactment of the 1946 Constitution. Now, sovereignty rested with the people (Article 1), the separation of powers was clearly established (Chapters 4, 5, and 6), and fundamental human rights were well respected and provided (Chapter 3), with the courts granted the power of constitutional review (Article 81). The conditions of pacifism also contained a provision for the renouncement of war, with the maintenance of armed forces being prohibited (Chapter 2, Article 9).

2.2.2 Human Rights Under the Constitution

Fundamental Human rights are provided in Chapter 3 of the 1946 Constitution. These rights can be classified or categorized as follows.[4]

First, there is a basic and comprehensive provision protecting Human rights and human dignity. Article 13 (Right of respect for individuals and life, freedom, and the pursuit of happiness) is considered to be part of this provision. It states that, 'All people shall be respected as individuals. Their rights to life, liberty, and the pursuit of happiness shall, to the extent that they do not interfere with public welfare, be the supreme consideration in legislation and in other governmental affairs.'

Second, 'equality rights' are protected under the Constitution. According to Article 14 (Equality under the law), paragraph 1, 'All people are equal under the law and there shall be no discrimination in political, economic or social relations because of race, creed, sex, social status or family origin.' There are also some related provisions in Article 24 (Equality of dignity of the individual and the sexes in family life) and Article 26 (Right to receive an equal education).

Third, a distinction is made between 'mental freedom' and 'economic freedom.' The former is related to personal freedom of the mind and its expression, such as freedom of thought and conscience (Article 19), freedom of religion (Article 20), freedom of assembly, association and expression (Article 21), and academic freedom (Article 23). The latter is related to the freedom to choose an occupation (Article 22) and the right to property (Article 29), both of which are generally considered to fall under the protection of economic freedom. It should be noted that mental freedoms

---

[3]Matsui (2011), p. 9.
[4]For details, see Matsui (2011), pp. 154–158; Oda (2009), pp. 90–108.

have stronger judicial protection than economic freedoms from the viewpoint of respecting human dignity and democratic society. The danger of infringement of the former is thus greater than for the latter.[5]

Fourth, there is a category called 'social rights', which requires the government to provide certain services, such as the right to live, the country's obligation to secure the right to live (Article 25), the right to receive education (Article 26), the right of labour, standards of working conditions, and the prohibition of child exploitation (Article 27), the worker's right to organize, the right to bargain collectively, and other rights to act collectively (Article 28).

Finally, there is a category called 'procedural rights', such as the voting right (Article 15), the right of access to a trial (Article 32), the rights of criminal suspects and defendants (Articles 31, 33 to 40), and the right to seek compensation for infringement of rights by the state and public entities (Article 17).

As described above, the 1946 Constitution develops the protection of human rights. However, it should be noted that these rights are not always considered an absolute right. As seen in Article 13 of the Constitution quoted above, human rights can be restricted 'to the extent that [they do] not interfere with public welfare.' As indicated by the Supreme Court in 1949, three years after the Constitution was enacted, this public welfare restriction may be applied to all of the human rights protected under the Constitution.[6]

2.3   The Structure of the Civil Code

The Civil Code in Japan is composed of five parts and more than 1000 articles. Following the German *Pandekten* system, it uses a logical process to derive specific rules from general principles and basic common rules. Part I of the code, the 'General Part', stipulates the basic rules of Civil law, covering the capacity of natural and juridical persons, juristic acts, agency and prescription. In Part I, the Civil Code provides some general principles in the form of a blanket clause. The court has broad discretion in the application of these principles, with the aim of reaching fair and equitable solutions. Both the 'good faith' principle in Article 1(2) and 'public policy or good morals' in Article 90 play an important role in the regulation of unfair terms. Part II of the code covers property and real security rights. Part III covers the law of rights and obligations resulting from contracts, management of another person's affairs (*negotiorum gestio*), unjust enrichment, and tort. Part IV, meanwhile, deals with family relations, and Part V prescribes the law of succession.

As mentioned above, the present civil code was enacted in 1898. It was only after World War II that Parts IV and V, dealing with family law and succession, respectively, were thoroughly amended, with a view to promoting democracy in family

---

[5]Matsui (2011), p. 157.
[6]Judgment of Supreme Court, Grand Bench, 18 May 1949, *Keishu* 3-839.

relationships and fostering gender equality. Parts I, II and III have not been substantially amended since their enactment. However, serious efforts have been made since 2006 to revise some related chapters of Part I and III dealing with Contract law. The 'Working Group on the Civil code (Law of Obligations)' was established in November 2009 under the Legislative Council of the Ministry of Justice. In March 2015, the 'Bill to Amend the Civil code' was finally submitted to the National Diet. Promulgated on June 2, 2017 it is set to take effect within three years from that day.

2.4 The Relationship Between the Constitution and the Civil Code

2.4.1 Primacy of the Constitution and Legislation

The Constitution is the supreme law of the nation (Article 98(1) of the 1946 Constitution). Therefore, no law, ordinance, imperial rescript or other act of government, or part thereof, contrary to the provisions hereof, shall have legal force or validity. Therefore, any comprehensive codes such as the Civil Code and any statutes are inferior to the Constitution. The superiority of the treaty over the Constitution is a source of debate. According to Article 98(2) of the 1946 Constitution, 'The treaties concluded by Japan and established laws of nations shall be faithfully observed.' However, it has become majority opinion that the Constitution is superior to treaties because the Constitution requires a strict revision procedure and cannot be easily abolished by a treaty.

Judges are expected to apply and interpret the law in each case, but not to create legal rules of their own. The doctrine of precedent (*Stare Decisis*) is not admitted in Japan. The binding force of judgment is limited, and the only provision referring to this point is found in Article 4 of the Court Act, which states that, 'A conclusion in a judgment of a higher instance court shall bind the lower instance courts with respect to the case concerned.' However, in practice, the judgment of the Supreme Court has a strong influence over subsequent judgments, either in the Supreme Court itself or in the lower courts.

2.4.2 The Question of Constitutional Effects Among Private Parties

In Japan, there is also a distinction between Public law and Private law. Public law, such as the Constitution, governs the relationship of state organizations with the nation and the people. Conversely, Private law, such as the Civil Code, governs the relationship between private parties. Whether or not the Constitution shall bind or be applied to private parties has thus long been a subject of debate[7] among constitutional scholars.[8] There are three theories about this:

(i) 'no direct application theory' (*Mukoryoku-setsu*), which supports the conclusion that the Constitution has no effect on private parties. This classical theory, which is based on the strict distinction between Public and Private law, assumes that there is no room for the Constitution to be applied to private parties;

(ii) 'direct application theory' (*Chokusetsu-Tekeiyo-Setsu*), which states that the provision of Fundamental rights under the Constitution shall be directly applied to disputes and relationships between private parties. This theory is based on the idea that the Human rights provisions of the Constitution should also affect private parties, as social power linked to the emergence of large-scale private organizations has been a phenomenon since the late nineteenth century;

(iii) 'indirect application theory' (*Kansetsu-Tekeiyo-Setsu*), which states that constitutional effects shall be indirectly applied to private parties through the application of the general provisions of the Civil Code. This theory assumes that, while respecting the distinction between Public law and Private law, the Constitution merely serves to govern the nation. The Constitution's human rights provisions will thus be applied to private parties through the application of private law. Conversely, this theory offers an intermediate perspective of theories (i) and (ii).

Not many constitutional scholars currently support 'no direct application theory'. The conclusion that there is no constitutional remedy in the field of Private law based on the public/private law distinction leads to both a denial of the Constitution as the upper norm of all laws and to the flouting of the purpose of Article 98 of the Constitution.

On the other hand, according to 'direct application theory', which allows the Constitution to take a direct effect in the field of Private law, the distinction between Public and Private law is inevitably ignored, with 'private autonomy'—the basic principle of Private law—being effectively denied. In addition, the conclusion that the court can derive relief directly from the constitution almost eliminates the legislative function of the Diet.

'Indirect application theory' is thus supported by case law[9] and the majority of constitutional scholars. According to this theory, the Constitution will provide the judicial review on judgments applied by the court under the general provisions of the Civil Code for private disputes. This is based on the principle that the Civil Code is also subject to the Constitution, while simultaneously respecting the distinction between Public and Private law.

---

[7]Matsui (2011), pp. 162–163.

[8]For a comprehensive and detailed study of this issue, see Kimizuka (2008).

[9]Judgment of Supreme Court, Grand Bench, 12 December 1973, *Minshu* 27-1536. See also Matsui (2011), pp. 162, 178.

2.4.3 The Response from Civil Law Scholars

However, most Civil law scholars are not interested in the above-mentioned issue discussed by constitutional scholars; neither do they share their opinions on the subject. The positions of several Civil law scholars are as follows.[10] First, that the Civil Code and the Constitution function in parallel[11]: they have the same substantial value and realize their own independent value in each area. Second, that the Civil Code and the Constitution overlap[12]: the Civil Code functions as the governing principle for society, while the Constitution functions as the governing principle of both the nation and society. Both of these opinions are based on the distinction between Public and Private law. However, unlike opinions held by constitutional scholars, these do not acknowledge the so-called priority relationship between the Constitution and the Civil Code.

However, an opinion[13] has recently emerged among Civil law scholars that it is not possible to ignore this priority relationship, and that the Civil Code is subject to the Constitution, as long as the Civil Code remains the law. Accordingly, the function of the Civil Code should be to manifest and specify the Fundamental rights under the Constitution. This opinion may be seen as linked to the 'indirect application theory' adopted by constitutional scholars.

3 Specific Issue: Regulation of Contracts by Public Policy

3.1 Justification for Applying Public Policy

Based on the above explanation of the Constitution and the Civil Code in Japan, this section will focus on the public policy or good morals provided in Article 90 of the Civil Code, with consideration given to the Human rights provisions in the 1946 Constitution.

3.1.1 The Drafter's Position

The drafters of the Civil Code in the Meiji period understood the contents of 'public policy or good morals' in a limited manner. That is, freedom of contract was taken as

---

[10]For an analysis of the major theories about the relationship between the Civil Code and the Constitution, see Miyazawa (2015).

[11]Hoshino (1994), p. 8; Hoshino and Higuchi (2001), p. 2; Hoshino (2006), pp. 27–28. See also Miyazawa (2015), p. 156.

[12]Omura (2001), p. 128; Omura (2009), p. 438. See also Miyazawa (2015), p. 156.

[13]Yamamoto (1998), p. 261; Yamamoto (2000b), p. 100; Yamamoto (2002), p. 232; Yamamoto (2004), p. 59. See also Miyazawa (2015), p. 158.

the guiding principle, with a contract becoming void for reasons of public policy or good morals only in exceptional circumstances. The scope of Article 90 of the Civil Code was hence limited to issues relating to administrative policy, justice and customs.

3.1.2 The Traditional View on Public Policy: Fundamental Ideal Theory

The theory which reversed the above principle and the exception was proposed by Dr. Suekawa[14] and Dr. Wagatsuma.[15] Public policy or good morals is not an exception that limits individual intention; rather, it is a fundamental idea governing the law, and freedom of contract is only recognized within that framework. This is known as 'fundamental ideal theory' (*Konpon Rinen Setsu*).

The background to this theory is the transformation of the philosophy of 'from individualism to communitarianism' by which individual freedom is accepted, as long as it adheres to the philosophy of the community. Public policy or good morals is thus not an exception that limits individual intentions; rather, it constitutes a principle by which the contents of freedom of contract are inherently defined by public policy or good morals. Alternatively, the fundamental principles—i.e., the philosophy of the national community—governing the law are conceived in the first instance, with the understanding that private autonomy and contractual freedom are incorporated into this philosophy.

3.2 Categorising Case Law on Public Policy or Good Morals

According to this view, the issue of public policy or good morals is required to clarify the demands of the community philosophy for each specific scenario. Dr. Wagatsuma has categorized related cases, and his examination of this national community philosophy resulted in the following seven types[16]:

Type 1. an act contrary to humanity
Type 2. an act against justice
Type 3. an act seeking excessive profits (*bouri koui*)
Type 4. an act that severely restricts personal freedom
Type 5. restrictions on freedom of business
Type 6. disposition of property that is the basis of survival
Type 7. gambling contracts

---

[14]Suekawa (1962, originally 1922), p. 11.

[15]Wagatsuma (1966, originally 1923), p. 121.

[16]Wagatsuma (1965), pp. 271–282.

3.2.1 The Development of Case Law

This is not a comprehensive list of every case involving public policy or good morals violation. In addition, as described later,[17] cases have emerged that do not fall under any of these types. However, the purpose of this chapter is not to introduce all types of public policy or good morals, but rather to clarify the relationship between the main types of public policy or good morals and the Human rights guaranteed by the Constitution. It is hence sufficient to use this list as a premise for discussion.

3.2.1.1 Type 1 (an Act Contrary to Humanity)

This type is primarily concerned with violations of parent-child court orders and marital status. As an example of the former,[18] the contract between the father and the child stating that the mother and the child do not live together after the parents' divorce was deemed contrary to public policy or good morals, and hence invalid. Most cases of the latter are related to mistress contracts (a contract for maintaining male-female relationships outside of marriage).

3.2.1.2 Type 2 (an Act Against Justice)

This type is related to contracts inducing, promoting or participating in crimes and other unlawful acts, such as money lending contracts for the purpose of illegal gambling, murder contracts, and the purchase of stolen goods.

3.2.1.3 Type 3 (an Act Seeking Excessive Profits)

Originally deriving from the doctrine of *laesio enormis*[19] in Roman law and subsequently codified in Article 138(2) of the German Civil Code (BGB), this is a specific doctrine established by case law in application of Article 90 that deems 'an act seeking excessive profits (*bouri koui*)' to be a transgression 'against public policy or good morals.' While there is no explicit provision in the Japanese Civil Code, the concept was introduced in the country by legal scholars[20] in the 1920s and eventually approved by a Judgment of the Great Court of Judicature on May 1st 1934.[21] According to this case, an act whereby a party 'obtains excessive profits by taking

---

[17]See Sect. 3.2.2.

[18]Judgment of the Great Court of Judicature, March 25, 1899, *Minroku* 5-3-37.

[19]For detail of *laesio enormis*, see, e.g., Zimmermann (1990, 1996), p. 259; Kötz and Flessner (1997), p. 130.

[20]Wagatsuma (1966, originally 1923), p. 150.

[21]Judgment of the Great Court of Judicature May 1, 1934, *Minshu* 13-875.

advantage of another person's poverty, carelessness, or non-experience' is considered against public policy or good morals, and consequentially declared void.
Nonetheless, it is necessary to satisfy both an objective requirement (*'obtaining
excessive profits'*) and a subjective requirement (*'taking advantage of another
person's poverty, carelessness, or non-experience'*) for such an act to be
rendered void.

This doctrine has been widely accepted and applied in several areas.[22] Traditionally, courts have emphasized its objective requirement. Loan contracts with extraor-
dinarily high interest rates and sales contracts with excessive liquidated damages or
penalties have been invalidated as a result. However, recently, in addition to the
above cases, courts have tended to emphasize the doctrine's subjective component.
For example, if there is unfairness in the method of concluding a contract, such as
unfair solicitation in the case of a consumer contract, the entire contract is deemed
invalid.[23]

3.2.1.4 Type 4 (an Act That Severely Restricts Personal Freedom)

A typical example of this type of act is a '*geishogi* (geisha and prostitutes) contract':
a compulsory labour contract for a young woman that was widely seen in Japanese
society until the 1950s. Under this contract, parents enter into loan agreements by
which borrowed money is repaid from the income that their daughter makes as a
geishogi. This contract relates partly to money lending and partly to employment.
Before World War II, the latter part was invalid, but the former part was considered
valid. However, since the parents' debt remained, this resulted in the conclusion of
another *geishogi* contract to repay the debt. In 1955, therefore, the Supreme Court[24]
also denied the money loan component of this type of contract. The request for the
return of money from the lender by applying the 'clean hand' principle under Article
708 of the Civil Code[25] was similarly denied.

3.2.1.5 Type 5 (Restrictions on Freedom of Business)

Prior to World War II, contracts restricting the freedom of business, such as a
covenant not to compete, were often an issue. The obligation to avoid competition
is normally concluded between companies and employees, or between employers

---

[22]For a detailed analysis of related case law, see, e.g., Omura (1995), pp. 273–358.

[23]Judgment of Supreme Court, May 29, 1986, *Hanji* 1196-102.

[24]Judgment of Supreme Court, October 7, 1955, *Minshu* 9-11-1616.

[25]Article 708 (Performance for Illegal Causes) of the Civil code: 'A person who has tendered
performance of an obligation for an illegal cause may not demand the return of the thing tendered;
provided, however, that this shall not apply if the illegal cause existed solely in relation to the
Beneficiary.'

and employees, and an employee is obliged not to operate the same type of business after retirement using the knowledge and experience gained in the course of their work. This obligation becomes an issue, as it limits the freedom of the employee's economic activities.

3.2.1.6 Type 6 (Disposition of Property Which Is the Basis of Survival)

There is one reported case which states that a contract to abandon irrigation water when payment of road repair expenses is delayed is against public policy or good morals.[26]

3.2.1.7 Type 7 (Contract on Gambling)

There are several cases related to speculative transactions and cases concerning monetary consumption and borrowing contracts related to gambling. Regarding the former,[27] public policy or good morals are not violated as long as the transactions do not violate laws such as the Exchange Act. Regarding the latter,[28] such contracts are against public policy or good morals.

3.2.2 The Transition to Case Law[29]

There were many pre-war cases affirming violations of public policy or good morals concerning Type 1 (an act contrary to humanity), Type 4 (an act that severely restricts personal freedom) and Type 7 (contract on gambling). However, while there are many cases relating to Type 3 (an act seeking excessive profits), the number of cases affirming violations is small.

After World War II, the number of cases featuring the above types decreased. Type 1, for instance, dropped to less than 10% of the total. In addition, the *geishogi* contract, as mentioned previously,[30] which was regarded as a Type 4 problem, was resolved by the 1955 Supreme Court decision. As such, Type 3 cases accounted for nearly half of the total, with nearly half of the cases affirming public policy or good morals violations relating to this type. In addition, affirmative cases of Type

---

[26]Judgment of the Great Court of Judicature, May 18, 1944, *Minshu* 23-308.

[27]Judgment of Osaka District Court, February 15, 1917 *Shinbun* 1238-25; Judgment of Osaka District Court, October 27, 1917, *Shinbun* 1334-21.

[28]Judgment of Appeal Court, July 27, 1921, *Shinbun* 1915-19; Judgment of the Great Court of Judicature, March 30, 1938, *Minshu* 17-578.

[29]For details, see Kimizuka (2008), pp. 30–31; Nakaya (1995), pp. 65–88; Yamamoto (2000a), pp. 123–190; Yamamoto (2005), pp. 389–393.

[30]See Sect. 3.2.1.4.

5 (restrictions on freedom of business) increased, mainly in relation to labour contracts.

Furthermore, there was a case in which acts that conflict with constitutional values—a new type, not on the existing list—were deemed a violation of public policy or good morals. In 1981, the Supreme Court[31] ruled that a different retirement age system depending on gender (60 for males and 55 for females) violated the principle of equality pursuant to Article 14 of the Constitution. Simultaneously, unreasonable discrimination based on gender was also recognized as a violation of public policy or good morals under Article 90 of the Civil Code. 'Equal Employment Opportunity Law' subsequently came into force in 1986, and discrimination against women based on gender was clearly prohibited under Article 8(1) of this law.

As described above, issues such as business or labour relations, formerly regarded as matters of public policy or good morals, have been recategorized as economic activities in recent years. New types of issue have also begun to emerge, such as Human rights conflicts. The scope of application of Article 90 of the Civil Code is thus expanding, and, as discussed below, academics have attempted to reconstruct the theory of public policy or good morals based on case law.

3.3 Two Recent Opinions: Reconstructing the Principles of Public Policy

In recent years, based on the recognition that the scope of public policy or good morals is expanding under case law, two theories have emerged that attempt to reconstruct this issue using a different justification. The first, advocated by Professor Omura, focuses on contractual justice and economic public policy.[32] The second, proposed by Professor Yamamoto, emphasizes the relationship with fundamental rights under the Constitution.[33]

3.3.1 Reconstruction Based on Contractual Justice

According to Professor Omura, public policy or good morals was originally an exceptional tool by which to restrict private autonomy and freedom of contract. Today, however, its scope of application is expanding. Therefore, he asserts, public policy or good morals violations are in place not only to limit the freedom of contract exceptionally—i.e., not only to protect political and family order—but also to ensure

[31]Judgment of Supreme Court, March 24, 1981, *Minshu* 35-2-300.
[32]For a summary, see Omura (2005), p. 15; Yamamoto (2005), pp. 394–396. For details, see Omura (1995); Omura (1999), pp. 163–204.
[33]Yamamoto (1993, 2000a, 2005).

fairness in the execution of contracts (contractual justice) and to protect the interests of the parties engaged in transaction and competition (economic public order).[34]

The purposes of protecting disadvantaged parties under 'contractual justice', and of maintaining trading order ('economic public theory'), are common to both Public and Private law, and may be seen as reinforcing one another.[35] Therefore, in cases where the provisions of Public law are violated, it may be necessary to deny the legal effect under Private law. In addition, the idea that Public law and Private law are not qualitatively different is linked to the concept of Contract justice. There is commonality, in that both should embody contractual justice. Therefore, as long as Public law regulations embody contract justice, it is actively incorporated into public policy or good morals.[36]

3.3.2 Reconstruction Based on Fundamental Rights

According to Professor Yamamoto, violations of public policy or good morals were originally considered as an exceptional case for maintaining social order. Today, however, the idea exists that it should be seen as actively playing the role of Fundamental rights protection.[37] A private person therefore has the right to demand the protection of their Fundamental rights by the state, with any contract which causes the infringement of these Fundamental rights being considered a public policy or good morals violation.[38]

3.3.2.1 Private Autonomy and Freedom of Contract

This theory reconstructs public policy or good morals from the viewpoint of guaranteeing the constitutional right (i.e., the Fundamental right). The key to its reconstruction is in understanding that Article 90 of the Civil Code limits private autonomy and freedom of contract. Professor Yamamoto presents a different stance to the conventionally held view of the relationship between private autonomy and contractual freedom.[39]

First, in Civil law, private autonomy has been understood traditionally as 'freedom for individuals to form their own legal relationships by their own will.' As juristic acts are the means by which this freedom is realized, private autonomy has therefore been equated with freedom of contract.

---

[34]Omura (2005), p. 16.

[35]Yamamoto (2005), p. 396.

[36]Omura (1999), pp. 201–202.

[37]Yamamoto (2000a), pp. 32–35; Yamamoto (2005), p. 398; Omura (2005), p. 16.

[38]Omura (2005), p. 16.

[39]Yamamoto (2005), pp. 396–398.

However, according to Professor Yamamoto, the starting point of private autonomy lies in 'determining oneself' in everyday life, which means 'freedom to form a self-living space actively'.[40] Therefore, if we reallocate the meaning of private autonomy in this broad sense, the justifications extend beyond Private law and are required by the Constitution. Conversely, private autonomy and self-determination rights can be regarded as Fundamental rights guaranteed by Article 13 of the Constitution (the right to pursue happiness).[41]

However, if nobody was permitted to infringe upon the private autonomy and self-determination rights of others, it would be impossible to do anything that was likely to affect others. In our society, it is impossible to ignore or not influence others when forming our living spaces. Consent is required, and the tool which makes it possible is a 'contract'. Freedom of contract can thus be positioned as the freedom to employ this type of contract system.[42]

As a result, freedom of contract is also regarded as constitutional freedom.[43] The passive aspect of freedom of contract is the realization of our freedom to formulate our own living spaces actively and by contract. Further, this formulation is based on private autonomy, which is a constitutional freedom. In addition, the positive aspect of freedom of contract, which approves the rights to ensure that the other party enforces contracts, is also a constitutional freedom to guarantee private autonomy. Private autonomy cannot be realized if the other party does not have to perform his or her contractual duty. In this sense, freedom of contract is hence a constitutional freedom pursuant to Article 13 of the Constitution.[44]

3.3.2.2 Position of Public Policy or Good Morals

If both private autonomy and freedom of contract are Fundamental rights under Article 13 of the Constitution, Article 90 of the Civil Code is regarded as legislation that restricts these fundamental rights.[45] As such, when courts interpret and apply public policy or good morals under Article 90, a constitutional interpretation is required. This is not deemed to be unreasonable intervention against private autonomy and freedom of contract, as these are considered a Fundamental right.

There are two reasons justifying this intervention.[46] First, the state has an obligation to protect the fundamental rights of individuals from infringement by others. Constraining the Fundamental rights of perpetrators to fulfil this state's obligation to protect the rights of others may also be justifiable. Second, the state

---

[40]Ibid., p. 397.
[41]Ibid., p. 397.
[42]Ibid., p. 398.
[43]Ibid., p. 398.
[44]Ibid., p. 398.
[45]Ibid., p. 398.
[46]Ibid., pp. 398–399.

has an obligation to take various measures to ensure that Fundamental rights are better realized, even if the rights of individuals are not infringed. This may also be a reason justifying the constraint of Fundamental rights. However, it is essential that the correct policymaking decisions are made regarding the extent to which these Fundamental rights are supported. In principle, legislators are required to make such decisions democratically.

3.4 Relationship with Constitutional Values

3.4.1 Criticisms of Yamamoto's Opinion

For the broader concerns addressed by this chapter, it is important to consider the appropriateness of Professor Yamamoto's above-mentioned stance.

Professor Yamamoto's opinion is linked to 'indirect application theory,[47]' whereby the function of Article 90 of the Civil Code is to manifest and specify fundamental human rights under the Constitution. More specifically, the provision of public policy or good morals in Article 90 is a tool by which to restrict private autonomy and freedom of contract. However, on the other hand, private autonomy is deemed to be an aspect of self-determination rights. Similarly, freedom of contract is considered a constitutional freedom. These are Fundamental rights guaranteed by Article 13 of the Constitution (right to pursue happiness).[48] Therefore, in applying Article 90 of the Civil Code, a constitutional interpretation is required to avoid unreasonable intervention affecting these fundamental rights.

Some criticisms have also been levelled against Professor Yamamoto's proposed framework that considers the Fundamental rights under the Constitution when judging public policy or good morals. First, constitutional scholars[49] have observed that Professor Yamamoto relies on Article 13 of the Constitution, which takes a comprehensive Fundamental right as the basis for adjusting public policy or good morals issues under the Constitution. However, it is rather the case that rationale for the protection for each Human right is separately prescribed by the Constitution.[50] For example, a contract to create a political association is guaranteed under Article 21 of the Constitution[51]; a contract concerning the family is guaranteed under Article 24[52]; and a contract to form a labour union is guaranteed under Article 28.[53] Moreover, the contents and nature of Human rights, the scope and extent of the

---

[47] See Sect. 2.4.2.

[48] See Sect. 2.2.2.

[49] Kimizuka (2008), pp. 202–205.

[50] Ibid., p. 203.

[51] See Sect. 2.2.2.

[52] See Sect. 2.2.2.

[53] See Sect. 2.2.2.

guarantee, and the criteria of the judicial review all differ according to the individual articles.[54] Nevertheless, Professor Yamamoto seeks to explain all issues pertaining to Article 90 of the Civil Code—an abstract, general provision—using Article 13 of the Constitution, which states the fundamental right in its most abstract terms.

Second, even assuming that not only Article 13 of the Constitution but all constitutional rights are considered, the question arises as to whether the constitutional fundamental rights correspond to the wide variety of social orders provided under Article 90 of the Civil Code.[55] For example, in the case of infringement of contract freedom, competition orders, labour orders and consumer orders may become issues, with the decision framework and consideration factors differing for each. Similarly, human rights are not necessarily confirmed, and there are strong rights and weak rights. In some cases, a right may be insufficiently developed to provide adequate legal protection to determine a social order. Therefore, while Human rights can be included in social orders, the inverse cannot be taken to be true.[56]

3.4.2 Case Law Analysis

Based on the above criticism, we will verify whether the Fundamental rights of the Constitution can correspond with a social order that is problematic in terms of public policy or good morals. Several related cases will be cited.

3.4.2.1 Article 24 of the Constitution

Article 24 (Equality of dignity of the individual and the sexes in family life) of the Constitution provides that '(1) Marriage shall be based only on the mutual consent of both sexes and it shall be maintained through mutual cooperation with the equal rights of husband and wife as a basis. (2) With regard to choice of spouse, property rights, inheritance, choice of domicile, divorce and other matters pertaining to marriage and the family, laws shall be enacted from the standpoint of individual dignity and the essential equality of the sexes.'

This provision is generally viewed as a declaration in support of monogamy. Therefore, according to Dr. Wagatsuma's list, Type 1 (an act contrary to humanity),[57] especially in cases of the violation of marital status, such as concluding a mistress contract, may also invalidate such a contract not only under Article 90 of the Civil Code but also under Article 24 of the Constitution. However, when examining related cases in detail, the decisions of the courts have not inevitably reflected this.

---

[54]Kimizuka (2008), p. 203.

[55]Morita (2003), p. 136.

[56]Ibid., p. 133.

[57]See Sect. 3.2.1.1.

While offering money aimed at continuing relations between males and females was deemed invalid,[58] similar offerings aimed at terminating relationships[59] or testamentary gifts aimed at preserving the lives of adulterous women[60] were deemed valid. It is hence not possible to justify all cases related to Type 1 above based on Article 24 of the Constitution.

3.4.2.2   Article 13 of the Constitution

Article 13 (Right of respect for individuals and life, freedom, and the pursuit of happiness) of the Constitution provides that, 'All people shall be respected as individuals. Their right to life, liberty, and the pursuit of happiness shall, to extent that it does not interfere with the public welfare, be the supreme consideration in legislation and in other governmental affairs.'

This provision attempts to secure the Human rights of life, liberty and the pursuit of happiness. Therefore, according to the list, acts related to Type 2 (an act against justice),[61] contracts related to murder and prostitution, and acts related to Type 6 (disposition of property which is the basis of survival)[62] can be understood as Human rights violations concerning life, body and health, as guaranteed under Article 13 of the Constitution.

Also, while not specifically included in Type 3 (an act seeking excessive profits),[63] there are some reported cases applying Article 90 to examine whether exemption clauses for transport companies are void. For example, there are cases applying Article 90 of the Civil Code to invalidate exemption clauses limiting the amount of damages for each passenger to 1 million yen,[64] or 6.15 million yen[65] in cases of fatal air transport accidents. These cases could be justified by Article 13 of the Constitution as violations of the Human right to life.

Generally, the above types of public policy or good morals violation are closely linked to the protection of Human rights guaranteed under Article 13 of the Constitution. These cases can also be easily justified under the Constitution.

---

[58]Judgment of the Great Court of Judicature, May 28, 1920, *Minroku* 26-773; Judgment of the Great Court of Judicature, October 23, 1934, *Shinbun* 3784-8.

[59]Judgment of the Great Court of Judicature, May 15, 1915, *Shinbun* 1031-27; Judgment of the Great Court of Judicature, March 25, 1899, *Minroku* 5-3-37.

[60]Judgment of Supreme Court, November 20, 1986, *Minshu* 40-7-1167.

[61]See Sect. 3.2.1.2.

[62]See Sect. 3.2.1.6.

[63]See Sect. 3.2.1.3.

[64]Judgment of Osaka District Court, June 12, 1967, *Kaminshu* 18-5=6-641.

[65]Judgment of Tokyo District Court, September 20, 1978, *Hanji* 911-14.

3.4.2.3   Article 18 of the Constitution

Article 18 (Freedom from slave restraint and hard labour) of the Constitution provides that, 'No person shall be held in bondage of any kind. Involuntary servitude, except as punishment for crime, is prohibited.'

As already mentioned in Type 4 (an act that severely restricts personal freedom),[66] the *geishogi* contract—the compulsory labour contract of a young woman—is rendered void by Article 90 of the Civil Code. However, it may also be possible to consider this contract 'unconstitutional' under Article 18 of the Constitution. Indeed, some constitutional scholars argue that there should be a direct application of Article 18 in this case, and that such a contract is unconstitutional as a result. However, this view is not necessarily shared by Civil law scholars and legal practitioners. Furthermore, even constitutional scholars who support indirect application theory do not believe that there is no need to allow the direct application of Article 18 of the Constitution. Rather, it is sufficient to invalidate these contracts based on Article 90 of the Civil Code or Article 5 of the Labour Standards Act.

3.4.2.4   Article 14(1) of the Constitution

Article 14 (1) of the Constitution provides for 'equality under the law' as follows: 'All people are equal under the law and there shall be no discrimination in political, economic or social relations because of race, creed, sex, social status or family origin.'

According to this provision, discrimination based on 'race, creed, sex, social status or family origin' shall be prohibited, as well as other forms of discrimination not explicitly listed in Article 14. However, those unlisted equality rights have weaker judicial protection than their listed equivalents.[67]

Regarding discrimination based on gender, which is a listed equality right, there are many reported cases in which different treatment according to gender shall render an employment contract void under Article 90 of the Civil Code,[68] including a marriage retirement system only for female employees[69]; a different retirement age system for male and female employees[70]; a different salary system for male and female employees[71]; and a different promotion system for male and female

---

[66]See Sect. 3.2.1.4.

[67]Kimizuka (2008), p. 285. See also Sect. 3.4.1.

[68]See also Sect. 3.2.2.

[69]Judgment of Tokyo District Court, December 20, 1966, *Rominshu* 17-6-1407.

[70]Judgment of Tokyo District Court, July 1, 1969, *Rominshu* 20-4-715; Judgment of Tokyo High Court, February 26, 1975, *Rominshu* 26-1-57; Judgment of Supreme Court, March 24, 1981, *Minshu* 35-2-300.

[71]Judgment of Sendai High Court, January 10, 1992, *Rominshu* 43-1-1.

employees.[72] In justification of these judgments, the courts also referred to Article 14 of the Constitution.

Regarding discrimination based on age, which is not a listed equality right, there are cases[73] in which the employment rule stipulating a retirement age of 55 years was deemed to not immediately violate Articles 13, 14, 25 and 27 of the Constitution, meaning it would therefore not be invalid according to Article 90 of the Civil Code. While this could be regarded as discrimination by age, it is difficult to argue that the constitution guarantees the right to employ the elderly without consideration of their advanced years.

Reference to these cases of discrimination in terms of gender and age allow us to conclude that the criteria of the Constitution and the Civil Code are in alignment.

3.4.2.5   Articles 22 and 29 of the Constitution

The Constitution protects the freedom to choose an occupation under Article 22 and the right to property under Article 29. These provisions are generally viewed as protecting economic freedom.[74]

Article 22 (1) provides that, 'Every person shall have freedom to choose and change his residence and to choose his occupation to the extent that it does not interfere with the public welfare.' Article 29 (1) provides that, 'The right to own or to hold property is inviolable.'

There are many reported cases related to Type 3 (an act seeking excessive profits),[75] which may also be considered a violation of economic freedom guaranteed by the Constitution. However, this constitutional value has never been subject to a court ruling in cases related to economic activities. These cases have been resolved exclusively based on an interpretation of the Civil Code and related special laws, without reference to the Constitution. As mentioned previously,[76] economic freedoms have weaker judicial protection than mental freedoms or equality rights. It is thus natural that the constitutional consideration has not been regarded as significant in the case of economic activity.

On the other hand, cases concerning Type 5 (restriction on freedom of business)[77] are also related to economic activities. However, these cases are discussed separately to the Type 3 cases above. Unlike ordinary commercial transactions, Type 5 is mainly targeted at labour contracts, and workers' retirement is often an issue. In these cases, the basic value of the Constitution and the Labour Law need to be

---

[72]Judgment of Tokyo District Court, July 4, 1990, *Rominshu* 41-4-513.

[73]Judgment of Tokyo District Court, September 29, 1994, *Hanji* 1509-3. See also Judgment of Supreme Court, Grand Bench, December 25, 1968, *Minshu* 22-13-3459.

[74]Matsui (2011), p. 157.

[75]See Sect. 3.2.1.3.

[76]See Sect. 2.2.2.

[77]See Sect. 3.2.1.5.

considered. For instance, there is a case[78] in which a promise of employment contracts restricting the employment of others was deemed to be against public policy or good morals under Articles 22, 27 and 13 of the Constitution. In another case,[79] an employee was dismissed 'when [he/she] tried to be hired elsewhere without approval by the company.' Again, the court deemed this to be in violation of public policy or good morals under Article 22 of the Constitution, and hence invalid. However, the courts have also ruled that restrictions on the region and the period for which business is forbidden are not against public policy or good morals.[80] Therefore, it is not possible to justify all cases related to Type 5 based only on Article 22 of the Constitution.

4 Conclusion

4.1 The General Issue

To analyse the impact of constitutional values on the Contract law dimension from a general point of view, it is necessary to examine the framework governing the national legal system, especially the priority relationship between the Constitution and the Civil Code. Therefore, the issue of 'constitutional effects among private parties'—i.e., whether or not the Constitution shall be bound or applied to private parties—becomes a point of debate.[81]

There are three main theories about this, with 'indirect application theory' being supported by case law and a majority of constitutional scholars. According to this theory, constitutional effects shall be indirectly applied to private parties through the application of general provisions in the Civil Code, and the Constitution will perform the judicial review of the judgment applied by the court to the general provisions of the Civil Code in the private dispute. This is based on the principle that the Civil Code is also subject to the Constitution, while respecting the distinction between Public and Private law.[82]

On the other hand, most Civil law scholars are not interested in this issue and do not share this opinion. The views expressed by several Civil law scholars are very simple. For instance, their position that the Civil Code and the Constitution enjoy a parallel or overlapping relationship. These opinions, which are based on the distinction between Public law and Private law, are not so conscious of the relationship

---

[78]Judgment of Hiroshima High Court, August 28, 1957, *Hanji* 132-16.

[79]Judgment of Tottori District Court, July 27, 1968, *Rominshu* 19-4-846.

[80]Judgment of the Great Court of Judicature, October 29, 1932, *Minshu* 11-1947; Judgment of Supreme Court, October 7, 1969, *Hanji* 575-35; Decision of Tokyo District Court, October 16, 1995, *Hanji* 1556-83.

[81]See Sect. 2.4.2.

[82]See Sect. 2.4.2.

between these two.[83] However, a new opinion has emerged stating that it is not possible to ignore this priority relationship, and that the Civil Code is subject to the Constitution as long as the former remains the law. Therefore, the civil code should function to manifest and specify Fundamental rights under the Constitution. This opinion is considered to be linked to the 'indirect application theory' frequently adopted by constitutional scholars.[84]

4.2 The Specific Issue

The regulation of contracts according to public policy or good morals under Article 90 of the Civil Code was our chosen topic by which to investigate the impact of Constitutional law on Contract law. This provision is one of the main tools for regulating unfair contracts or unfair terms. However, it is a general provision, the application of which is subject to judicial discretion. In recent years, the question of what constitutes a matter of public policy or good morals has led to the incorporation of economic activities including business relations and labour relations. New categories have also emerged, such as Human rights conflicts. Thus, the scope of application of Article 90 is expanding, and academics have attempted to reconstruct public policy or good morals based on existing case law.[85]

According to Professor Yamamoto, the provision of public policy or good morals in Article 90 of the Civil Code is a tool by which to restrict private autonomy and freedom of contract. However, on the other hand, private autonomy is considered a function of self-determination rights. Similarly, freedom of contract is considered a constitutional freedom. These are fundamental rights guaranteed by Article 13 of the Constitution (the right to pursue happiness). Therefore, in applying Article 90 of the Civil Code, a constitutional interpretation is required to avoid unreasonable intervention that may contravene these fundamental rights. Professor Yamamoto's opinion is also linked to the above-mentioned 'indirect application theory'.[86]

Criticisms have also been levelled against Professor Yamamoto's proposed framework.[87] The first of these is that he seeks to explain all problems relating to Article 90 of the Civil Code—an abstract, general provision—using Article 13 of the Constitution, which gives the fundamental right in its most abstract terms.[88] The second concerns the question of whether the constitutional Fundamental right corresponds to the wide variety of social orders governed by Article 90 of the Civil Code. Human rights are not necessarily confirmed. There are also strong rights

---

[83]See Sect. 2.4.3.

[84]See Sect. 2.4.3.

[85]See Sect. 3.2.2.

[86]See Sect. 4.1.

[87]See Sect. 3.4.1.

[88]See Sect. 3.4.1.

and weak rights. Therefore, while Human rights can be included in social orders, the inverse is not the case.[89]

Case law analysis[90] reveals that some types of public policy or good morals violations are closely linked to the protection of Human rights guaranteed under Article 13 (the right to life, liberty, and the pursuit of happiness) of the Constitution. These cases can also be easily justified under the constitution.[91] Similarly, it may be possible to consider a compulsory labour contract as unconstitutional in terms of Article 18 (Freedom from slave restraint and hard labour) of the Constitution.[92] However, according to indirect application theory, such a contract may be invalidated based on Article 90 of the Civil Code or Article 5 of the Labour Standards Act.

Regarding equality rights guaranteed by Article 14 of the Constitution, there are both strong (listed) and weak (unlisted) rights.[93] From our examination of cases of discrimination in terms of gender and age, it can be concluded that the criteria of the Constitution and the Civil Code are in alignment.[94] However, while equality rights for family life guaranteed by Article 24 of the Constitution constitute a declaration of support for monogamy, not all cases of mistress contracts are void under Article 90 of the Civil Code,[95] although such a contract is a violation of marital status and considered unconstitutional under Article 24.

Other types exist that it is not possible to justify in all instances based on the Constitution. As for the type relating to economic activities, which may also be considered a violation of economic freedom as guaranteed by the Constitution, these cases have been resolved via the interpretation of the Civil Code and related special laws, without reference to the Constitution.[96] However, unlike ordinary commercial transactions, an employment contract restricting the employment of others may be deemed invalid and unconstitutional. However, restrictions on the region and the period for which business is forbidden are not deemed to be against public policy or good morals. Therefore, all cases related to type 5 cannot be justified based on the Constitution.[97]

In summary, both the constitutional provisions for Fundamental rights and the general provision in the Civil Code have an inherently abstract character. While there are areas where certain types of violation concerning public policy or good morals are closely linked to the protection of Fundamental rights guaranteed under the Constitution, it is also true that not all types of violation can be justified by these

---

[89]See Sect. 3.4.1.
[90]See Sect. 3.4.2.
[91]See Sect. 3.4.2.2.
[92]See Sect. 3.4.2.3.
[93]See Sect. 3.4.1.
[94]See Sect. 3.4.2.4.
[95]See Sect. 3.4.2.1.
[96]See Sect. 3.4.2.5.
[97]See Sect. 3.4.2.5.

Fundamental rights. While some types of violation may be considered unconstitutional, both the courts and a majority of academics who support the indirect application theory tend to solve issues without reference to the Constitution (see, for instance, cases of an act seeking excessive profits and compulsory labour contracts).

References

Hoshino E (1994) Minpo to Kenpo - Minpo kara Shuppatsu shite (The Civil law and the constitution - departing from Civil law). Hogaku Kyoshitsu 171(8):6–13

Hoshino E (2006) Minpo no Mouhitotsu no Manabikata (Another way to learn Civil law), revised edition. Yuhikaku, Tokyo

Hoshino E, Higuchi Y (2001) Shakai no Kihonho to Kokka no Kihonho (Fundamental law of society and fundamental law of state). Jurisuto 1192(2):2–22

Kimizuka M (2008) Kenpo no Shijinkan Kouryoku Ron (A study on the constitutional effects among private parties). Yuyusha, Tokyo

Kötz H, Flessner A (1997) European contract law volume one: formation, validity, and content of contracts; contract and third parties (trans: Weir T). OUP, New York

Matsui S (2011) The constitution of Japan. A contextual analysis. Hart Publishing, Oregon

Miyazawa T (2015) Minpo to Kenpo no Kankei no Hotekikosei to Bunseki - Kyotsu no Shiza no Kochiku o Mezashite (Classification and analysis of the legal structure of the relationship between the civil code and the constitution - toward building a common viewpoint). Yokohama Hogaku 24(1):153–196

Morita O (2003) Article 90 (2003). In: Kawashima T, Hirai Y (eds) Shinpan Chushaku Minpo (3) Sosoku (3) (New Edition Commentary of Civil Code (3), General Provisions (3)). Yuhikaku, Tokyo, pp 94–219

Nakaya H (1995) Sengo Hanrei ni okeru Kojo Ryozoku (Public policy or good morals in the postwar cases). In: Tsubaki T, Ito S (eds) Kojo Ryozoku Ihan no Kenkyu – Minpo ni okeru Sogoteki Kento (A study on public policy or good morals violation - comprehensive examination in Civil law). Nihon Hyoron Sha, Tokyo, pp 65–88

Oda H (2009) Japanese law, 3rd edn. OUP, New York

Omura A (1995) Kojo Ryozoku to Keiyaku Seigi (Public policy good morals and contractual justice). Yuhikaku, Tokyo

Omura A (1999, originally 1993) Torihiki to Kojo (Transaction and public policy). In: Omura A (ed) Keiyakuho kara Shouhishaho he (From contract law to consumer law). Tokyo Daigaku Shuppankai, Tokyo, pp 163–204

Omura A (2001) Minpo Soron (Introduction to Civil law). Iwanami-shoten, Tokyo

Omura A (2005) Mohitotsu no Kihon Minpo I (Another basic Civil law I). Yuhikaku, Tokyo

Omura A (2009) Atarashi Nihon no Minpogaku he (Toward a new Civil law in Japan). Tokyo Daigaku Shuppankai, Tokyo

Suekawa H (1962, originally 1922) Kojo Ryozoku no Gainen – Minpo 90 jo ni tsuite (Concept of public policy or good morals – about Article 90 of the civil code). In: Suekawa H (ed) Zoku Minpo Ronshu (Civil law essay collection – continued). Hyoron Sha, Tokyo, pp 11–40

Wagatsuma S (1965) Shitei Minpo Sosoku (General provisions of civil code, new revised edition). Iwanami Shoten, Tokyo

Wagatsuma S (1966, originally 1923) Hanrei yori mitaru Oyake no Chitsujyo Zenryo no Fuzoku (Public policy or good morals found in case law). In: Wagatsuma S (ed) Minpo Kenkyu II Sousoku (Civil law studies II general provisions). Yuhikaku, Tokyo, pp 121–156

Yamamoto K (1993) Gendai Shakai ni okeru Riberarizumu to Shiteki Jichi (1)(2) –Shiho Kankei ni okeru Kenpo Genri no Shototsu (Liberalism and private autonomy in modern society (1)(2) –

conflict of constitution principle in private law relations). Hogaku Ronso 133(4):1–20, 133 (5):1–29

Yamamoto K (1998) Kihonho to shite no Minpo (Civil law as a fundamental law). Jurist 1126:261–269

Yamamoto K (2000a) Kojo Ryozoku Ron no Saikosei (Reconstruction of public policy or good morals theory). Yuhikaku, Tokyo

Yamamoto K (2000b) Kihonken no Hogo to Shiho no Yakuwari (Protection of fundamental rights and the role of private law). Koho Kenkyu 65:100–115

Yamamoto K (2002) Article 1-2. In: Taniguchi T, Ishida K (eds) Shinpan Chushaku Minpo (1) Sosoku (1), revised edition (New edition commentary of civil code (1), general provisions (1)). Yuhikaku, Tokyo, pp 225–246

Yamamoto K (2004) Kenpo Shisutemu ni okeru Shiho no Yakuwari (The role of private law in the constitutional system). Horitsu Jiho 76(2):59–70

Yamamoto K (2005) Minpo ni okeru Kojo Ryozoku Ron no Genkyo to Kadai (Current status and issues of public policy or good morals in the Civil law). Minshoho Zasshi 133(3):385–421

Zimmermann R (1990, 1996) The law of obligations: Roman foundations of the Civilian Tradition. OUP, New York

Somali Contract Law: Constitutional and Comparative Perspectives

Salvatore Mancuso

Abstract The Somali legal system had a very peculiar development. After colonisation, the independent country adopted a Civil law based legal system largely influenced by Italian law. The Civil Code adopted in 1973 was modeled on the Egyptian homologue enriched with other influences, mainly Italian. From the constitutional perspective, the country had three constitutions before the collapse of the state, followed recently by a provisional constitution that introduces a federal system to try to keep the unity of the State under the federal umbrella. The 1973 Somali Civil Code is formally still in force, as after the fall of Siad Barre the state failure brought with it the lack of any authority capable of updating or changing the legal system. This contribution first examines the Somali constitutional development, then gives a brief overview of Contract law in the Somali Civil Code in a comparative perspective. Thereafter, it frames this Contract law regime in the new federal (provisional) constitution, with emphasis on how this could affect possible future changes in the contract law regulation. This investigation also considers other federal experiences on the African Continent.

1 Constitutional Developments in Somalia

1.1 The Legal System of the Independent Somalia

In 1960, the territories of the Italian and the British Somali colonies became independent and were unified in the new Somali state. From the legal point of view, the formation of a unified Somali state created a system largely based on the

S. Mancuso (✉)
Comparative Law, University of Palermo, Palermo, Italy

African Law, Xiangtan University, Xiangtan, China

University of Paris I Panthéon-Sorbonne, Paris, France

© Springer Nature Switzerland AG 2019
L. Siliquini-Cinelli, A. Hutchison (eds.), *More Constitutional Dimensions of Contract Law*, https://doi.org/10.1007/978-3-030-15107-2_5

Civil law legal tradition.[1] In particular, the civil procedure code was based on the Italian code, while the Civil code was inspired by its Egyptian homologue (with some infusion coming from the Italian one).[2] In the criminal sector, the penal code was an almost identical copy of the 1942 Italian penal code, while the procedural code[3] followed the British pattern (through the homologue Indian code), with some elements borrowed again from the Italian code.[4]

The strength of *xeer* (traditional law) was enough to resist the marginalisation that the official law attempted to create; while, on the other side, traditional law had to adapt itself to the presence of the state law and find some space in the gaps left open there.[5]

Official state law and *sharī'a* have—during this period—a controversial relation.

If the exclusion clause represented by the compliance with the public order was, during the colonial period, a way to escape from the strict implementation of the *sharī'a* tenets, this possibility ended with the establishment of the sovereign state. This is because the recognition of the limit represented by the public order would have implied recognition of the existence of a further order, which would have been also potentially conflicting with *sharī'a*; situations which are both inadmissible according to the tenets of Islamic law.[6]

1.2   The 1960 Constitution

Moving to consider the constitutional framework, the first document to be considered is the 1960 Constitution, a liberal document modelled on the 1948 Italian Constitution. It is soaked with the illuminist principles of classic western liberal democracy, and was drafted without taking into consideration whether or not these tenets where coherent to the reality and the needs of the new country.

This Constitution is actually a copy of the 1948 Italian Constitution, apart from some exceptions related to unicameralism, the elimination of regional autonomies, and the central role given to the Islamic religion. The principles on which this constitution is based are the separation of powers, a parliamentary system of government, an extreme multi-party system, and the protection of Fundamental rights. No one considered that Somalia is, first of all, an African country, and that the African culture conceives of power based on its unity where the head of the state

---

[1]On the problems of the integration of the two legal systems arising from the unification of the two colonies see Contini (1967).

[2]Such codes are collected, together with the fundamental legislation in the private law sector, in Hassan (1978).

[3]Legislative Decree 1 June 1963 n. 1, as modified by the Law 12 December 1972 n. 84.

[4]Contini (1969); the code was commented on by Singh and Hassan (1978).

[5]For a few examples see Mancuso (2014b).

[6]Sacco (1973), p. 28.

holds all the powers. A chief without real or effective powers, as well as the presence of other constitutional entities which can concur with the head of the state to the division and the exercise of the state powers, are unconceivable situations in African culture.[7] The African concept of power does not imply that the power is exercised by the chief in an authoritative or despotic way. The chief is chosen among those who possess leadership, wisdom and a sense of justice and impartiality; he governs through the council of the elders, chosen by the community where all important issues related to community life are democratically debated, and frequent are the cases where he is outvoted and follows the decision of the majority. The chief who governs despotically is normally dismissed and a new chief is appointed.

Despite the efforts of the Italian authors to present the Constitution as suitable for the Somali reality and the needs of a new and modern country,[8] the principles set forth there were revealed to be unsuited to the social and cultural reality of Somalia, as well as to its legal culture. The separation of powers principle soon became a source of conflicts among the different arms of state. The head of the state was not accepting of his constitutional role of "president-notary", continuously invading the competence area of the executive power. On the other side, the prime minister was exercising prerogatives that the Constitution reserved for the legislative and executive powers, which soon became auxiliary bodies of the executive. The multiparty system, conceived to favour the development of a pluralist democracy, was used as an instrument to facilitate national disaggregation and clan division, since any clan, sub-clan or group could create its own party in the name of the freedom of political association granted by Article 12 of the Constitution.[9]

In the 1960 Constitution, Islam played a central role,[10] representing—in particular—the main source of law,[11] and therefore directing the enactment of subsequent laws, which have been channelled, formally, in the same direction. For example, some Islamic legal tenets have been incorporated by the legislator in the Somali penal code (for the rest largely copied from the Italian code in force at that time), for example, maintaining the death penalty in cases of murder,[12] and the introduction of criminal offences for the consumption and sale of alcoholic beverages, with both applying only to Muslim citizens.[13] The presence of specialised judges granted the *sharī'a* the possibility of being effectively applied in judicial cases.

At the birth of the Somali state, Islamic law was adopted officially for the first time in the normative order; not only as the ultimate source to fill legislative gaps, but, above all, to give legitimacy to the new institutional system.

---

[7]See more in detail Kamto (1987).

[8]Costanzo (1962) and Angeloni (1964).

[9]A clear sign of this situation can be seen in the 1969 election, where lists of 88 different "political parties" were presented.

[10]Ad es., secondo l'Art. 71 comma 1, uno dei requisiti di eleggibilità del Presidente della Repubblica era quello di essere musulmano.

[11]Art. 50 Cost. del 1960.

[12]Art. 434 c. p. In this respect see Angeloni (1967).

[13]Artt. 411 e 412 c.p. See also Mantovani (1973).

1.3   The 1979 Constitution

On 21 October 1969, a bloodless military coup terminated the experiment of pluralist democracy in Somalia and established a military regime led by Mohamed Siad Barre. Following a pattern already rooted in the African countries, the military group renamed itself Supreme Revolutionary Council,[14] and repealed the 1960 Constitution on 24 February 1970.[15] From this moment, the 1969 Revolutionary CHart Publishing, together with the law on the juridical order of the country,[16] acted as the Somali Constitution, to which the 1971 Second Revolutionary Chart and the 1976 Third Revolutionary Chart were subsequently added. Those normative acts served as constitutional instruments, according to which power was exercised and the country was governed, at least formally, after the military coup. The socialist option was a one-party system. The unification of the powers in the hands of the chief of the state, with the consequent adoption of the presidential system, were among those principles with constitutional value which were operating in the country and needed only to be formalised.

The result was the 1979 Constitution of the Somali Democratic Republic, a socialist document supporting Fundamental rights, in line with the trends of the African constitutionalism at that time which were posing the head of the state as the centre of the administration. Examples indicating the socialist characteristic of the Constitution include: the definition of the republic as a socialist state led by the working class (Art. 1), the proclamation of the democratic centralism as the principle to organise the party and the state activities (Art. 14), the different kinds of ownership contemplated in the Constitution (Art. 41), the importance given to economic planning (Art. 43), and putting the socialist option out of the constitutional revision (Art. 112). On the other hand, the recognition of the citizen's political, economic, social and cultural rights (Art. 20 and ff.), the recognition of the judge as the only competent state entity to decide on matters of individual freedom (Art. 26), the proclamation of the independence of the judge in exercising his or her functions (Art. 96) are among the rules protecting Fundamental rights.

Very soon, the constitutional principles were abandoned in favour of a purely presidential power administration. The resuming of the Supreme Revolutionary Council effected in October 1980, the changing of the constitution to extend the presidential mandate from six to seven years and the disappearance of activity of the constitutional entities of the state (People's Assembly, Council of Ministers, judiciary) and of the party (Party's Central Committee, Party's Political Committee)—which remained in place only formally—were the steps through which Barre created a monocratic regime. All state powers were concentrated in the president's hands.

It has already been mentioned how the formal role of traditional law has been drastically reduced, up to be annulled, with the taking of power from Siad Barre,

---

[14]Law 21 October 1969 n. 1.

[15]Supreme Revolutionary Council Decree of 24 February 1970 n. 70.

[16]Law 21 October 1969 n. 1.

whose choice of the socialist option determined the need to create a highly centralised state. Therefore, the 1979 Somali Constitution eliminated any form of tribalism, and religion was no longer regulated in detail there. That Constitution affirmed that Islam is the state religion[17] and the freedom of religious choice.[18] On the other side, the Constitution was nevertheless considered the supreme source of law, without any reference to the *sharī'a* as the main source of law as it was in Article 50 of the 1960 Constitution. The purpose behind this change was to eliminate any traditional or religious tenet from the scene, which could have been contrary to the revolution. The subsequent legislation was necessarily developed along this line.[19] The power-management which Siad Barre based on clan membership, together with the scarce enforcement of the official law, are among those factors that allowed the tradition to maintain its strength in managing the daily lives of Somali society, in which the state and its law penetrated only superficially.

1.4   The 1990 Constitution

With an institutional framework like the one described before, the economic, political and social situation of the country seriously deteriorated up to the beginning of the civil war ignited in certain regions in 1988.

In order to try to keep the power and to give to the country a different and more modern system, which would have implied the abandonment of the socialist option, Siad Barre decided to introduce a new constitution inspired by liberal principles. The constitution would be in line with the African constitutionalism movement of the 1990s, and inspired by the rejection of the first liberal constitutionalism introduced by the former colonial powers in the 1960s, by the failure of the socialist option in Africa, and by the catastrophic experience of African presidentialism.[20]

The 1990 Somali Constitution opted for a semi-presidential system where the president of the republic would be elected directly by the people and exercised a specific series of important powers: the appointment and removal of ministers under recommendation of the prime minister, the sharing of the executive power with the government (Art. 86), the legislative (Art. 68 par. 1) and constitutional revision initiatives (Art. 118), and the power to dissolve the People's Assembly where it did not correctly exercise its functions (Art. 60).

The Constitution distinguished between the president and the government by clearly defining the related competences.[21] The government was spearheaded by the

---

[17]Article 3 of 1979 Somali Constitution.

[18]Article 31 of 1979 Somali Constitution.

[19]On the 1979 Somali Constitution see Ajani (1982).

[20]On the 1990 Somali Constitution see Bootan (1995).

[21]See Art. 87, 92 and 93 of the 1990 Constitution.

prime minister: the highest executive and administrative body of the state.[22] Within the government the prime minister boasted the central role, being responsible for government policies and of the coordination of the ministries' activities.[23] The People's Assembly was conceived as the state's legislative authority (Art. 57), and the Constitution introduced a moderate multi-party system with formal recognition of the role of the opposition as "an important pillar of the political and democratic life of the country" (Art. 8), forbidding the creation of any party based on tribal or clan division (Art. 18 par. 2), and introducing a 5% minimum threshold for a party to be admitted to the assembly. The Constitution also provided for a judiciary independent from the political power (Art. 106-112).

In this Constitution, *sharī'a* was identified as "an important normative source,"[24] and all legislative instruments had to comply with the "general principles of Islam" other than the Constitution itself.[25] On the other hand, there is no mention about traditional law in this Constitution. The 1990 iteration did not have enough operational time to leave traces: the serious riots which developed in Mogadishu and in the rest of the country during the same year already prevented the new constitution from having any impact on the juridical life of the country.

2   The Collapse of the Somali State

On January 27, 1991, Siad Barre was overthrown and a long and bloody phase started, characterised by the total absence of a central state and of organs able to exercise control over the territory and the state's essential functions (leading to its description as a 'failed state')—a phase which only now the country is trying—very hard—to get out of.[26] If the legal system in force at the time of Barre's fall remained formally in force, the total lack of institutions able to exercise legislative and judicial functions led to their disappearance, and to which the civil war, the closure of the Somali National University, the destruction of almost all written sources of Somali law because of the war itself significantly contributed.

Meanwhile, a model of alternative justice was developed, which strengthened over time when the functioning of all institutions was definitively compromised by the conflict.[27] Such alternative justice models, based on clanic grounds, were not

---

[22] Art. 87 par. 1, 1990 Constitution.

[23] Art. 93 par. 1, 1990 Constitution.

[24] Art. 3, 1990 Constitution.

[25] Art. 113, 1990 Constitution.

[26] On the fall of the Siad Barre's regime and the opening of the failed state phase see Issa-Salwe (1994).

[27] Battera (2005), p. 27.

suitable to disputes (such as commercial ones) unknown to the mere clanic relationship since they present phenomena unknown to the traditional systems.[28]

The result was a system developed on completely different principles from those to which a Western scholar is used, made necessary in a reality in which the component represented by the state is completely absent. The following examples are worth mentioning. In the absence of bodies in charge of the constitution and registration of companies, Somalis have used companies established abroad (usually in Dubai), thereby importing foreign rules and concepts for the operation of such companies which were adapted to the Somali context, in the absence of local rules, and practiced there. In the absence of any government since 1991, three companies have been established to offer mobile phone and internet services: the lack of the government license filter to enter the market made possible that it developed on pure market competition with prices that have been the lowest in Africa, lacking both state control of market access (with the consequent cost of obtaining and maintaining operating licenses) and the risk of distortions caused by the entry into the market of a state-controlled company, as well as, more generally, the imposition of taxes. But what is more significant is the fact that, despite the total absence of a system of official law and a functioning judicial system, the level of contractual non-performance was virtually non-existent, since the payments and the fulfillment of contractual obligations were secured using traditional dispute resolution and solidarity systems.[29] Here too the contractual models used were borrowed from other jurisdictions and used in the Somali context.

In this historical period, religious law continued to be applied and strengthened, between spontaneous observance and fundamentalist tendencies. Religious courts more or less administer orthodox *sharī'a* law, sometimes intertwined with traditional rules, others in a form that is claimed to be pure and strictly observant only of the principles derived from the reading of the Holy Scripture.

Meanwhile, the need to prevent the instability of the territory after the disintegration of the Somali state was immediately recognised in the former British Somaliland. Then, a conference where the various local clans participated was held in Borama (a city of Somaliland) to discuss the future of the territory. On 18 May 1993, Somaliland proclaimed itself as an independent and sovereign state, the Republic of Somaliland,[30] but until now the new state has not gained international recognition.[31]

Here, the lack of international recognition has not prevented the emergence of state structures that have applied, and still apply, a legal system of religious,

---

[28]Nemova and Hartford (2004).

[29]Winter (2004).

[30]On the process that brought Somaliland to proclaim independence, and on the recent history of the territory, see Lewis (2008).

[31]On the issue of the lack of international recognition of Somaliland see Government of Somaliland, Briefing Paper. The Case for Somaliland's International Recognition as an Independent State, (2007) Hargeisa, Ministry of Foreign Affairs (unsure how to cite this source).

traditional, Somali pre-1991 law and Somaliland law in a mixture of written and non-written rules in which it is not easy to get oriented, where the essential feature is the institutionalisation of the components of traditional law within the official system.[32]

3   Contract Law in the 1973 Somali Civil Code

3.1   The Egyptian Civil Code and the Somali Civil Code

An essential element of the Civil law legal system is the theory of obligation. This category includes a set of rules regarding legal persons, the different kinds of performance, the objects, the different kind of legal obligations (generic, alternative, optional), and the ways to create, modify and extinguish them.

Sharī'a knows about legal obligations and contracts and has the necessary instruments to cope with all the related issues. *Sharī'a* and Civil law are closely related in this area.

After independence, the Italian rules contained in the Italian Civil code as extended to Somalia needed to be replaced. Therefore, when Somalia looked for a new law of obligations and contracts, it had three models from which to choose: the Turkish (a code modeled on the Swiss one), the Tunisian (a code which is a melding of the Maliki tenets with Civil law foundations)[33] and the Egyptian.

In 1875, Egypt adopted a code based on the French model, modified to comply with Islamic tenets.[34] Among the rules related to obligations and contracts that are worth mentioning are the right of the purchaser to inspect the good he wants to buy, the rule according to which a sale contract entered into during the last illness of one party is assimilated to a will, the rules on the appearance of a new defect on a good already affected by a previous defects and the introduction of specific contracts to receive an income from *awqāf* goods.[35] The Egyptian Civil Code has been amended several times: at the beginning of the last century several articles from the German and the Swiss codes were introduced, and after 1942, other articles were introduced from the Italian Civil Code. Solutions elaborated by the schools and the courts (both Egyptian and Europeans) were also included. The 1948 version was the one in force when Somalia codified its own.

In 1973 (the year of the enactment of the Somali Civil Code) Somalia made the choice already made by other countries in Africa (such as Libya in, 1954, and Sudan,

---

[32]Mancuso (2014a).

[33]This code was drafted by a famous Islamist, D. Santillana.

[34]The code was prepared by the French scholar M. Manoury.

[35]See Sanhoury (1938), pp. 621–642; D'Emilia (1976), pp. 543–568.

in 1971)[36] and chose to introduce a code that—apart from a few small variations—identically reflects the Egyptian Civil Code. The Somali Code is therefore one based on the French Civil Code with the abovementioned alterations originating from the German, Swiss and Italian experiences, and further adaptation to the dictates of the *sharī'a*. For reasons already mentioned, when Somalia codified the move from the application of the 1942 Italian Civil Code to the new Somali version, it did not represent an achievement. Somalia had adopted a code whose recent version was updated with the enactment of the code it was setting aside; it therefore lost the opportunity to adopt a more modern code with the newest available solutions at that time.[37]

3.2   Obligations and Contracts in the Somali Civil Code

As in the other Civil codes of Civil law countries, the Somali code contains a general part regarding the law of obligations. Here the main peculiarities are indicated.

In the Somali code the natural obligation[38] is a source of a civil obligation, while the non-performance of an obligation is a source of compensation for the damages suffered by the victim unless the non-performance is caused by an event out of the debtor's control.[39] Despite the prohibition of *riba* in Islamic law, default interests are set forth and regulated by the code.[40] Subrogation, Paulian and misrepresentation actions are provided for to protect the creditor.[41]

A group of norms are dedicated to alternative, optional, joint and several, indivisible obligations.[42] Following the French pattern, solidarity between debtors

---

[36]After taking power, the Nimeiri regime, which looked to Nasser's government in Egypt as a model, formed a commission to review the Sudanese legal systems dominated by twelve Egyptian jurists. In 1970 this commission unveiled a new Civil code of 917 sections, copied in large part from the Egyptian Civil code of 1949, with slight modifications based on the Civil codes of other Arab countries. This major change in Sudanese legal system was controversial because it disregarded existing laws and customs, introduced many new legal terms and concepts from Egyptian law without source material necessary to interpret the codes, and presented serious problems for legal education and training. Following a 1971 abortive coup attempt against the Nimeiri government and increasing political disillusionment with Egypt, the minister of justice formed a committee of Sudanese lawyers to re-examine the Egyptian-based codes (draft commercial and penal codes were also published in 1971). In 1973 the government repealed these codes, returning the country's legal system to its pre-1970 common-law basis. On such events see Guadagni (1976), pp. 183–198. On the Sudanese Civil code see Khalil (1971), pp. 624–644.

[37]Sacco (1985), p. 197.

[38]Arts. 197–199. As noted by Sacco (1985), p. 198, this solution is borrowed by the French code, while the solution chosen by the Italian legislator was different.

[39]Art. 212.

[40]Arts. 223–229.

[41]Arts. 232–242.

[42]Arts. 272–299.

is not presumed.[43] Credit rights are transferable through a specific agreement and the assignment becomes effective for the debtor through its notice or acceptance by the same debtor.[44] Debts are transferable as well.[45]

Performance can be made by a third party with all related effects in terms of restitution and subrogation.[46] A specific section deals with time and place of performance, as well as to the appropriation of payment.[47] Following the continental law pattern, the Somali Civil Code provides for the entire set of ways of discharging obligations apart from their performance.[48] A specific section is dedicated to the statute of limitations,[49] as well as for the proof of the obligation.[50]

The Somali code, borrowing from the French, Italian, and Egyptian patterns, includes the contract among the sources of obligations. Formation of contract[51] is copied from the Egyptian code.[52] Contract involves an offer, that is effective when it is known by the other party and can be revoked,[53] and an acceptance, that can be express or by conduct.[54] Unless a specific form is expressly required by law, contracts may be entered into by any means.[55] In line with the Italian and the Egyptian patterns,[56] even the Somali code recognises the preliminary contract.[57]

Mistake, fraud and duress are regulated following French law as transposed in the Egyptian code,[58] while the abuse of specific personal conditions of the counterpart to obtain better contractual conditions follows the Swiss model, as mimicked by the Egyptian code.[59] Contracts can be void and voidable, with a clear influence of the Italian formulation.[60] Specific chapters are dedicated to the effects and termination

---

[43] Art. 276.

[44] Arts. 300–311.

[45] Arts. 312–319.

[46] Arts. 320–329.

[47] Arts. 338–346.

[48] Arts. 347–369.

[49] Arts. 371–385.

[50] Arts. 386–414.

[51] Arts. 88–99.

[52] Arts. 89–100 of the Egyptian code.

[53] Arts. 88, 90, 93 and 96.

[54] Arts. 89 n. 2 and 97.

[55] Art. 89.

[56] Art. 1351 Italian Civil code and 101 Egyptian Civil code. See also Art. 22 of the Swiss Code of Obligations.

[57] Art. 100.

[58] Arts. 119–126 Somali Civil code and 120–127 Egyptian Civil code.

[59] Art. 127 Somali Civil code and 129 Egyptian Civil code. See Sacco (1985), p. 201.

[60] Arts. 135–141. In the Egyptian code the matter is covered by Arts. 138–144.

of contracts[61]: both are also copied from the Egyptian code,[62] and the influence of Italian law is again evident here too.[63]

A specific section is dedicated to the different types of contracts.[64] It is not within the scope of the present work to describe them. Here, it is enough to remember that the Somali legislator has regulated the following contracts: sale, barter, donation, company, loan, settlement, rent, gratuitous loan for use, work,[65] agency, deposit, escrow,[66] gaming and betting, insurance,[67] and guarantee.

4   The Present Somali Constitution(s)

The intention for the future of the new Somali state is to form a federal state. The reason is clear: more than 20 years of total absence of a central state led to the epiphany of more-or-less strong forms of autonomy, the centrifugal force of which would be incompatible, in any case, with their reduction into a unique, centralised state.

In April 2012, pending the full set up of the federal state, the autonomous region of Puntland approved its constitution declaring the territory an autonomous state of the future Somali Federal Republic. Here *sharī'a* assumes the role of the guiding principle on which the political system of Puntland is based,[68] while the Islam is the only religion allowed in the territory of the autonomous state.[69] However, what is interesting to acknowledge is the content of Art. 101, entitled "Recognition of Traditional Rules and Uses." The norm is opened with the declamation that the

---

[61]Arts. 142–153 and 154–158.

[62]Arts. 145–156 and 157–161 Egyptian Civil Code.

[63]Sacco (1985), p. 201.

[64]Arts. 415–680.

[65]The term "work" is hereby used to identify a contract whereby the contractor undertakes to produce a work under payment of a compensation by the principal. This type of contract is identified as *contrat d'entreprise* in French or *contratto d'appalto* in Italian, but a similar type of contract does not exist in common law jurisdictions in such general terms, where the need for a specific consideration brings to identify specific applications of it, like the procurement or the building contracts.

[66]Here the pattern used is the Swiss. See Art. 480 of the Swiss Code of Obligations, after Art. 729 of the Egyptian Civil code and Art. 634 of the Somali Civil code.

[67]Against the Islamic prohibition of aleatory contracts, the insurance contract is fully recognised in the Somali Civil code (Arts. 644–650), even if in a less detailed way than the Egyptian Civil code (Arts. 747–771) where different kind of insurance contracts were specifically regulated. On the relation between Islamic law and the insurance contract see Kettani and Sacco (1982), pp. 387–406 and the authors cited therein.

[68]Art. 3 par. 6. Its primacy in the hierarchy of legislative sources infers from the first paragraph of Art. 101, where it is indicated as the first regulatory instrument to which traditional rules must comply.

[69]Art. 8.

Constitution recognises traditional rules that are not in conflict with *sharī'a*, the
same Constitution and the laws of Puntland (recalling, to a certain extent, the
colonial conformity clause), and with the express acknowledgment that legitimate
(according to traditional rules) elders are considered the custodians of the traditional
authority.[70] The central role of the traditional authorities can be easily detected in the
next three successive paragraphs: in the case of disputes or "misunderstandings" that
may threaten peace between clans or sub-clans, the elders will be called to give an
opinion or find a peaceful solution. The decision taken by the elders applying the
traditional rules is recognised as valid by any authority, which must provide its
support for the execution of the decision; such decision must also be registered with
the District Magistrate Court in which the case was resolved. If we consider that,
according to the traditional rules, basically all disputes are at the level of clan or
sub-clan relations, the impact that the rule in question may—potentially—have in
the settlement of disputes becomes immediately clear.

A similar situation is also present in Somaliland. There the Constitution (designed
for the recognition of the territory as an independent state) recognises *sharī'a* as the
supreme source of law even above the Constitution itself.[71] Despite the absence of a
constitutional rule similar to that previously seen for Puntland, elders often request
the state judge to settle disputes directly, and the same judges favor this out-of-court
settlement based on the consent of the parties. In the civil sector, this can be done at
any level of judgment by using Articles 117 and 239 of the Somali Civil Procedure
Code. According to the aforementioned Articles, borrowed from the homologue
Italian Code, the judge may invite the parties to find an out-of-court settlement of the
dispute, being the interpretation given to these articles which always allows the
parties to find a solution to the dispute by applying traditional rules and methods.
Here the judge doesn't apply traditional law, he merely takes notice of the settlement
of the dispute made by the competent authorities by using traditional law. The parties
register the agreement with the official court only to close the file, since the same
enforcement of the agreement is left to the mechanisms provided for by traditional
law. The same phenomenon also occurs in the criminal field. Here, judges consider
this to settle disputes regarding an application of the Islamic law principle that the
offender (or his heirs) has the right to choose whether the perpetrator of the offense
should be punished personally or whether the matter should be solved by paying the
diya through compensation. In this case, the judge accepts the extra-judicial decision
taken by the elders, imposing a symbolic penalty representing the punishment of the
offence against the state.[72]

The Constitution of the Jubaland State, also considered the State of the future
Federal Somalia, is worth mentioning. Even in this document, *sharī'a* is considered
the supreme source of the law to which all normative acts—including the

---

[70]To preserve their impartiality and dignity, the rule prohibits them from being part of political
associations or parties.

[71]Art. 5 Somaliland Const.

[72]More details in Mancuso (2014b).

Constitution—must comply.[73] What is interesting to note is the central role given to traditional law, as the source on which the Constitution is based, together with the *sharī'a*.[74]

The provisional Constitution of the new Federal Republic of Somalia of August 1, 2012 reaffirms the primacy of the Islamic religion and of the *sharī'a* as a supreme source of law with which all state laws must be in line,[75] and to which the Constitution itself is declared to be compliant and subordinate.[76] It confirms the bicameral system,[77] and has specific provisions for the separation of powers.[78]

Regarding traditional law, there are no specific provisions. The provisional Constitution merely sets out a general recognition of the "positive traditions and cultural practices of the Somali people", prescribing the removal of those that could adversely affect the unity and well-being of the population.[79]

It is also necessary to mention the provision of Art. 139, which provides for the principle of continuity in the application of the laws in force prior to the entry into force of the provisional constitution. If the norm may seem almost obvious from a purely technical point of view, the consequences of its application are currently totally unpredictable if one considers that the norms to which the constitutional rule refers are those of the first Somali state, since after the fall of Siad Barre and the dissolution of the central state, no authority could legitimately intervene to modify them. Therefore, the problems of reconstructing the applicable legal rules can easily be imagined, particularly given that the territories of Somaliland and Puntland have proceeded with autonomous legislative activities, whose fate shall be established in the context of a Somali federal state that still needs to be built.

The scope of this work is clearly not to go into the question of federalism and its presence in Africa[80]; rather it is to understand how regulating Contract law can be affected at constitutional level. Federalism is an issue in the case of Somalia since the state chose the federal option to try to go out from the phase of the failed state.

The matter lays upon the division of legislative competences between the central and the local legislative bodies. The past experiences tell us that every time an issue at central level fundamentally puts into question the interests or the political orientations of one of the states or overlaps in some ways with the local legislative prerogatives, the legislative machine is blocked.[81] It is therefore essential that the

---

[73]Arts. 2 and 3 Jubaland Const.

[74]Art. 2 par. 2 Jubaland Const.

[75]Art. 2 Somali prov. Const.

[76]Art. 3 par. 1, and 4 par. 1 Somali prov. Const.

[77]Art. 55 identifies two houses of parliament, the House of People and the Upper House.

[78]Legislative competence is vested in the parliament (Art. 71); the executive power is entrusted to the prime minister, assisted by the deputy prime minister and the minister running all together the council of ministers (Art. 97); while the judicial function is vested in the courts (Art. 106).

[79]Art. 31 Somali prov. Constitution.

[80]On federalism in Africa see Nwabueze (2013) and Thiam (1972).

[81]Thiam (1972), p. 86.

respective competences of the central and local legislative bodies are clearly identified at a constitutional level. We do not yet have any such division in the 2012
Somali (Provisional) Constitution.

If we look at other federal experiences in Africa, and, in particular, those having a
continental law legal system, the situation appears to be similar almost everywhere.

In Ethiopia, the creation of the federal state is subsequent to the enactment of the
Civil code, being the first made with the 1994 Constitution (entered into force in
1995), while the Civil code dates 1960. The entering into force of the Constitution
has not affected the validity of the 1960 Civil code where Contract law is regulated,
and in the 1994 Constitution the legislative competence in the areas covered by the
classic codes of Civil law countries stays at federal level.[82]

In the Comoros (a republic made by the union of autonomous islands),[83] the
competence of the autonomous islands is clearly identified by the Constitution that
lists the matters left to their competence, leaving all the others to the central state.[84]
Here too the formation of the "federal" state is subsequent to the enforcement of the
civil code (that is the French *Code Napoléon* extended there during colonial times) in
the country. Moreover, Comoros is a member of OHADA and all the activities
related to the preparation and the enactment of OHADA Uniform Acts have been
made at central level.[85]

As far as common law jurisdictions are concerned, Nigeria and Sudan are the two
federal jurisdictions in Africa.

In Nigeria there has been virtually total legislative inactivity in the area of the
general principles of Contract law, so the related regulation is left to the case law and
the application of common law and equity principles.[86] Therefore, this situation does
not have direct constitutional implications.

In Sudan, federalism was introduced in 1991 with the 4th Constitutional Decree,
and sanctioned finally in the 1998 Constitution, where there is a list of exclusive
federal, exclusive state and concurrent legislative powers.[87] All those not mentioned
in the list are considered concurrent.[88] From the list of powers indicated in the
Constitution, it can be inferred that the main legislative powers have been vested in
the federal government,[89] even if there is no reference whatsoever to matters related
to Contract law. Contract law in Sudan was regulated before the adoption of the

---

[82]See Art. 55 of the Ethiopian Const. There the Civil Code is not expressly indicated, but from the
wording of n. 6 of the Article ("Civil laws which the Federal Council deems necessary to maintain
and sustain one economic community") the fact that (at least) contract law must be regulated at
federal level can be easily inferred. See also Arts. 51 and 52 of the same Const.

[83]Art. 1 Comorian Const.

[84]Art. 9 Comorian Const.

[85]On the legal framework of Comores see Mancuso (2012), pp. 73–93.

[86]See J. C. Onyemere, The Law of Contract and Contractual Relationship, (2012) Owerri, Odesaa at
10; I. E. Sagay, Nigerian Law of Contract, (1985) London, Sweet & Maxwell, at vi.

[87]Respectively Arts. 110, 111 and 112 Sudanese Const.

[88]Art. 112 par. 3, Sudanese Const.

[89]This is the opinion of Ali Gasmelseid (2006), p. 179.

federal option through the Sudan Law of Contract 1974, which is a codification of the common law doctrines and principles as applied in the Condominium period and therefore until 1971 when the Civil code was enacted to be repealed immediately after, in 1973.[90] Thus, English law will be referred to as the origin of the Sudan Law of Contract 1974. Such legislation has not been touched after the adoption of the federal system and Contract law remains fundamentally regulated by the principles of common law and equity.

5 By Way of Conclusion

If the centrality of *shari'a* is not formally questioned (the future characteristics of the new Somali state will tell us the real position it will assume), the role of traditional law seems to be more controversial. If, as seen before, the "constitutional" charts of Somaliland, Puntland and Jubaland recognise—though in a different form—the centrality of tradition, the same does not happen in the new provisional Somali Constitution. There is no doubt that, beyond mere formal recognition (it will be necessary to see what the final constitution will provide in this regard), the essence of tradition is in the daily lives of the Somali people. The issue will be how to deal with the issue of pluralism, and the need to rebuild the legal system of the new Somalia could be a unique opportunity, albeit in the consciousness of the lack of solutions that can magically solve the problem definitively.

   Of course, the stratification of the sources of law and the legal pluralism presently existing could be considered an important resource for the institutional and legal development of Somalia. Moreover, this will largely depend on the ability of the *shari'a* to carve out a central space but non-oppressive of other normative systems, as well as on the role that traditional law (both in its traditional-clanic and spontaneous-urban forms) will have. Moreover, it shall be necessary to understand the extent to which traditional law can be integrated into the official legal system in a long-term perspective, and in a dynamic form in which the mechanisms of interaction of the various normative orders develop in a cooperative and non-conflicting way of seeking the best possible solution for each case.

   As far as Contract law is concerned, the core of the matter stays in the division of the legislative competencies at federal and state level. Here it is advisable that Contract law should be regulated in future in a new, more modern, Civil code at federal level that will be applied in the entire Somali territory to secure uniformity of contract regulation in the country. Other federal experiences within Africa and beyond are heading in this direction and no drawbacks are reported for such a choice.

---

[90]On the Sudanese contract law see El-Hassan (1985); on the enactment and subsequent repeal of the civil code see Guadagni (1976).

For Somalia, winning this challenge would represent the discovery of its own constitutional pattern that will facilitate new political and institutional stability in the country.

Acknowledgement The preparation of the present chapter has been possible also thanks to the grant of the Van Calker Research Fellowship at the Swiss Institute of Comparative Law in Lausanne (Switzerland) for the period May–June 2017.

References

Ajani G (1982) The 1979 Somali constitution: the socialist and the African patterns and the European style. Rev Socialist Law 8:259–269

Ali Gasmelseid OA (2006) Federalism as conflict-management device for multiethnic and multi-cultural societies: the case of Sudan. Helbing & Lichtenhahn, Başel

Angeloni R (1964) Diritto costituzionale somalo. Giuffrè, Milan

Angeloni R (1967) Codice penale somalo commentato ed annotato. Giuffré, Milan

Battera F (2005) State-building e diritto consuetudinario in Somalia. In: Baldin S (ed) Diritti tradizionali e religiosi in alcuni ordinamenti contemporanei. EUT, Trieste, pp 27–47

Bootan AA (1995) La costituzione somala del 1990. In: Grande E (ed) Transplants, innovation and legal tradition in the Horn of Africa. L'Harmattan, Turin, pp 131–165

Contini P (1967) Integration of legal systems in the Somali Republic. Int Comp Law Q 16:1088–1105

Contini P (1969) The Somali Republic: an experiment in legal integration. Frank Cass, London

Costanzo GA (1962) Problemi costituzionali della Somalia nella preparazione all'indipendenza (1957–1960). Giuffrè, Milan

D'Emilia A (1976) Il diritto musulmano e il codice civile egiziano. In: D'Emilia A (ed) Scritti di diritto islamico. Istituto per l'Oriente, Rome, pp 543–568

El-Hassan AEWA (1985) Freedom of contract, the doctrine of frustration, and sanctity of contracts in Sudan law and Islamic law. Arab Law Q 1(1):51–59

Guadagni M (1976) La riforma del diritto privato nel Sudan. In: Raccolta per il cinquantesimo anniversario dell'Università di Trieste. Del Bianco, Udine, pp 183–198

Hassan SI (1978) I codici e le leggi civili della. Somalia, Mogadishu

Issa-Salwe AM (1994) The collapse of the Somali state. Haan Associates, London

Kamto M (1987) Pouvoir and droit en Afrique noire. LGDJ, Paris

Kettani A, Sacco R (1982) L'assicurazione in Marocco. Giur. Comm, pp 387–406

Khalil I (1971) The legal system of the Sudan. Int Comp Law Q 20(4):624–644

Lewis IM (2008) Understanding Somalia and Somaliland. Hurst, London

Mancuso S (2012) La diversité des sources du droit aux Comores: entre droit occidental, droit islamique et droit coutumier. Revue Juridique Océan Indien 15:73–93

Mancuso S (2014a) Short notes on the legal pluralism(s) in Somaliland. In: Donlan DP, Heckendorn Urscheler L (eds) Concepts of la: Comparative, jurisprudential, and social Science perspectives. Ashgate, London

Mancuso S (2014b) Pluralismo giuridico in Somalia. Trascorsi storici e sviluppi recenti. Iura Gentium 9:140–163

Mantovani F (1973) I codici e le leggi penali somali. Angeloni, Mogadishu

Nemova CT, Hartford T (2004) Anarchy and invention. How does Somalia's private sector cope without government? The World Bank Group – Private Sector Development Vice-Presidency, November 2004

Nwabueze B (2013) Federalism: its application in Africa as a constitutional device for creating a nation and furthering democracy. Gold Press Ltd, Ibadan

Onyemere JC (2012) The law of contract and contractual relationship. Odessa, Owerri

Sacco R (1973) Introduzione al diritto privato somalo. Giappichelli, Turin

Sacco R (1985) Le grandi linee del sistema giuridico somalo. Giuffré, Milan

Sagay IE (1985) Nigerian law of contract. Sweet & Maxwell, London

Sanhoury EA (1938) Le droit musulman comme élément de refonte du code civil égyptien. In: Recueil d'études en l'honneur d'Edouard Lambert, vol 2. LGDJ, Paris, pp 621–642

Singh I, Hassan M (1978) Commentary on the Criminal Procedure Code. Somalia, Mogadishu

Thiam D (1972) Le fédéralisme africain. Présence Africaine, Paris

Winter J (2004) Telecoms thriving in lawless Somalia. http://news.bbc.co.uk/2/hi/africa/4020259.stm. Accessed 17 May 2017

Engaging with Qualifying Principles in Nigerian Contract Law

Ada Ordor and Ngozi Oluchukwu Odiaka

Abstract The principles of Contract law are among the oldest firmly established principles of law across legal systems generally. This is no different in Nigerian Contract law which is substantively based on longstanding common law principles. Over time, however, the claims of various normative paradigms have contributed to the reshaping, in some respects, of the formal body of law recognised as the law of contract. These influential paradigms include employment rights ethos, the imperative of consumer protection and the pluralism presented by the prior claims of customary law. These, rather than the Constitution simpliciter, are among the key agents that influence, inform, define and redefine the direction of legal development. This chapter specifically discusses a number of considerations that have been introduced to Contract law principles in Nigeria in ways that qualify the operation of these principles. These developments are identified in public service employment, consumer protection and customary law. Although the common law foundation of formal Nigerian Contract law remains intact, it is interesting, instructive and important to note how the superstructure may have altered over time in response to these agents of change. This exploration is what this chapter undertakes.

1 Introduction

It is the general position in the law of contract that in the absence of fraud, duress, misrepresentation or other forms of illegality, courts will not question the adequacy of consideration or other terms of a contractual agreement. A contract will not be

A. Ordor (✉)
Department of Commercial Law, Faculty of Law, University of Cape Town, Cape Town, South Africa
e-mail: ada.ordor@uct.ac.za

N. O. Odiaka
Department of Commercial Law, Faculty of Law, University of Cape Town, Cape Town, South Africa

College of Law, Afe Babalola University, Ado-Ekiti, Nigeria
e-mail: odkngo001@myuct.ac.za

© Springer Nature Switzerland AG 2019
L. Siliquini-Cinelli, A. Hutchison (eds.), *More Constitutional Dimensions of Contract Law*, https://doi.org/10.1007/978-3-030-15107-2_6

declared invalid simply because one party gets a better bargain than the other. This principle which underpins the concept of freedom of contract is predicated on the fact that the parties involved are of full legal capacity. In Nigeria, contracts have generally been administered according to these common law principles.[1] However, certain categories of contracts have attracted statutory intervention which subsequently presented the opportunity for judicial pronouncements on those statutory qualifications. Statutory and judicial input into contracting is mainly informed by the need to protect weaker parties in a contract, as well as the imperative of establishing certainty in a variety of transactions concluded under plural legal environments. It is often not the case in Nigerian Contract law that there is a direct import of constitutional provisions into the consideration of these issues in judicial and administrative processes. Rather, compelling issues arise from plural normative systems, social justice imperatives, dynamic informal systems and the demands of expediency in ways that call for resolution. Of course, all these issues are comprised in the bedrock of the social contract sought to be captured in the Constitution. In this regard, a number of areas stand out in the context of Nigerian law, three of which are considered pertinent to the subject matter of this chapter. These are contractual transactions under contracts of employment, consumer law and customary law. It is not unusual for qualifying principles to be imposed on contractual terms on grounds founded in these areas and this chapter concisely discusses each of them in turn. However, to place this discussion in context, it is necessary to describe the make-up of the Nigerian legal system as this has substantively shaped its juridical evolution, and not least the character of its Contract law.

2 Overview of the Nigerian Legal System

The annexation of Lagos in 1861 marked the commencement of British colonial rule in the geographical area now known as Nigeria. This was the precursor to the introduction of the English court system into the country in 1862, when English lawyers admitted to practice as barristers and solicitors in Britain became eligible for enrolment to practice in Nigeria.[2] Then followed the training of the first Nigerian lawyers in England, over the next few decades by private sponsorship as there were no government scholarships for the training of lawyers.[3] Similar to the policy in other African colonies, the training of lawyers was not a priority of the colonial government and while formal fields of study such as agriculture and medicine

---

[1]Ezike (2015), p. 4, discusses the bindingness and freedom of contract and cites cases in which this position has been recently reinforced to include *SAIC Ltd v Ministry of Finance Inc* [2014] 10 NWLR (Pt 1416) 515 and *Golden Construction Co Ltd v Stateco (Nig) Ltd* [2014] 8 NWLR (Pt 1408) 171.

[2]Okonkwo (2000), pp. 1–2.

[3]Ibid. at 3.

pioneered in the 1940s, starting with the establishment of the University of Ibadan, law was only introduced as a course of study in the 1960s, after independence.[4]

Concerning its international law commitments, the constitutional requirement for a treaty to be enacted into law by the national assembly before it comes into force makes Nigeria a dualist state.[5] Nonetheless, this has not stopped its courts from referring to international treaties signed by Nigeria, as well as comparative jurisprudence from the common law world in arriving at its decisions.[6] However, the trend, given the consistent growth of local jurisprudence over the years, is to stay with domestic precedents, which are considered more relevant to local realities. This is the case in many fields of law, as often observed by authors in their introductory chapters.[7]

The body of law in Nigeria is therefore made up of the received English law, Nigerian statutes and case law, customary law and in some jurisdictions, Muslim personal and succession law. The received English law is comprised of the common law, principles of equity and statutes of general application in England as of 1 January 1900. Since then, post-independence legislation and case law have significantly transformed the corpus juris, adding great value in very definitive ways such as clarifying the application of the received English law and defining the scope of customary law.[8]

The deep legal pluralism that is the outcome of this history recognises the Constitution as the grundnorm, not in a rigid exclusive sense that fastidiously dictates boundaries, but in a highly nuanced and inclusive way that admits of other normative systems that do not contradict the spirit of the Constitution. In a mutually reinforcing recognition and interplay of value, the constitutional is located in, and admits of, the plural and the plural allows, enables and subscribes to the constitutional. Indeed, the constitutional development of the country has come a long way from the inaugural Constitution of 1922 in which the local people had no official representation in government.[9] The trajectory shows a move to minimal local representation in the legislature under the 1946 Constitution, partial self-governance under the 1951 Constitution, internal self-rule under the 1954 Constitution and independence in 1960 with the 1960 Constitution.[10]

1963 brought a republican Constitution followed by a military interregnum which yielded the 1979 presidential Constitution and 20 years later, the 1999 Constitution,

---

[4]Okonkwo (2000), pp. 3–6.

[5]See Section 12(1), 1999 Constitution of the Federal Republic of Nigeria, Lagos, Nigeria: Federal Government Press.

[6]Okeke (2015) cites *Ibidapo v Lufthansa Airlines* (1997) 4 NWLR (Pt 498) 124 and *Ogugu v the State* (1994) 9 NWLR (Pt 366) as examples of the former and *Agbakoba v Director State Security Services* (1994) 6 NWLR (Pts 351) as an example of the latter.

[7]See for example Monye (2006), pp. 2–4; See also the preface to Ezejiofor (1997), p. v.

[8]See Ordor (2014).

[9]Nwabueze (1982), p. 34, observes that prior to this time, governance was done by letters patent and orders-in-council.

[10]Nigeria's constitutional development is discussed extensively in Nwabueze (1982), ch 2.

where the constitutional development seems to have berthed for the moment. This chequered constitutional history notwithstanding, there is no discernible direct constitutional influence on the underlying principles of Contract law. Conversely, provided there is no illegality or offence to public policy, contractual terms will be enforced.[11] Likewise, parties are still free to choose whom to contract with, provided that choice is not exercised in a way that offends the long-standing constitutional provision against discrimination.[12] This minimal direct constitutional influence is implied only because the provision against discrimination is a clear constitutional right which has been in place along with other civil and political rights since 1958. A bill of rights was introduced into the 1958 amendment of the 1954 Constitution preparatory to independence in 1960, in response to the representations of minority ethnic groups concerned about post-independence domination by majority ethnic populations.[13] Given that socio-economic rights were not included in the original bill of rights and were only later expressed as fundamental objectives and directive principles of state policy in the Constitutions of 1979 and 1999 respectively, they are not considered directly justiciable and for that reason, have very little influence in the adjudication of contractual disputes.[14] However, this has not stopped civil society organisations from asserting citizens' rights to the realisation of socio-economic entitlements implied in the social contract.[15]

In subsequent sections of this chapter, three key qualifications to established Contract law principles in Nigeria are concisely discussed. As indicated in the introduction, this discussion commences with a focus on the incursion made by employment law into the general post-colonial concept of public employment being at the pleasure of the state. The employment contracts section traces the progression from that state of affairs to the recognition, by case law, that employment to a position created by statute cannot be terminated unilaterally. At the very least, the statutory procedure for termination and the rules of natural justice must be complied with.

Following this is the section on consumer law which highlights the encroaching effect of consumer-protection statutes, as well as various industry-specific grievance

---

[11]*Alfotrin v Attorney General of the Federation* (1996) NWLR (Pt. 475) 634; *SAIC Ltd v Ministry of Finance Inc* [2014] 10 NWLR (Pt 1416) 515.

[12]See Ezike (2015). Section 42(1) and (2) of the Constitution of the Federal Republic of Nigeria 1999 provides for the right to freedom from discrimination on grounds of membership of a particular community, ethnic group, place of origin, sex, religion, political opinion or circumstances of birth.

[13]Nwabueze (1982), pp. 116–117.

[14]Chapter 2 of the 1999 Constitution sets out fundamental objectives and directive principles of state policy which include national ethics, duties of citizens, obligation of the mass media, cultural directives, as well as political, economic, social, educational, foreign policy and environmental objectives.

[15]See for instance the 2010 case *Socio-Economic Rights and Accountability Project (SERAP) v Federal Republic of Nigeria and Universal Basic Education Commission* ECW/CCJ/JUD/07/10, Available via https://www.escr-net.org/sites/default/files/SERAP_v_Nigeria.pdf. Accessed 26 Sept 2018.

mechanisms on contractual freedom. Constructed holistically, this development constitutes an implied import of supplemental terms into the contract between the provider of goods or services and the customer or consumer.

Perhaps the most far-reaching shifts in the application of common law principles of contract have occurred in response to the recognition of customary law norms. This is discussed in the section on customary contractual practices, illustrated by relevant cases. Although the engagement between customary law and common law has generated a large number of cases, the greater majority of these cases do not make it through the courts into law reports, as various customary dispute resolution methods are unrelentingly brought to bear on parties at different stages of litigation.[16]

More detailed treatment of other developments in Nigerian Contract law including the recognition of the validity of pre-contractual agreements by the Supreme Court,[17] the definition of the concept of unjust enrichment, the growth of new remedies and the impact of online contracts has been undertaken in other texts.[18]

2.1 Employment Contracts

The employment relationship in Nigeria is rooted in the common law doctrine of contract which underscores equality between parties.[19] Consequently, the courts have repeatedly ruled that employment terms are to be interpreted primarily within the provisions of the contract.[20] The basis for this is the sacrosanct principle of law that parties have the unimpeded freedom to enter into contracts, which must be respected.[21] As reiterated in *Onyiuke v Okeke*,[22] except in certain circumstances, the courts will neither inquire into the circumstances of the contract nor make contracts for parties. This principle is underscored by the rule of *pacta sunt servanda* which binds parties to keep the terms of an agreement.[23] As Blum observes, "The power to

---

[16]Ezejiofor (1997), p. 22, acknowledges this when he makes reference to the popularity of customary law arbitration, which is characteristically oral in nature.

[17]See *BFI Group Corporation v Bureau of Public Enterprises* [2012] 18 NWLR (Pt 1332) 209.

[18]See for example, Ezike (2015), chs 1, 20, 22 and 23.

[19]Agomo (1997), p. 95; Adeogun (1969, 1986).

[20]*Chukwuma v Shell Petroleum Development Co. of Nigeria Ltd* (1993) 4 NWLR 512; *Daniels v Shell B.P Petroleum Development Co.* (1962) 1 All NLR 19; *Ahuruonye v University College Hospital Ibadan* (1959) W.N.L.R 232; *Obo v Commissioner of Education, Bendel State and Anor* (2001) 9 WRN 1; *Fakuade v Obafemi Awolowo University Teaching Hospital Complex Management Board* (1992) 5 NWLR 47.

[21]This was reinforced in *Unilife Development Company Ltd v. Adeshigbin* (2001) 2 SC 43.

[22]*Chief A.N. Onyiuke III v. G.F. Okeke* (Unreported) Supreme Court of Nigeria, Suit No: SC/430/74 delivered on 5th May 1976.

[23]Reiterated in the Arbitral Award in *Sapphire v. National Iranian Company* (1963), I.L.R 1967, 136 at 181. Delivered 15 Mar 1967.

enter contracts and to formulate the terms of a contractual relationship is regarded in our legal system as an exercise of individual autonomy – an integral part of personal liberty."[24] This assertion, made in respect of US Contract law, also reflects the general position of Nigerian contract law as the cases cited in this section so far indicate. Further, in *Alfotrin v Attorney-General of the Federation*,[25] the Nigerian Supreme Court restated the essential elements of a contract to include freedom of contract, *consensus ad idem*, intention to create legal obligations and a concluded bargain which has settled all essential conditions and leaves no vital term or condition unsettled.[26]

A line of authories agree that since courts cannot rewrite a contract, parties are bound by the terms agreed upon and because contracts of employment are regulated and protected by law, courts are duty bound to enforce the intentions revealed in the contract.[27] Depending on the nature of the occupation, employment is governed by the contract of employment, supplemented by a variety of statutes which provide minimum standards. These statutes are principally the Labour Act,[28] the Employee Compensation Act,[29] the Trade Unions (Amendment) Act,[30] the Trade Disputes Act[31] and the Factories Act,[32] together with the bill of rights enshrined in the Constitution.[33] In addition, public service employment is primarily governed by the Public Service Rules[34] and the Pension Reform Act.[35] It is in public service employment, where statutorily created positions are usually found, that employment contracts encounter the keenest qualifications, as discussed in this section.

By way of background, public servants in colonial Nigeria were employed at the pleasure of the Crown in line with the principles established in *Dunn v The Queen*[36] and *Shenton v Smith*.[37] Since the employment of the public servant was to serve the public good, the crown had the discretion to terminate and dispense with such an appointment if it considered that it no longer served the good of the public. Based on

---

[24]Brian (2007), p. 8.

[25](1996) NWLR (Pt. 475) 634.

[26]Above note 11.

[27]*Cooperative Development Bank Plc v Arc. Mfon Ekanem* (2009) 16 NWLR (Pt. 1168) 585; *Shell Petroleum Development Company of Nigeria Limited v Monday Amadi* (CA) (2010) 13 NWLR (Pt. 1210) 83; *Aprofim Engineering Ltd v Bigouret and Anor* (2015) 52 N.L.L.R (Pt.173)1 CA. See also Yekini and Anjorin (2015).

[28]Chapter L1, Laws of the Federation of Nigeria 2004 ("Labour Act").

[29]2010 No 13 A 1281.

[30]2005 Laws of the Federation of Nigeria 1999.

[31]CAP T8 Laws of the Federation of Nigeria 2004.

[32]Cap. F1 Laws of the Federation of Nigeria 2004.

[33]The Constitution of the Federal Republic of Nigeria 1999.

[34]Public Service Rules 2008 Edition Gazette No. 57, Vol. 96, 2009 Available via https://www. nama.gov.ng/PublicServiceRules.pdf.

[35]P 4 Laws of the Federation of Nigeria 2004.

[36](1896) QB 116.

[37](1895) AC 229.

inherited common law jurisprudence, the idea of being employed at the pleasure of the state continued in Nigeria after independence in 1960, with the implication that public servants had no fixed tenure of office and could be dismissed from service at will, without receiving a fair hearing.[38] The rationale was that "as the person having the power of dismissal need not have anything against the officer, he need not give any reason".[39] In *Martins v Federal Administrator-General*,[40] following the dismissal of a public servant, the court re-affirmed this common law position as the applicable law in Nigeria. In the subsequent case of *Briggs v Attorney-General*,[41] the Supreme Court left undecided the issue whether the status of Nigeria as a republic had altered the legal position and the employment of public officers continued to be at the pleasure of the government.

This was the position until the Supreme Court judgment in the case of *Shitta-Bey v Federal Public Service Commission*.[42] In that case, the appellant who was removed from his position as Legal Adviser in the Federal Ministry of Justice, sought and obtained a declaratory judgment from the High Court of Lagos State on the ground that his removal from office was not in accordance with the Civil Service Rules. On seeking to enforce the judgment, the court of first instance held that the Commission acted lawfully by refusing to reinstate him. However, on appeal, the Supreme Court held that the 1974 Civil Service Rules made pursuant to the 1963 Constitution provided the conditions of service of federal public servants. According to the court, the Civil Service Rules had constitutional backing and vested the public servant with legal status, which made his relationship with the respondent a relationship beyond mere master and servant. The court further held that Nigeria, being a republic and no longer under the crown, was not subject to the pleasure of the crown in its public service employment. The court, making recourse to the provisions of the Civil Service Rules, held that the applicant was entitled to reinstatement to his position as a Legal Adviser as his appointment could not be determined without reference to the rules.

With this decision, the concept of employment at the pleasure of the crown or the state came to an end. Employment of a public servant was no longer at the whims and caprices of the state but was subject to the Civil Service Rules with authority derived from the Constitution. It was no longer the rule that public servants could be dismissed without reasons or without an opportunity to defend themselves.[43] The court in reaching this decision, observed that a public servant in the established pensionable cadre of the Federal Public Service has a legal status and *ex hypothesi*, a right to remain in the service until properly removed in accordance with the applicable Civil Service Rules. Thus, the category of employment with statutory

---

[38]Akpan (2000).

[39]Per Lord Reid in *Ridge v Baldwin* (1964) AC 40 at 65–66.

[40](1963) LLR 65.

[41]Unreported PHC/38/1972.

[42](1985) 2 NWLR (Pt 9) 599.

[43]Akpan (2000), p. 259.

flavour was officially recognised in Nigeria in response to the human right imperatives of due statutory process and rules of natural justice.

Subsequently, a string of cases applied the decision in Shitta-Bey to employment in different kinds of public institutions, including universities,[44] a state-owned research institute,[45] a state-owned broadcasting service,[46] diplomatic service,[47] among others, thus establishing what became the new position of the law. While the collective impact of these employment contract cases has long been absorbed into the jurisprudence on contracts of employment, more recent developments are unfolding in the field of consumer law, as the next section shows.

2.2   The Dynamics of Consumer Law

Consumer law presents another area in which contractual freedom may be encroached upon to achieve outcomes that prevent the exploitation of parties. Much of the body of consumer law in Nigeria is captured by the Consumer Protection Council Act 1992 which, among other goals, seeks to provide redress to aggrieved consumers and monitor the market for unwholesome products.[48] A consumer, as defined by the Consumer Protection Council Act, is 'an individual who purchases, uses, maintains or disposes of products or services'.[49] The Act seems to include sellers of goods and services in its definition of a consumer, by the inclusion of a person who ". . . disposes of products."[50]

The Act provides for a council charged with the responsibility of addressing consumer complaints through mediation, conciliation and negotiation.[51] However, it does not create substantive rights in a consumer although it preserves a consumer's right of action in court[52] and criminalises certain conduct of manufacturers and distributors, including the sale of unsafe goods, as well as misleading advertising.[53] Essentially, the Act establishes a one-stop shop alternative dispute resolution mechanism for all kinds of consumer grievances regardless of the nature of the claim. This

---

[44]*Olaniyan & 2 ors v University of Lagos & Anor* (1985) 2 NWLR 599; *Essien v University of Calabar* (1990) 1 AK-CRJ 26; *University of Calabar v Inyang* (1993) 5NWLR (pt 291) 100; *Adeniyi v Governing Council, Yaba College of Technology* (1993) 6 NWLR Pt 300, p. 428.

[45]*Olatunbosun v Nigerian Institute of Social and Economic Research Council* (1988) 3 NWLR (Pt 80) p. 26.

[46]*Osumah v Edo State Broadcasting Service* (2005) All FWLR Pt 253, 773.

[47]*Federal Civil Service Commission and Ors v J.L Laoye* (1989) 2 NWLR (Part 106) 632.

[48]Section 2 Consumer Protection Council Act 1992 Cap C25 Laws of the Federation of Nigeria 2004.

[49]Section 32.

[50]Section 32.

[51]Section 2 (a).

[52]Section 8.

[53]Sections 9–12.

is irrespective of whether the transaction is in goods or services. However, the Act does not replace industry-specific consumer complaint-redress mechanisms such as the Central Bank of Nigeria's consumer protection mechanism, the Bankers' Committee and the Consumer Affairs Bureau of the Nigerian Communications Commission.[54]

Industry-specific consumer protection mechanisms are typically found in regulatory institutions such as government ministries, agencies and departments in Nigeria. For example, the Nigerian Electricity Regulation Commission requires that a distribution company must have a consumer complaints unit in place to handle consumers' complaints.[55] Similarly, the Nigerian banking industry applies the *Code of Conduct in the Nigerian Banking Industry (Professional Code of Ethics & Business Conduct)*.[56] Among other things, the code sets out a list of bank customers' rights such as the obligation to provide customers with all relevant information regarding the products offered by the bank, as well as the obligation to protect customers' data, deduct only lawful charges on customers' accounts, inform customers of such deductions and so on.[57] The procedure for seeking redress is also spelt out in the Code.[58]

On 7 November 2016, the Central Bank of Nigeria issued a Consumer Protection Framework 'to ensure that consumers of financial services are adequately protected and treated fairly.'[59] The Framework recognises nine key principles of consumer protection and makes these the pillars of its provisions.[60] The Framework further creates obligations around these principles and mandates banks to establish consumer complaint channels to handle consumer grievances.[61] A dissatisfied consumer can follow the redress procedure all the way through to the Consumer Protection Department of the Central Bank of Nigeria.

Similarly, the Nigerian Communications Commission (NCC) pursuant to its powers under section 75 (2) of the Nigerian Communications Act 2003, issued a

---

[54]The Nigerian Communications Commission was established by the Nigerian Communications Act 19 of 2003 which repealed the Nigerian Communications Commission Act 1992.

[55]Section 3 of the Nigerian Electricity Regulation Commission Consumer Complaint Handling: Standards and Procedures.

[56]Approved by the Bankers' Committee and issued by the Chartered Institute of Bankers.

[57]Section 3 Code of Conduct in the Nigerian Banking Industry (Professional Code of Conduct and Business Ethics).

[58]Article 3.6 Code of Conduct in the Nigerian Banking Industry (Professional Code of Ethics & Business Conduct).

[59]Paragraph 2, Preamble to the Central Bank of Nigeria Consumer Protection Framework (The Framework), issued on 7 November 2016.

[60]Articles 2.1–2.9 Central Bank of Nigeria Consumer Protection Framework. These principles are: 1. Legal, regulatory and supervisory structures; 2. Responsible business conduct; 3. Disclosure and transparency; 4. Consumer financial education; 5. Fair treatment; 6. Protection of consumer assets, data and privacy; 7. Complaints handling and redress; 8. Competition; and 9. Enforcement.

[61]Article 2.7 The Consumer Protection Framework, the Central Bank of Nigeria. 7 November 2016.

set of guidelines establishing a dispute resolution channel specifically for the resolution of small claims.[62] The NCC dispute resolution model operates by arbitration and mediation and the guidelines do not circumscribe the type of complaints that may be laid. This implies that any matter arising from the service provision of a telecommunications company can be addressed through this channel, provided it qualifies as a small claim, being claims not exceeding one million naira.

Predating these contemporary developments is the statutory consumer protection found in the Sale of Goods Act 1893 which provides for the duties, obligations and rights of sellers and buyers of goods.[63] The Act also sets out implied terms in a contract of sale of goods, such as the warranties of merchantability, fitness for purpose and correspondence with description.[64] Further, the Sale of Goods Act defines goods to include *"all chattels personal other than things and money; and including emblements, industrial growing crops, and things attached to or forming part of the land which are agreed to be severed before sale or under the contract of Sale"*.[65] However, the Sale of Goods Act does not apply to contracts relating to interest in land and unlike the Consumer Protection Council Act, it does not apply to contracts for the provision of services.

Generally, an action in negligence or a claim for breach of a seller's or manufacturer's implied term can be maintained where injury arises from the use or patronage of goods or services.[66] Alternatively, an aggrieved consumer may decide to use an industry-specific dispute resolution channel or to approach the Consumer Protection Council. The choice of one option does not foreclose the possibility of pursuing an alternative (Fig. 1).

Where consumers do not consider alternative avenues of redress satisfactory, they are free to resort to litigation. In *Fijabi Adebo Holdings Ltd & Anor vs. Nigeria Bottling Company Plc,*[67] the plaintiff sued the Nigerian Bottling Company (NBC), for breach of its duty of care in manufacturing its *Fanta* products, alleging that the product was unfit for human consumption. The claim arose out of the claimant's export of the products to the United Kingdom. The products were confiscated and destroyed by the UK standards authority on the ground that the constituent ingredients of the product failed to meet the standard for consumption in the UK. However, the plaintiff's claims for general and special damages failed, as the court upheld

---

[62]Nigerian Communications Commission Dispute Resolution Guidelines issued in September 2004. This document is currently being revised. Explanatory notes in the guidelines referred to small claims as disputes involving sums not in excess of one million naira.

[63]The Sale of Goods Act is an English statute of general application which apples in most parts of Nigeria, with its derivative, the Sale of Goods Law 1958, applying in the western part of the country.

[64]Sale of Goods Act, sections 14(2), 14(1) and 13 respectively.

[65]Sale of Goods Act section 62.

[66]In relation to the Sale of Goods Act, the cause of action can only be in respect of the sale of goods and not services.

[67]LD/13/2008—*Fijabi Adebo Holdings Ltd & Anor vs. Nigeria Bottling Company* PLC, Judgment of Oyebanji J., High Court of Lagos State, Nigeria.

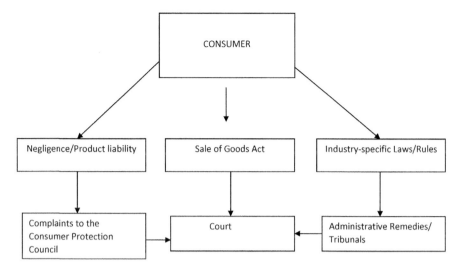

Fig. 1 Flowchart of consumer rights redress. Diagram courtesy of Abimbola Eniola, who provided research assistance for this chapter

NBC's contention that the product met the standard set by the responsible Nigerian institution, namely the National Agency for Food and Drug Administration and Control (NAFDAC).[68] It was therefore the decision of the court that the defendant had not breached its duty of care in manufacturing the product.

It is clear from this and an earlier line of cases that the court will not hold a manufacturer to a general duty of care.[69] The standard of care required of a manufacturer in a product liability or negligence case is that set by the responsible agency, statute or regulation applicable to the manufacture of the product, not the common law's reasonable person's test. Consequently, industry-specific dispute resolution channels seem better suited for addressing contractual dissatisfaction with providers of various services.

Having considered the influence of certain principles of employment law and consumer law on contractual relationships and transactions, the next section highlights another important influence on common law notions of contract in Nigeria, emanating from a variety of customary contractual practices.

---

[68]CAP N1 Laws of the Federation of Nigeria 2004.

[69]*NBC Plc. v. Okwejiminor & Anor* (1998) 8 NWLR 295; *Nathaniel Ebelamu vs. Guinness Nig. Plc* (1983) 1 FNLR 42; *Boardman v Guinness* (Nig) Ltd (1980) NCLR 109.

2.3 Customary Contractual Practices

Generally, the making of a contract in customary transactions can be through a formal or informal process. However, in the absence of a statutory provision, the validity of a contract cannot be affected by the form.[70] In customary contracts, it is common practice to bargain or haggle over the terms of the contract and once this produces an agreement, the transaction comes into effect.[71] A contract will not be declared invalid simply because one party has got a better bargain than the other. Parties to a contract are at liberty to include terms which they consider necessary provided they are well spelt out.[72] The principle of freedom of contract is anchored on the fact that the parties involved are of full capacity.[73] When disputes arise between contracting parties, they are resolved through various means, many of which emphasise compromise and integration.[74]

Nigerian customary jurisprudence recognises various settlement mechanisms, but typically, disputing members of a community take their private matters before independent people for settlement[75] These independent figures may be heads of families, elders or chiefs, and the disputing parties usually accept the decisions of these mutually constituted arbiters whose authority is derived from their acceptance by the community as binding.[76] Customary arbitration practices are not necessarily uniform but are grounded in the customs and traditions of each community, which exert strong regulatory influence deriving from communal recognition.[77]

Therefore, customary arbitration consists of local governance systems in which disputes are submitted to communal authorities for settlement.[78] These authorities may be formal, semi-formal or informal and the outcomes of their arbitration processes are valid and enforceable. As noted in *Okoye v Obiaso*,[79] where the Supreme Court had to determine the legal consequences of pleading the facts of customary arbitration, once it is established that parties voluntarily submitted the dispute to arbitration, the decision of the arbitrators is treated as final and binding.[80]

---

[70] Sagay (2009).

[71] Ben-Shahar (2008).

[72] Ezejiofor (1997), p. 33.

[73] Sagay (2009), p. 73.

[74] Mary (1999), pp. 8–9.

[75] Elias (1956) pp. 212–272; David and Brierly (1985), pp. 547–563.

[76] Akanbi (2007), p. 462.

[77] Silungwe (1988), p. 79.

[78] Nwocha (2016), p. 441.

[79] (2010) 41 NSCQR 955.

[80] This reiterates the position of the law earlier stated in an assortment of cases, including *Njoku v Ekeocha & Anor* (1972) 2 ECSLR 199; *Mgbagbu v Agochukwu* (1993) 3 ECSLR (Pt.) 90; *Ofomata v Anoka* (1974) 4 ECSLR 251; *Ojibah* (1991) 22 NSCC (Pt. 2) 130; *Ohiaeri v Akabeze* (1992) 23 NCC (Pt. 1) 139; *Nkado v Obiano* (1993) 4 NWLR 6; *Igbokwe v Nlemchi* (1996) 2 NWLR (Pt. 429) 185.

In the next segment, three types of contracts under customary law are highlighted to illustrate the influence of non-common law principles and practices on contractual transactions and other processes that transmit proprietary interest. These are contracts involving customary land tenure, pledges for loan and matters of devolution of certain kinds of property.

2.4 Customary Land Tenure

Traditional land tenure is one of the most resilient features of customary law in Africa as a whole. The preservation and conservation of the customary land tenure system were hinged on the dominant ancient conception of land as belonging compositely to all—the ancestors in the past, the living in the present and the unborn in the future. In some cultures, land is considered mystical and deified.[81] Therefore land was not typically the object of sale, but a shared asset to which licence could be granted on an egalitarian basis.[82] Members of a family or community were allotted land for farming, building and other purposes and in this cultural context, land was not the object of speculation and commercialisation.[83] Even the revolutionary Land Use Act 1978 tacitly recognises the inalienability of traditional lands by virtue of the restrictive provisions it places on the acquisition of rural lands.[84] The Land Use Act 1978 took the pivotal step of vesting all lands within each state in the Governor of the State and making the alienation of land subject to the consent of the Governor.[85] This was the culmination of a process initiated by the military government of the time to make it easier for the government to control the use and occupation of land.[86] Before this development which replaced absolute ownership with a statutory right of occupancy,[87] communal and family lands were managed customarily.[88] This primacy of traditional authority is still very present for even after a parcel of land has been acquired compulsorily by the government, permission is usually sought from the leadership of the land-owning family or community before entry and acts of possession are exercised on the land.[89] With urbanisation and commercialisation, the value of land as an economic asset largely displaced the worldview of land as a social

---

[81]Ibidapo-Obe (2005), p. 52.

[82]Adigun (1991).

[83]Ibid. at 52; See also *Amodu Tijani v Secretary, Southern Nigeria* (1921) A.C. 399; *Otugbola v Okeluwa* (1981) 6–7 S.C 99; *Chukwueke v Nwankwo* (1985) 2 W.L.R. 195.

[84]Sections 36 and 37 Land Use Act 1978.

[85]Sections 1 and 22, Land Use Act 1978.

[86]Oluyede (1989).

[87]Or customary right of occupancy, also known as deemed right of occupancy, in respect of land in rural areas.

[88]Ilegbune (1978), Banire (1988), Olawoyin (1974) and Emiola (1977).

[89]Ibidapo-Obe (2005), p. 53.

and spiritual construct.[90] Consequently, a prospective purchaser of land may negotiate a sale with the vendor, who may be an individual owner by gift,[91] by partition of
family land,[92] by inheritance or by purchase.[93] The purchaser must then take steps to
ascertain the size and quality of the land, the authenticity of the vendor's title, and in
respect of family land, the identity of the head and principal members of the family,
before making payment.[94] In many cases, dispositions are largely based on trust and
are often not evidenced by receipts or reduced to writing, but are conducted before
witnesses.[95] Increasingly however, transactions in respect of rural lands are subsequently captured in writing. Often this happens when the purchaser commences the
process of complying with the Land Use Act requirement of securing the Governor's
consent by registering the transaction with the local government authority.

2.5   Loan Procurement Through Pledges

In the past, pledges for loans were secured by means of various culturally derived
socio-economic mechanisms such as the *ito na mbe* practice in eastern Nigeria
similar to the *iwofa* practice in western Nigeria culture which was a system of
indentured servitude involving the indentured labour of another person, usually a
dependant of the debtor as collateral for a loan.[96] Over time, farm produce, land and
personal property replaced indentured labour as security for customary pledges.
Where a debtor pledges land to secure a debt and is unable to redeem the debt, the
creditor is entitled to continue farming on the land or put it to any other beneficial
use, but must not build immovable structures on the land.[97] Economic gains on the
land can be appropriated as interest, but where interest is not paid at all or in full, the
pledgor can only sue for it—unpaid interest cannot debar the pledgor from the
redemption of his property once the original debt is repaid.[98]

In *Mustafa Ekundayo Leragun & others v Funlayo*,[99] the plaintiff claimed for the
recovery of land which the defendant admitted had originally been pledged to her for

---

[90]Obioha (2008).

[91]*Imah v. Okegbe* (1993) 12 SCNJ 57.

[92]*Abraham v. Olorunfunmi* (1991) 1 NWLR (Pt. 165) 53.

[93]*Adesanya v. Aderonmu* (2000) FWLR (Pt. 15) 2492.

[94]Ordor and Oniekoro (2011), p. 260. See also *Ekpendu v. Erika* (1959) 4 FSC 79; *Adewuyin
v. Ishola* (1958) WRNLR 110; *Okonkwo v. Okonkwo* (1998) 10 NWLR (Pt. 571) 35.

[95]Ordor and Oniekoro (2011), p. 265.

[96]Johnson notes that *iwofa* has no English equivalent. See Johnson (2010), pp. 1–39; See also
Adeniyi (1985); IWOFA: The Stubborn Afrikan available at https://thestubbornafrikan.wordpress.
com/tag/iwofa/ accessed on 19 May 2018.

[97]Ajibola (1982). See also James and Kasunmu (1966).

[98]Ibid.

[99]W.R.N.L.R 1955–1956, 167.

the sum of 12.10 pounds. The defendant also claimed that the land was later sold to her for an additional sum of 8 pounds, but there was no evidence of such a sale. The plaintiffs were granted possession of the land by the court of first instance, following which the defendant appealed. It was held that the planting of permanent crops on the land is not itself conclusive proof of ownership. It was further held that lapse of time, in this case over 30 years, was not a bar to the recovery of land which was the subject matter of a pledge. Also, in *Jimo Amoo v Rufayi Adigun*,[100] the plaintiff claimed an account of rents collected by the defendant during his possession of the plaintiff's shop as pledge in respect of a loan made by the defendant to the plaintiff. The court held that the transaction was an 'indigenous mortgage' or pledge of land and that the plaintiff was entitled to credit for the defendant's exploitation of the premises while in possession.

A person alleging a pledge must establish a number of things including the parties to the pledge, the pledged sum, the witnesses to the pledge and the agreed mode of redemption.[101] Furthermore, a pledge does not mature into a right of occupancy and is perpetually redeemable. In *Okoro v Nwachukwu*,[102] the respondent successfully brought an action at the customary court in which he claimed an entitlement to recover his grandfather's land pledged as security for a loan to a member of the appellant's family many years earlier. The appellant's appeals against the judgment of the customary court failed both at the Customary Court of Appeal and at the Court of Appeal as both appellate courts upheld the decision of the customary court.

2.6   Contracts Affecting Customary Succession Principles

Even with the Governor's consent and all other requirements for the transfer of an interest in land under the Land Use Act being met, there remains a category of property that is inalienable. This consists of property which, under the relevant customary law, is intended to be preserved in the family by inheritance. In many communities, the rule of male primogeniture operates to confer on the eldest son of a family, the natal homestead, which similarly devolves by inheritance to subsequent generations. Consequently, any transaction that purports to alienate the homestead, including disposition by will, is invalid and this position has been upheld by the Supreme Court.[103] In *Idehen v Idehen*,[104] a testator made a will in which he devised two properties which constituted the homestead to his eldest son, who then

---

[100] 1957 W.R.N.L.R 55.

[101] *Ezike v Egbuaba* (2008) 11 NWLR (Pt 1099) 627.

[102] (2007) 4 NWLR (Pt 1024) 285.

[103] See *Idehen v Idehen* (1991) 6 NWLR (Pt 198) 382; *Lawal-Osula v Lawal-Osula* (1993) 2 NWLR (Pt 274) 148.

[104] (1991) 6 NWLR (Pt 198) 382.

predeceased the testator. Following the testator's death, the will was challenged on various grounds, including the fact that the testator could not devise his principal residence or homestead, known as *igi-ogbe* under Bini customary law to anyone as it simply enures to the eldest surviving son by operation of customary law. The Supreme Court held that under the applicable Wills Law,[105] the right of a testator to dispose of his property as he wishes is subject to the customary law relating to that property.

Closely related to this is the sale of family land. Title to family land is vested in all members of the family, while management of the land is vested in the head of the family, who holds the land in trust for all the family members.[106] Family land cannot be validly alienated without the consent of the head and principal members of the family.[107] However, a unilateral sale of family land by the head of the family is voidable, but becomes valid if the principal members of the family do not promptly apply to have it set aside.[108] Given that land and landed property constitute the subject matter of a vast proportion of commercial contracts and considering that most land is comprised in rural and semi-urban areas where customary law is very present and operational, these highly nuanced qualifications to Contract law, which also vary from one community to another, have widespread relevance and are of crucial importance.

3   Conclusion

The concept of a constitutional Contract law is one which is yet to be theorised in Nigerian jurisprudence. In an environment where legal concepts and subjects remain consistently compartmentalised, the intersection of concepts and cross-fertilisation of jurisprudential thought across those compartments have yet to crystallise into analytical theories on the subject of constitutional Contract law. The doctrine of freedom of contract, hinged as it is on the presumption of equal standing of contracting parties before the law, makes the courts disinclined to interpret contractual terms widely for the advancement of constitutional goals. This is no doubt reinforced by the fact that socio-economic rights in the Nigerian Constitution are not justiciable, but are expressed as fundamental objectives and directive principles of state policy.[109] However, there seems to now be a ready judicial response to the

---

[105] Section 3(1) of the Wills Law of Western Nigeria applicable in the old Bendel State.

[106] See Ordor and Oniekoro (2011), p. 261.

[107] *Ekpendu v Erika* (1959) 4 FSC 79; *Coker v Oguntola* (1985) 2 NWLR [Pt 5]; *Adeleke v Iyanda* (2001) 13 NWLR [Pt 729] 1.

[108] *Okonkwo v Okonkwo* (1998) 10 NWLR [Pt. 571] 35; *Adewuyin v Ishola* (1958) WRNLR 110.

[109] Chapter 2, Constitution of the Federal Republic of Nigeria.

discriminatory impact of factors over which people have no control such as gender, ethnicity and place of origin.[110]

Nonetheless, when people agree to do things in a particular way, captured in a contract, the inclination of the courts has been to uphold the terms of the contract and only in a few instances will they depart from this position. In this chapter, the few strands of jurisprudential reasoning that may qualify this position in Nigerian law were identified in employment law, consumer law and customary land contracts. In summary, employment contracts in respect of statutorily created positions cannot be terminated without recourse to statutory procedure and the rules of natural justice; statutory and industry-specific consumer grievance redress mechanisms import extraneous terms into commercial contracts; and customary law principles, coupled with statutory state fiat over land, significantly influence contracts of sale of landed property.

Perhaps what the summary discussion in this chapter demonstrates is a mutating law of contract, shaped by a number of things, the fundamental one being its location within plural normative systems, which necessitates the inclusion of cultural principles. Furthermore, certain laws impose non-negotiable duties on contracting parties, particularly in the area of appointment to statutorily constituted positions. Even more targeted are provisions in consumer law, including soft law and alternative dispute resolution provisions, which import additional terms into commercial transactions. Although the state of affairs created by these dynamics is not entirely contained within the rubric of established theories of Contract law and outcomes are not always in line with common law principles of contract, the terrain of Contract law in Nigeria is well defined and the principles of contract law are well established.

References

Adeniyi EO (1985) Iwofa: an historical survey of the Yoruba Institution of Indenture. Afr Econ Hist (14):75–106
Adeogun AA (1969) The legal framework of industrial relations in Nigeria. Nigerian Law J 3 (13):13
Adeogun AA (1986) From contract to status in quest for security. Inaugural Lecture, University of Lagos
Adigun O (1991) An egalitarian land policy for Nigeria. In: Omotola JA (ed) Issues in Nigerian law. University of Lagos Press, Lagos, pp 19–25
Agomo CK (1997) Natural justice and individual employment law in Nigeria. In: Agbede IO, Akanki EO (eds) (1997) Current themes in Nigerian law. Faculty of Law - University of Lagos, Lagos, pp 2–15
Akanbi MM (2007) A critical assessment of the history and law of domestic arbitration in Nigeria. In: Oluduro et al (eds) Trends in Nigeria law: essays in Honour of *Oba DVF Olateru-Olagbegi III*. Constellation (Nig.) Publishers, Ondo, pp 462–472

---

[110]Demonstrated in the 2014 Supreme Court's categorical decision in *Ukeje and Anor. v Ukeje* (2014) 11 NWLR 1154; (2014) All FWLR Pt 730 p. 1154 upholding women's inheritance rights.

Akpan GS (2000) The public servant and security employment: a comparative study. Singapore J Int Comp Law 4:252–279

Ajibola JO (ed) (1982) Administration of justice in the customary courts of Yorubaland. University Press Ltd, Ibadan

Banire MA (1988) Critical appraisal of the democratic principles enshrined in the management of corporate real property under customary law. In: Agbede IO, Akanki EO (eds) Current themes in Nigerian law. Faculty of Law – University of Lagos, Lagos, pp 78–93

Ben-Shahar O (2008) A bargaining power theory of gap-filling. Coase-Sandor working paper series in law and economics, University of Chicago Law School, Chicago

Brian A (2007) Blum contracts: examples and explanations, 4th edn. Aspen Publishers, USA

David R, Brierly J (1985) Major legal systems of the world today. Stevens, London, pp 547–563

Elias TO (1956) Nature of African customary laws. Manchester University Press, Manchester

Emiola A (1977) Principles of African customary law. Emiola Publishers, Lagos

Ezejiofor G (1997) The law of arbitration in Nigeria. Longman Nigeria Plc, Ikeja

Ezike E (2015) Nigerian contract law. LexisNexis, Durban

Ibidapo-Obe A (2005) A synthesis of African law. Concept Publications Limited, Lagos

Ilegbune CU (1978) Family property and its alienation under the Land Use Act. TNJLR 3:24–36

IWOFA. The stubborn Afrikan. https://thestubbornafrikan.wordpress.com/tag/iwofa/. Accessed 19 May 2018

James RW, Kasunmu AB (1966) Alienation of family property in Southern Nigeria. Ibadan University Press, Ibadan

Johnson S (2010) The history of the *Yorubas*: from the earliest times to the beginning of the British Protectorate. CUP, Cambridge

Mary PF (1999) Constructive conflict. In: Oyewo AT (ed) Issues in African judicial process with particular reference to the customary courts of Southern-Western Nigeria. Jato Publishing Co, Nigeria, pp 1464–3731

Monye F (2006) Commercial law: sale of goods, hire-purchase, carriage of goods by sea. Chenglo Ltd, Enugu

Nwabueze BO (1982) A constitutional history of Nigeria. Longman, Essex

Nwocha ME (2016) Customary law, social development and administration of justice in Nigeria. BLR 7(4):430–442

Obioha EE (2008) Change in tenure pattern and customary land practices among Igbo Community in Southeastern Nigeria. Anthropologist 10(1):45–53

Okeke CN (2015) Methodological approaches to comparative legal studies in Africa. In: Mancuso S, Fombad CM (eds) Comparative law in Africa – methodologies and concepts. Juta, Cape Town, pp 34–54

Okonkwo CO (2000) A historical overview of legal education in Nigeria. In: Ayua IA, Guobadia DA (eds) Legal education for twenty-first century Nigeria. Nigerian Institute of Advanced Legal Studies, Lagos, pp 160–178

Olawoyin CO (1974) Title to land in Nigeria. Evans Bros. Ltd, Lagos

Oluyede PAO (1989) A decade of a statutory monster: the Land Use Act. In: Ajomo MA (ed) New dimensions in Nigerian law, vol 3, NIALS Law Series. Lagos, pp 127–133

Ordor A (2014) Associational life and women's constitutional rights in Africa. In: Röhrs S, Smythe D, Hsieh A, de Souza, M (eds) In search of equality: women, law and society in Africa. UCT Press, Cape Town, pp 208–241

Ordor A, Oniekoro F (2011) Source book on drafting, property law and practice in Nigeria. Snaap Press Ltd, Enugu

Sagay IE (2009) Nigerian law of contract, 2nd edn. Spectrum Books Limited, Ibadan

Silungwe (1988) The need for and prospects of alternative or additional legal methods of dispensing justice in common law Africa. In: The common law in the Africa context. Report of the proceedings of the Second Commonwealth Judicial Conference. 8–12 August 1988 (Pub. Court of Appeal. Tanzania), pp 2411–3001

Yekini A, Anjorin A (2015) Non-compete clauses in contracts of employment in Nigeria: a critical evaluation of the decision in Aprofim Engineering Ltd v Bigouret. J Law Policy Glob 56:101–108

The Disabled Consumer and Educational Services Contracts in Brazil

Lucas Abreu Barroso and Marcos Catalan

Abstract In the legal systematisation of the first Brazilian Civil Code (1916), a person with mental, intellectual or sensory disability was considered absolutely incapable of performing personally the acts of civil life (Article 5), which deprived such person of the power to act according to private autonomy. A person with mental, intellectual or sensory disability was often seen as a burden to his family; since such person required special care, showed no signs of social and/or economic return and because of this was even kept invisible to the community. The current Federal Constitution, promulgated in 1988, albeit recognised as the most plural in Brazilian political history, did not reap immediate results regarding the protection of Fundamental rights of people with disabilities. Even with the edition of the current Civil Code (2002), and after almost a decade and a half of its validity, the legal status of the disabled person had not reached a standard of human dignity compatible with the democratic rule of law. That is because the second Brazilian Civil Code repeated the guidelines on absolute incapacity regarding people with mental, intellectual or sensory disabilities (Article 3). Moreover, a set of constitutional provisions does not mean effectiveness of its legal content in the social fabric. The best possible expectations were renewed with the publication of Law 13,146 of 06.07.2015, establishing the Statute on Persons with Disabilities, to ensure and promote, on equal terms, the exercise of the rights and freedoms of disabled people, aiming at their social inclusion and citizenship. Yet, before the law fulfilled its *vacatio legis,* the National Confederation of Educational Institutions (CONFENEN) filed in the Federal Supreme Court (STF) the direct action of unconstitutionality (ADI) 5357/DF to repeal § 1 of its Article 28 which prohibits private institutions of any level and

L. A. Barroso (✉)
Civil Law, Universidade Federal do Espírito Santo, Vitória, Brazil

Civil Law, Universidade Vila Velha, Vila Velha, Brazil

Research Group "Civil Law in Legal Post-modernity", Vitória, Brazil

M. Catalan
Consumer Law, Universidade La Salle, Canoas, Brasil

Civil Law, Unisinos, São Leopoldo, Brazil

Research Group "Legal Social Theories", Canoas, Brazil

© Springer Nature Switzerland AG 2019   129
L. Siliquini-Cinelli, A. Hutchison (eds.), *More Constitutional Dimensions of Contract Law*, https://doi.org/10.1007/978-3-030-15107-2_7

type of education to seek additional payment of any kind on their tuition, annual and enrolment fees. However, the highest court of the Brazilian judiciary enforced the Human rights of the disabled consumer concerning contracts for provision of educational services.

1 The Disabled Person in Search of Identity and Inclusion in the Consumer Society

The affirmation of the identity of the disabled person in the consumer society is linked to the notion of *man*, as elaborated by Social Psychology, once the identity process is constructed "through a dialectic between the self and the other".[1] Man is a socio-historical being, "product and producer of culture", constituted in it and by it.[2]

Man is inseparable from society and his constitution takes place in the "process of socialisation" from culture, which establishes the mediation among (in)dividuals; therefore, the individual "is the fruit of this mediation [...] and the product of culture".[3] This mediation occurs through language ("discourse that stems from culture"), which highlights two factors: the first, objective, as "organiser of reality for a collectivity"; the second, subjective, because "the meanings produced historically by the social group acquire, for the individual, a 'personal sense'".[4]

It is through communication, the "tension between the objective and subjective factors of language", that man "structures his world",[5] whereas society seeks to "categorise people" and to establish the common traits of each category.[6] Man is socially inserted into a certain class because of his attributes and receives an identity based on the "perspective of normality", with expectations that he is supposed to fulfil or not.[7]

This inevitably leads to the reproduction of the "ideology of normalisation", as well as its maintenance.[8] Categorisation determines who is or is not within the "normality established by the social order"; those who do not conform to the standard of normality will necessarily be marginalised, devalued and excluded, and will also become victims of prejudice, because of fear, anguish and weakness.[9]

What is sought is the maintenance of the social order, by "keeping away the frightening individual, the abnormal one [...] considered dangerous by—and to—

---

[1]Iglesias (2017), p. 21.
[2]Iglesias (2017), p. 21.
[3]Iglesias (2017), p. 21.
[4]Iglesias (2017), pp. 21–22.
[5]Iglesias (2017), p. 22.
[6]Iglesias (2017), p. 22.
[7]Iglesias (2017), p. 22.
[8]Iglesias (2017), p. 22.
[9]Iglesias (2017), pp. 23–24.

society being necessary to exercise control and dominion over him".[10] From the point of view of the disabled person, the relationship with the non-disabled person (mixed interaction) is no less difficult. This is because, "such individual feels exposed, and feels that his stigma, his weakness - imputed by society - is highlighted".[11]

To avoid categorisation, the disabled person often tries to conceal his condition, intending to conform to "normality". There are two explanations for such. Aiming to remain unchanged, society determines that the person with a disability "behaves in a normal way, hiding the disability", avoiding the discomfort of contact and critical reflection, in the mixed interaction.[12] Moreover, when society encourages the person with the disability to assume it, "it does so in order to maintain the *status quo*", for assuming the stigma leads to feeling normal, avoiding the encounter between the *normal* being and the *abnormal* one.[13]

To categorise [(in)dividuals and things] "is necessary for the ordering of reality so that it may be understood with ease".[14] The categorisation of the individual occurs through the generalisation of his characteristics before the group to which he belongs and can be modified. Also his relation with the group can change, "according to the present socio-historical context".[15]

Simultaneously, stereotypes arise, which sustain prejudice and reduce human complexity, "according to the spirit of the age".[16] It is not an easy task to remove prejudice, rooted in man by beliefs and attitudes "incorporated and shared by his group".[17] It must also be remembered that the relation of man to his group is not definitive. Hence, we speak of reference groups, since the member of a group can identify himself more, on certain aspects, with another group.

At the limit, this can cause a member to repudiate the group into which he is inserted (endo-group), seeking reference in the group that represents the "normalised standard". Not infrequently, this is the case with the disabled person, as he seeks reference in the culturally dominant group of non-disabled (in)dividuals.[18] Both groups (endo-group and reference group) are preponderant for the *constitution of the (in)dividual*. In addition to inclusive practices, social interaction between people with and without disabilities will cause "the anguish of this contact and a critical reflection", indispensable to overcoming prejudice; and inclusion through education plays an important role in this context.[19]

---

[10]Iglesias (2017), p. 24.

[11]Iglesias (2017), p. 24.

[12]Iglesias (2017), pp. 24–25.

[13]Iglesias (2017), p. 25.

[14]Iglesias (2017), p. 25.

[15]Iglesias (2017), pp. 25–26.

[16]Iglesias (2017), p. 26.

[17]Iglesias (2017), p. 28.

[18]Iglesias (2017), p. 28.

[19]Iglesias (2017), p. 29.

In the field of education, "inclusion institutes insertion in a more radical, complete and systematic way, whose primary goal is to leave no one outside of regular education from the outset".[20] The educational system shall be structured based on the needs of the students, reflecting the contemporary concept of inclusion as a bilateral process by which society adapts itself to receive in the social system the disabled person who, at the same time, prepares to assume his role in the social environment.[21]

The influence of education on the course of the inclusion of people with disabilities was historically striking. However, the decisive moment for a new treatment on the subject only occurred with the International Convention on the Rights of Persons with Disabilities (CRPD), adopted by the UN General Assembly in 2006.[22]

One of the most significant points of the CRPD is related to the understanding of disability, changing "totally and profoundly the understanding and the legislative treatment of the matter",[23] by establishing the *social model* overcoming the *medical model* of deficiency in force according to the scientific standards of modernity.[24]

The Federal Constitution of 1988 had not given the issue of human disability such breadth, despite the treatment of the socially vulnerable. In particular, it regulated the protection of work, assistance and social security, education and accessibility.[25] These norms are more focused on the integration of people with disabilities, with a constitutional orientation still pending on their inclusion.[26]

With Brazil's accession to the CRPD and its Optional Protocol in 2007, ratified by the National Congress through Legislative Decree n. 186/2008 and promulgated by Decree no. 6,949/2009, there was a radical constitutional re-dimensioning of the legal protection of persons with disabilities,[27] "by placing [such protection] at the level of human rights and adopting the commonly named social model of disability".[28] According to the social model, "disability is considered as another characteristic of human diversity".[29]

---

[20]Barboza and Almeida (2017), p. 22.

[21]Sassaki (1997), p. 41.

[22]Barboza and Almeida (2017), p. 22.

[23]Barboza and Almeida (2017), p. 23.

[24]Barboza and Almeida (2017), p. 25.

[25]Federal Constitution of 1988, among others, articles 7, XXXI; 23, II; 24, XIV; 37, VIII; 40, § 4, I; 100, § 2; 201, § 1; 203, IV e V; 208, III; 227, § 1, II, e § 2; 244. See at: http://livraria.camara.leg.br/constitution-of-the-federative-republic-of-brazil.html.

[26]Barboza and Almeida (2017), p. 20.

[27]Federal Constitution of 1988, article 5, paragraph 3: "International human rights treaties and conventions which are approved in each House of the National Congress, in two rounds of voting, by three fifths of the votes of the respective members shall be equivalent to constitutional amendments".

[28]Barboza and Almeida (2017), p. 18.

[29]Lopes (2016), p. 47. "It should be stressed that disability should not be treated as a minority issue. According to the world report on disability, 15% of the world's population, about one billion

The Brazilian Law on the Inclusion of Persons with Disabilities (Law No. 13,146/2015) or, as it is better known, the Statute of the Persons with Disabilities (EPD [in Portuguese]) was designed according to the pre-constitutional guidelines of the CRPD[30] and the alterations caused by it in the constitutional internal order, so as to enshrine the social model of disability in Brazilian law. Thus, disability becomes a social problem to be considered by the whole community.

The social model is therefore based on Human rights and causes a re-understanding of the meaning of persons with disabilities, recognising them as the holders of rights, demanding "an active role of the State, society and the disabled people themselves".[31] The biomedical view gave way to a bio-psychosocial approach based on Human rights.[32]

This may even be the main effect of acceptance of the social model, turning deficiency from an individual problem into a bilateral relationship, in which society has "legal duties to fulfil".[33] Following the line that disability is the result of the interaction between a personal impediment and a social barrier, Article 2 of the EPD provides: "Persons with disabilities are those with a long-term physical, mental, intellectual or sensory impediment, which, in interaction with one or more barriers, can obstruct their full and effective participation in society on an equal basis with other people".

However, no less important was the configuration of the bilateral relationship by the social model, turning the EPD into the "main tool for the effective implementation of the social model, by convening public and private institutions for the inclusion process", at the same time as "all sectors of society, collectively or individually are called on" [to participate].[34] Hence, "society is co-responsible for the inclusion of people with disabilities",[35] as in the case of education (article 8 of the EPD).[36]

---

people, has some kind of disability. In 2010, in Brazil about 24% of the population, something around 46 million people, fell into this category" (Barboza and Almeida 2017, p. 23).

[30]"(e) It is recognised that disability is an evolving concept and that disability results from the interaction between people with disabilities and barriers to attitudes and the environment which prevent their full and effective participation in society on an equal basis with other people".

[31]Lopes (2016), p. 43.

[32]Lopes (2016), p. 43.

[33]Barboza and Almeida (2017), p. 27.

[34]Barboza and Almeida (2017), p. 28.

[35]Lopes (2016), p. 43.

[36]"Art. 8: It is the duty of the State, society and the family to ensure the disabled, with priority, the realization of the rights related to life, health, sexuality, paternity and maternity, food, housing, education, professionalisation, work, social security, habilitation and rehabilitation, transport, accessibility, culture, sport, tourism, leisure, information, communication, scientific and technological advances, dignity, respect, liberty, family and community coexistence, among others arising from the Federal Constitution, the Convention on the Rights of Persons with Disabilities and its Optional Protocol, and the laws and other norms that guarantee their personal, social and economic well-being".

Among the various Fundamental rights (re) affirmed in Title II of the EPD, the right to education is highlighted. Article 27 of this legal micro-system provides: "Education constitutes a right of the disabled; [and] an inclusive educational system in all levels and lifelong learning is ensured to achieve the maximum possible development of their physical, sensory, intellectual and social talents and abilities according to their characteristics, interests and learning needs".

In the sole paragraph, the same law sets forth: "It is the duty of the State, the family, the school community and society to ensure quality education for persons with disabilities and to safeguard them from all forms of violence, neglect and discrimination". The normative guideline of this legal provision of the EPD seeks to align with that of article 24 of the CRPD.

In turn, paragraph 1 of art. 28 of the EPD reads: "The provisions of items I, II, III, V, VII, VIII, IX, X, XI, XII, XIII, XIV, XV, XVI, XVII and XVIII of the chapeau of this article shall apply to private institutions of any level and type of education, being prohibited the charge of additional amounts of any nature in their monthly payments, yearly payments and enrolments in compliance with these determinations".

At the end of paragraph 1 of Article 28 of the EPD lies the problem which is the topic of this paper. The charge of additional amounts (of whatever nature) of the disabled consumer in the provision of educational services was prohibited when complying with the determinations contained in the various sections of Article 28, the chapeau, except for items IV and VI.[37] In Sect. 3 below, there is an analysis of the main outcome of this legal determination in the civil area,[38] the ruling of the Federal Supreme Court (STF [in Portuguese])[39] of the Direct Action of Unconstitutionality (ADI [in Portuguese]) n. 5,357/DF.[40]

It is true that in the consumer society the inclusion of the disabled consumer "is necessarily linked to the question of the right to access".[41] Accessibility "is an essential attribute of the environment that guarantees the improvement of people's

---

[37]See: http://www.planalto.gov.br/ccivil_03/_ato2015-2018/2015/lei/l13146.htm.

[38]In the criminal sphere, the EPD amended the wording of art. 8, I, of Law no. 7,853/1989, which became effective as follows: "Article 8 It is a crime punishable by imprisonment of two (2) to five (5) years and a fine: I – to refuse, levy additional amounts to, suspend, procrastinate, cancel or terminate student enrolment in any educational establishment or degree, public or private, because of the student's disability".

[39]The Federal Supreme Court is the highest court in the Brazilian judiciary.

[40]STF, *Legal Glossary*, available at http://www.stf.jus.br/portal/glossario/: "Direct Action of Unconstitutionality (ADI): Action that aims to declare that a law or part of it is unconstitutional, that is, contrary to the Federal Constitution. The ADI is one of the tools of what jurists call 'concentrated control' of constitutionality of laws (or abstract control). In short, it is a direct contestation to the norm itself in theory. Another form of concentrated control is the Declaratory Action of Constitutionality. The opposite of the 'concentrated control' is 'diffuse control' in which unconstitutional laws are questioned indirectly through the analysis of concrete situations". (translation ours).

[41]Nishiyama (2016), p. 197.

quality of life".[42] Article 53 of the EPD sets forth that "accessibility is the right that guarantees persons with disabilities or with reduced mobility to live independently and exercise their rights of citizenship and social participation." Some economic-contractual barriers may make it difficult or impossible for disabled consumers to access education, such as "charge of additional amounts of any kind in their monthly fees, yearly payments and enrolments" (Article 28, § 1, of the EPD).

The Federal Constitution of 1988, when addressing the Fundamental rights and guarantees, specifically in the chapter on individual and collective rights and duties (Article 5), stipulated that "the State shall promote, in the form of the law, consumer protection" (item XXXII). In addition, in the title dealing with the economic and financial order, consumer protection is regarded as a general principle of economic activity (Article 170, item V).

In the chapter on social rights, the Federal Constitution of 1988 opens Article 6 by raising education to the level of a right and a fundamental guarantee: "The following are social rights: education, health, food, work, housing, transportation, leisure, security, social security, protection of motherhood and childhood, and assistance to the destitute, as set forth by this Constitution".

In the title dealing with social order, the Federal Constitution of 1988 reserved a section of a chapter about education, imposing in Article 205 that: "Education, which is the right of all and duty of the State and of the family, shall be promoted and fostered with the cooperation of society, with a view to the full development of the person, his preparation for the exercise of citizenship and his qualification for work". In turn, Article 208, item III provides that "the duty of the State toward education shall be fulfilled by ensuring specialised schooling for the disabled, preferably in the regular school system".

As seen, the EPD is a special legislation "aimed at ensuring and promoting on an equal basis the exercise of Fundamental rights and freedoms by persons with disabilities, with a view to their social inclusion and citizenship" (Article 1). In consumer relations involving people with disabilities, this implies the recognition of a new modality of consumer vulnerability, the vulnerability of access,[43] that the contracts for the provision of educational services are a problematic example.

2   The Intertextuality Between the Statute of the Disabled Person and the Consumer Defence Code

Carvalho points out that "within a framework of pluralism of positive systems, we will find varied specific guidelines for the development of the hermeneutics of norm production".[44] The encounter here provoked is between two legal micro-systems,

---

[42]http://www.pessoacomdeficiencia.gov.br/app/acessibilidade-0.

[43]Nishiyama and Araújo (2016), unpaged.

[44]Carvalho (2018), p. 87.

therefore, with (even more) specific guidelines. The intention is to establish a communication between the EPD and the Consumer Protection Code (CDC [in Portuguese], Law No. 8,078/1990).

Considering that legal knowledge is invariably presented as a language (in terms of form and meaning of the text), we stress the actual experience "of inner intertextuality, [internal or intra-juridical] and exterior inter-textuality [external or extra-juridical] in regards to law, without which the act of interpretation would prove impracticable".[45] Therefore, there is no way to sustain a disciplinary isolation between the EPD and the CDC, "without directly hurting" the inter-textuality,[46] as it is not appropriate to speak of inter-disciplinarity "without taking into account the individual value of the disciplines related, which means to recognise the two-fold implication of these concepts".[47]

The advent of a new law, with the impact of the EPD, establishes "a complex and extensive network of legal and extra-juridical communications",[48] imposing on the strictly legal level (internal or intra-juridical inter-textuality) a close dialogue with past, present and future texts, "regardless of the dependency relations established among them".[49] In current legal hermeneutics, the subject of knowledge has to *construct* the meaning that is hidden in the text, "in function of its ideology and, mainly, within the limits of his 'world', that is, of his universe of language".[50]

There is no doubt that "the Brazilian legal system determines the protection of people with disabilities in consumer relations".[51] It is a stepped hierarchical protection, decreasing from the 1988 Federal Constitution. When it reaches the CDC—the main infra-constitutional set of consumer protection rules—it does not distinguish between "persons with or without disabilities" in consumer relations, as the Code focuses on consumer vulnerability.[52]

Consumer vulnerability consisting of the "state of the person, an inherent state of risk or a sign of excessive confrontation of interests identified in the market, is a permanent or provisional, individual or collective situation that weakens the subject of rights, unbalancing the relationship".[53] There has long been talk of hyper-vulnerability or aggravated consumer vulnerability, which "stems from social, factual and objective situations, which aggravate the vulnerability of the consumer

---

[45]Carvalho (2018), p. 89.

[46]Carvalho (2018), p. 89. "[. . .] inter-textuality is the constitutive process, or rather, the elementary procedure for the composition of the text, which, drawing from two or more textual materials, draws and updates the meaning in that particular situation of inter-discursivity" (Carvalho 2018, p. 90).

[47]Carvalho (2018), p. 90.

[48]Carvalho (2018), p. 92.

[49]Carvalho (2018), p. 92.

[50]Carvalho (2018), p. 93. "According to the standards of the modern Science of Interpretation, the subject of knowledge does not 'extract' or 'discover' the meaning that was hidden in the text" (Carvalho 2018, p. 93).

[51]Nishiyama and Araújo (2016), unpaged.

[52]Nishiyama and Araújo (2016), unpaged.

[53]Marques and Miragem (2012), p. 117.

[human] person, due to personal circumstances, be they permanent (prodigal, inca-pacitated, physically or mentally disabled consumers) or temporary (illness, preg-nancy, illiteracy, age)".[54]

The hyper-vulnerability of people with disabilities in consumer relations can be perceived in their "difficult access to consumer goods, because in many cases, their social integration depends on the facilitation of their movement, regardless of the help from third parties, and the need for specific goods and services, which are dispensable for non-disabled consumers".[55]

Prior to the adoption of the EPD, Law no. 10,048/2000 and Law no. 1,098/2000, regulated by Decree no. 5,296/2004, respectively, guaranteed the right of access and priority attention to people with disabilities in public transport, as well as greater accessibility to places of consumption and communication and signalling systems.[56] With the CDPD there has been a huge advance in the use of universal design in products, services, equipment and facilities, as well as in the participation of people with disabilities in cultural life, recreation, leisure and sport.[57]

After the EPD entered into force, there has been a growing protection of people with disabilities in consumer relations, beginning with the express reference to the *consumer with a disability*.[58] "Art. 69. The public authority shall ensure the avail-ability of correct and clear information on the different products and services offered, by any means of communication employed, including in virtual environment, containing the correct specification of quantity, quality, characteristics, composition and price, as well as and on the possible risks to the health and safety of the disabled consumer, in case of their use, observing, where applicable, Articles 30 to 41 of Law No. 8,078 of September 11, 1990 [Code of Consumer Protection]".

The EPD's justified concern about access to information led it to change the CDC (Article 6) to include it among basic consumer rights: "Sole paragraph. The infor-mation referred to in item III of the chapeau of this article must be accessible to the person with a disability, observing the provisions of regulation".[59]

It also caused the amendment of the CDC to include Paragraph 6 in Article 43: "All information referred to in the *chapeau* of this article shall be made available in accessible formats to all, including the disabled person, upon request of the consumer".[60]

---

[54]Oliveira and Fassbinder (2016), p. 407.

[55]Oliveira and Fassbinder (2016), p. 408.

[56]Nishiyama and Araújo (2016), unpaged.

[57]Nishiyama and Araújo (2016), unpaged.

[58]Nishiyama and Araújo (2016), unpaged.

[59]"Art. 6. The following are basic consumer rights: III - adequate and clear information about different products and services, with correct specification of quantity, characteristics, composition, quality, price and taxes, as well as the risks presented".

[60]"Art. 43. The consumer, without prejudice to the provisions of art. 86, shall have access to the information contained in registers, records, personal and consumer data filed on him, as well as on their respective sources".

Despite the application of the CDC to any consumer relation, whether the consumer is a disabled person or not, there is clearly an increase of sense with the emergence of EPD in Brazilian law: accessible information on products and services. Recent decisions of several Brazilian courts bear out this finding, for instance, this case of the Superior Court of Justice (STJ)[61]: "The *Braille* method is official and compulsory in the national territory for use in the writing and reading of the visually impaired, and its non-use during the entire banking agreement prevents the hyper-vulnerable consumer from exercising, under equal conditions, basic rights, consubstantiating, besides intolerable discrimination and evident violation of the duties of adequate information, violation of the human dignity of the disabled person".[62]

In fact, among the different types of violation to which the consumer is subject, the informational vulnerability is especially highlighted in a "consumer world that is increasingly visual, fast and risky".[63] Information may sometimes exist, may even be abundant, but flawed, manipulated, controlled or unnecessary.[64]

In the case of Article 69 and paragraphs[65] of the EPD, the legislator sought "to protect people with disabilities regarding the provision of products and services in the media, while also highlighting the Internet, so that the information provided is correct not only so that the disabled consumer may know the correct specification of quantity, quality, characteristics, composition and price, but also be protected against possible risks to his health and his safety".[66]

The change caused by Article 100 of the EPD, with respect to the sole paragraph of Article 6 of the CDC, still awaits regulation, despite the possibility (and necessity) of its compliance in consumer practices. On the contrary, the change proposed by

---

[61]"The Superior Court of Justice (STJ) is the court responsible for standardizing the interpretation of federal law throughout Brazil. It is responsible for the definitive solution to civil and criminal cases that do not involve constitutional matter nor specialised justice". Available at: http://www.stj.jus.br/sites/STJ/default/pt_BR/Institucional/Atribui%C3%A7%C3%B5es.

[62]"Special appeal. Public civil action. Consumer. Person with visual deficiency. Hipervulnerable. Bank contracts. The *Braille* method. Necessity. Duty of full and adequate information. Effects of the ruling. Protection of different and collective interests *stricto sensu*. Ruling that produces effects in relation to all consumers with visual deficiency who have established or come to sign contractual relationship with the financial institution demanded in the entire national territory. Indivisibility of the right guaranteed. Collective moral damage. Non-occurance." (Special Appeal 1,349,188 - RJ, Rapporteur, Justice Luis Felipe Salomão, Judgment: 10/05/2016).

[63]Marques (2005), p. 329.

[64]Marques (2005), p. 329.

[65]"Paragraph 1: The virtual commercialization channels and the advertisements in the written press, on the Internet, on the radio, on television and in the other means of communication, open or by subscription, shall make available, according to the compatibility of the means, the accessibility resources provided for in art. 67 of this Law, at the expense of the supplier of the product or service, without prejudice to compliance with the provisions of articles 36 to 38 of Law No. 8,078 of September 11, 1990. [Code of Consumer Defence and Protection]

Paragraph 2: Suppliers shall make available, on request, copies of package inserts, leaflets, texts or any other type of promotional material in an accessible format".

[66]Nishiyama and Araújo (2016), unpaged.

Article 100 of the EPD regarding paragraph 6 of Article 43 of the CDC is fully effective before legal consumer relations.

In summary, there was "concern of the legislator about the informational vulnerability of people with disabilities".[67] However, is it possible to have the same understanding regarding the vulnerability of access? In the case of consumers with disabilities, the "existence of obstacles placed by suppliers in the consumer market"[68] seems unquestionable, which allows to infer that the EPD legislator's role in the specific protection of the disabled consumer was rather limited.

Nevertheless, the inter-textuality between the CDC (hyper-vulnerability or aggravated vulnerability) and the EPD (accessibility) allows the construction of this new meaning, the disabled person's vulnerability of access. The inclusion of the disabled consumer in the consumer society depends directly on accessible places, information, products, services and technical assistance, to guarantee greater individual autonomy and freedom of choice. It is a matter of equality and the exercise of citizenship.[69]

All this is very well aligned with the fundamental objectives of the Federative Republic of Brazil (Article 3 of the Federal Constitution of 1988): to build a free, just and solidary society; to promote the well-being of all without prejudice and any other forms of discrimination.

3 Contracts for the Provision of Educational Services and Non-discrimination Against Consumers with Disabilities

It seems appropriate to present the central discussion of this study from the provocative insight of Andrew Solomon: "There is no such thing as reproduction. When two people decide to have a baby, they engage in an act of 'production', and the widespread use of the word 'reproduction' for this activity [...] is at best a euphemism for comforting future parents before they get into something they cannot control".[70]

The American writer continues: "In the subconscious fantasies that make the conception seem so seductive, we would often like to see ourselves, living forever, not as someone with a personality of their own. [...] Children whose defining traits annihilate the fantasy of immortality are a particular insult: we must love them for themselves, not for the best of ourselves in them, and this is much harder to do".[71]

---

[67]Nishiyama and Araújo (2016), unpaged.

[68]Nishiyama and Araújo (2016), unpaged.

[69]Nishiyama and Araújo (2016), unpaged.

[70]Solomon (2013), unpaged.

[71]Solomon (2013), unpaged.

Love and care require parents and caregivers to educate, at all levels, from the familiar to the institutional, in the public or private education system.

In fact, as mentioned before, the EPD did not neglect the Fundamental right to education (Articles 27 to 30), ratifying the social right provided for in Article 6 of the Federal Constitution of 1988. It was also previously stated that the Brazilian Constitution has a section in a specific chapter to deal with this matter (Articles 205 to 214). Articles 206, item I, 208, item III, and 209, item I[72] are now highlighted.

Law no. 9,394/1996 (LDB [in Portuguese]) established the guidelines and bases of national education. From it, it is important to emphasise Article 4, III: "Art. 4 The duty of the State as to public school education shall be fulfilled by guaranteeing: III – free specialised educational services for students with disabilities, global developmental delay and high skills or giftedness, transverse to all levels, stages and modalities, preferably in the regular network of education". Article 58 provides as follows: "For the purposes of this Law, special education is understood as the form of school education offered preferably in the regular network of education, for students with disabilities, global developmental disorders and high skills or giftedness". The following article states: "Art. 59. Education systems shall provide learners with disabilities, developmental disorders, and high skills or giftedness with: I – specific curricula, methods, techniques, educational resources and organisation to meet their needs; II – specific completion for those who cannot reach the level required for the completion of elementary education, due to their deficiencies, and acceleration to complete the school program for the gifted in a shorter time; III – teachers with adequate specialisation at the intermediate or higher level, for specialised care, as well as special education for work, with a view to their effective integration into life in society, including suitable conditions for those who are not able to enter into competitive work, through cooperation with the related official bodies, as well as for those who present a superior ability in the artistic, intellectual or psychomotor areas; V – equal access to the benefits of supplementary social programs available for the respective level of regular education". In the end, Article 60 prescribes: "[...] Sole paragraph. The public power shall adopt, as a preferred alternative, the expansion of care for students with disabilities, global developmental disorders and high skills or giftedness in the regular public school network, regardless of the support provided to the institutions set forth in this article".

Even before the emergence of LDB and EPD, Law no. 7,853/1989, providing support for persons with disabilities and their social integration, among other

---

[72]"Article 206 Education shall be provided on the basis of the following principles:
I – equal conditions of access and permanence in school;
[...]
Article 208 The duty of the State towards education shall be fulfilled by ensuring the following
III – specialised schooling for the handicapped, preferably in the regular school system;
[...]
Article 209 Teaching is open to private enterprise, provided that the following conditions are met:
I – compliance with the general rules of national education".

subjects, set forth in Article 2: "The Government and its bodies shall ensure that persons with disabilities fully exercise their basic rights, including the rights to education, health, work, leisure, social security, child protection and maternity, and others that stem from the Constitution and the laws and foster their personal, social and economic well-being". It further defined as criminal offense the conduct described in Article 8, I: "Art. 8. It is a crime punishable by imprisonment from 1 (one) to 4 (four) years, and a fine: I – to refuse, suspend, procrastinate, cancel or terminate, without just cause, the enrolment of a student in an educational institution of any course or degree, public or private, for reasons derived from the disability the person has". Currently, this provision of Law no. 7,853/1989, as amended by Article 98 of the EPD, reads as follows: "Art. 8. It is a crime punishable by imprisonment of two (2) to five (5) years and a fine: I - to refuse, levy additional amounts, suspend, procrastinate, cancel or terminate student enrolment in any educational establishment or degree, public or private, because of their disability".[73]

Law no. 8,069/1990, the Statute of the Child and Adolescent (ECA [in Portuguese]), protects the material right to the education of disabled people in Article 54, III: "Art. 54 It is the duty of the State to provide the child and adolescent with: [...] III - specialised educational services for the disabled, preferably in the regular educational network". It also registered a procedural protection in Article 208, II: "Art. 208. The provisions of this Law govern liability suits regarding offenses against the rights granted to children and adolescents, as to the non-offer or irregular offer of: [...] II – specialised educational services for the disabled".

Returning to the EPD, especially regarding contracts for the provision of educational services, it is necessary to ratify what is regulated in § 1, of Article 28. Private institutions, at any level and type of education, are obliged to comply with the provisions of this law,[74] except for items IV and VI,[75] and are prohibited from

---

[73]Decree n. 3,298/1999 regulated Law no. 7,853/1989, in particular Articles 2 and 24.

[74]"Certainly, an evolution in the infra-constitutional legislation, especially because it imposes on private institutions the great majority of the obligations set forth in art. 28 of the law, destined to the public power" (Rocha 2016, unpaged).

[75]"Art. 28. The government shall ensure, create, develop, implement, encourage, monitor and evaluate: I - inclusive educational system at all levels and modalities, as well as lifelong learning; II - improvement of educational systems, aiming to guarantee conditions of access, permanence, participation and learning, by offering services and accessibility resources that eliminate barriers and promote full inclusion; III - pedagogical project that institutionalises the specialized educational service, as well as other services and reasonable adaptations to meet the characteristics of students with disabilities and ensure their full access to the curriculum on an equal footing, promoting the achievement and exercise of their autonomy; *IV - provision of bilingual education in Libras as the first language and in the written Portuguese as a second language in schools and bilingual classes and in inclusive schools;* V - adoption of individualised and collective measures in environments that maximise academic and social development of students with disabilities, favouring access, permanence, participation and learning in educational institutions; *VI - research focused on the development of new pedagogical methods and techniques, teaching materials, equipment and assistive technology resources;* VII - planning of a case study, elaboration of a plan for specialised educational services, organization of resources and services for accessibility and availability and pedagogical usability of assistive technology resources; VIII - participation of students with

collecting additional amounts of any kind in their monthly payments, yearly payments and registration by virtue of such normative prescriptions.

However, the norms contained in this second part of § 1, Article 28, of the EPD, whose intention of the legislator was to prevent discrimination against disabled consumers in private institutions,[76] led to the filing of the Direct Action of Unconstitutionality (ADI) n. 5,357/DF by the National Confederation of Educational Institutions (CONFENEN [in Portuguese]) before the Federal Supreme Court (STF).[77]

The ADI 5,357/DF was assigned to the Rapporteur, Justice Edson Fachin, on 08/05/2015, who issued a notice the following day: "It is a Direct Action of Unconstitutionality, with request for precautionary measures, proposed by the National Confederation of Educational Institutions - CONFENEN, in view of paragraph 1 of Articles 28 and Article 30, the chapeau, of Law 13,146/2015, which establishes the Brazilian Law on the Inclusion of Persons with Disabilities

---

disabilities and their families in various instances of action by the school community; IX - adoption of support measures that foster the development of linguistic, cultural, vocational and professional aspects, taking into account the talent, creativity, skills and interests of students with disabilities X - adoption of inclusive pedagogical practices by initial and continuing training programs for teachers and provision of continuing education for specialised educational services; XI - training and provision of teachers for specialised educational services, translators and interpreters from Libras, interpreter-guides and support professionals; XII - offer of the teaching of Libras, the Braille System and the use of assistive technology resources, in order to extend students' functional abilities, promoting their autonomy and participation; XIII - access to higher education and vocational and technological education in equal opportunities and conditions with other persons; XIV - inclusion in curricular contents, in courses of higher level and of technical and technological professional education, of subjects related to the person with the disability in their respective fields of knowledge; XV - access of persons with disabilities, under equal conditions, to games and recreational, sports and leisure activities, in the school system; XVII - accessibility for all students, education workers and other members of the school community to the buildings, environments and activities concerning all modalities, stages and levels of education XVII - offer of school support professionals XVIII – inter-sector articulation in the implementation of public policies". In Ferreira's view, "it is certain that it is a faculty, and the private institution may also conduct research or offer bilingual education" (Ferreira 2016, p. 168). To Farias et al. (2016, p. 114), "the reason for the caveat is not known, especially when other measures, which were much more difficult to implement, were included".

[76]Private institutions are the categories described in article 20 of the LDB: "Art. 20. Private educational institutions shall be classified into the following categories: I - private in the strict sense, understood as those that are instituted and maintained by one or more individuals or legal entities of private law that do not have the characteristics of the items below; II - community, including those which are established by groups of natural persons or by one or more legal persons, including educational cooperatives, non-profit making organisations that include representatives of the community; III - confessional, that is to say, those which are instituted by groups of natural persons or by one or more juridical persons that attend to a specific confessional orientation and ideology and to the provisions of the previous item; IV - philanthropic, as defined by law".

[77]In this respect, the relevance of Barbosa's warning stands out: "In countries with a history of diverse inequalities such as Brazil, norms such as Law no. 13,146/2015 are of extreme importance. To make it effective, on the other hand, is a task that is completed in everyday life" (Barbosa 2016, p. 832).

(Statute of Persons with Disabilities)." On November 11, 2015, the injunction was rejected in a sole decision by the Reporting Justice Edson Fachin.[78]

On November 30, 2015, the Federal Public Ministry expressed its opinion regarding ADI n. 5,357/DF.[79] The relevant arguments of the Attorney General of the Republic, Rodrigo Janot are shown below.

---

[78]"Direct action of unconstitutionality. Precautionary measure. Law 13,146/2015. Statute of the disabled person. Inclusive education. International convention on the rights of persons with disabilities. Dismissal.

1. The International Covenant on the Rights of Persons with Disabilities implements the principle of equality as the foundation of a democratic society which respects human dignity.
2. In the light of the Convention and, consequently, of the Constitution of the Republic itself, inclusive education at all levels is not a reality foreign to the legal system of the country, but rather an explicit rule.
3. Law 13,146/2015 indicates the ethical commitment to reception and democratic plurality adopted by the Constitution by requiring that not only public schools, but also private institutions should guide their educational services from all facets and potentialities that the fundamental right to education entails and are solidified in its Chapter IV.
4. Injunction dismissed".

[79]"Constitutional and educational. Direct action of unconstitutionality. Arts. 28, § 1, E 30, Chapeau, of law 13,146/2015 (statute of people with disabilities). Right to education of the disabled. Duties of private institutions of teaching. Viabilizing measures of the inclusive educational system. Duty to attend to the disabled in regular education. Freedom of initiative of private schools. Compliance with legislation. No affront to the right of property and its social function. Constitutional, conventional and legal rules. Danger in the procedure. Inexistence. Dismissal of the injunction.

1. The freedom of initiative of private educational institutions is conditional on compliance with national legislation on education. Precedents.
2. The right to property and the social function of property are not violated by the determination to enrol students with disabilities in accordance with the inclusive educational system adopted by the constitutional, conventional and legal order, with the approval of the International Convention on the Rights of Persons with Disabilities (New York Convention - Decree 6,949/2009), which has constitutional rule status.
3. There is only an inclusive educational system if it is implemented in the public and private spheres. Providing education to people with disabilities is not exclusively a responsibility of the State.
4. Determining that private educational institutions adopt measures to implement an inclusive educational system and accept enrolment of persons with disabilities promotes values that are dear to the constitutional order, such as material equality, citizenship and human dignity.
5. It is important that an expert's report, certificate or report, prepared by a qualified professional, be presented to the school indicating the needs and adaptations demanded by the student with a disability, in order for the institution to carry out the reasonable adjustments.
6. Danger in the process not shown. Suspension of the effectiveness of the provisions carries the risk of inverse damage, since the enrolment of thousands of students with disabilities would be impossible. There have been legal norms since the 1980s that require the inclusion of persons with disabilities, including in the education system. The precautionary measure is rendered inappropriate because these legal provisions are not recent.
7. Opinion in favour of the decision rejecting the injunction".

(i) The determinations contained in the legal rules questioned do not violate the provisions of Article 209, I, of the Federal Constitution of 1988, nor do they violate the right to property and the social function of property (Articles 5, XXII and XXIII, and 170, II and III, of the Federal Constitution of 1988). In fact, "the precepts of inclusive education concretise the social function of the property employed in educational activity, rather than violating it".[80]

(ii) The right to education of persons with disabilities is not limited to the State's duty to guarantee specialised educational services, preferably in the regular educational system (Article 208, III, of the Federal Constitution of 1988). There is also specific regulation in the Guatemala Convention [CRDP], the ECA and Law No. 7,853/1989.

(iii) The filing of ADI 5,357/DF is a cultural barrier as it seeks to hinder or prevent the access of disabled consumers to regular education, considering exclusively economic factors. "It is true that private entrepreneurs of educational establishments must have an economically viable activity, but the action does not demonstrate that the inclusion of persons with disabilities is an insurmountable economic burden".[81]

(iv) It would be paradoxical to allow the "coexistence of distinct educational systems, one public and inclusive and another private and exclusive".[82] The social inclusion of consumers with disabilities must take place in the public and private spheres, otherwise, "it will not be possible to recognise effective inclusion".[83]

On 9 June 2016, the Justices of the Federal Supreme Court unanimously agreed in a Plenary Session to convert the judgment of the injunction into a judgment of merit, by majority vote, according to the opinion of the Reporting Justice Edson Fachin, who dismissed the ADI n. 5,357/DF.[84]

---

[80]Ministério Público Federal (2015), pp. 14–15.

[81]Ministério Público Federal (2015), p. 20.

[82]Ministério Público Federal (2015), p. 31.

[83]Ministério Público Federal (2015), p. 31.

[84]"Direct action of unconstitutionality. Law 13,146/2015. Statute of the disabled person. Inclusive teaching. International convention on the rights of the disabled person. Dismissal of the injunction. Constitutionality of law 13.146/2015 (articles 28, § 1 and 30, caput, of Law 13,146/2015).

1. The International Convention on the Rights of Persons with Disabilities implements the principle of equality as the foundation of a democratic society which respects human dignity.

2. In the light of the Convention and, consequently, of the Constitution of the Republic itself, inclusive education at all levels is not a reality extraneous to the legal system of the country, but rather an explicit rule.

3. In this regard, the Constitution of the Republic provides for the protection of persons with disabilities, as verified in articles 7, XXXI, 23, II, 24, XIV, 37, VIII, 40, § 4, I, 201, § 1, 203, IV and V, 208, III, 227, §1, II, and §2, and 244.

4. Plurality and equality are two sides of the same coin. Respect for plurality does not preclude respect for the principle of equality. And in the current historical period, a reading focused only on its formal aspect does not satisfy the completeness that the principle requires. Thus, equality

From the Reporting Justice's opinion, the following may be regarded as the principal grounds.

(i) Paragraph 1 of Article 28 of the EPD "establishes the obligation for private schools to promote the inclusion of persons with disabilities in regular education and to provide the necessary adaptation measures without the financial burden being passed on to tuition, yearly payments and registration fees".[85]

(ii) Paragraph 1 of Article 28 of the EPD seems to assume "an ethical commitment to reception when it demands that not only public schools, but also private institutions shall guide their educational performance from all facets and potentialities that the fundamental right to education entails and are solidified in Chapter IV".[86]

(iii) Private institutions should prepare themselves to welcome the disabled consumer, providing educational services designed "from appropriate spaces, environments and resources to overcome barriers - the real deficiencies of our society".[87]

(iv) Had the injunction or merit of ADI n. 5.357/DF been accepted there would be "the risk of creating to the private educational institutions the odious privilege from which the other economic agents cannot evade. [It is an] odious privilege because it officialises discrimination".[88]

The outcome of the judgement of the ADI n. 5,357/DF has impeded a clear social backlash and affront to quality education (Article 206, VII, of the Federal Constitution of 1988), [which could occur] at the time of formation and execution of contracts for the provision of educational services to consumers with disabilities in Brazil. The charge of additional amounts of any kind in their monthly fees, yearly

---

is not exhausted with the legal provision for equal access to legal interests, but also includes the normative provision for measures that effectively enable such access and its concrete realisation.

5. Enclosure in the face of what is different steals the colour of daily life, depriving us of the stupefaction before that what is new and different.

6. It is only with through coexistence with the difference and with its necessary reception that there can be the construction of a free, just and solidary society, in which the good of all is promoted without prejudices of race, gender, colour, age and any other forms of discrimination (Article 3, I and IV, Federal Constitution).

7. Law 13,146/2015 indicates the ethical commitment to reception and democratic plurality adopted by the Constitution by requiring that not only public schools but also private individuals shall guide their educational activities from all facets and potentialities that the fundamental right to education entails and are solidified in its Chapter IV.

8. Injunction dismissed.

9. Conversion of the judgment of the referendum of the dismissal of the injunction, by unanimity, into a final judgment of merit, adjudged, by majority and in the terms of the Opinion of the Reporting Justice Edson Fachin, to dismiss this direct unconstitutionality action".

[85] Brasil (2016), p. 5.
[86] Brasil (2016), p. 7.
[87] Brasil (2016), p. 10.
[88] Brasil (2016), p. 10.

payments and enrolments would open the opportunity for the return of practices of rejection and make it difficult for the disabled student-consumer to benefit from formal education in the regular school system.

Acknowledgment The authors thank Kennedy Matos for the translation of the text from Portuguese into English.

References

Barbosa FN (2016) Democracia e participação: o direito da pessoa com deficiência à educação e sua inclusão nas instituições de ensino superior. In: Menezes JB (ed) Direito das pessoas com deficiência psíquica e intelectual nas relações privadas: convenção sobre os direitos da pessoa com deficiência e lei brasileira de inclusão. Processo, Rio de Janeiro, pp 815–833
Barboza HH, Almeida VA Jr (2017) Reconhecimento e inclusão das pessoas com deficiência. RBDCivil 13:17–37
Brasil, Supremo Tribunal Federal (2016) Referendo na Medida Cautelar na Ação Direta de Inconstitucionalidade 5.357 Distrito Federal. T. Pleno. http://portal.stf.jus.br/processos/detalhe.asp?incidente=4818214. Accessed 13 mayo 2018
Carvalho PB (2018) Hermenêutica no direito. In: Leite GS, Streck LL (eds) Interpretação, retórica e linguagem. JusPodivm, Salvador, pp 71–94
Farias CC, Cunha RS, Pinto RB (2016) Estatuto da pessoa com deficiência comentado, 2 rd edn. JusPodivm, Salvador
Ferreira LAM (2016) Arts. 27 a 30. In: Leite FPA, Ribeiro LLG, Costa Filho WM (eds) Comentários ao estatuto da pessoa com deficiência. Saraiva, São Paulo, pp 150–171
Iglesias VDO (2017) Pessoa com deficiência e sua identidade para si na sociedade atual. Juruá, Curitiba
Lopes LF (2016) Arts. 1° a 3°. In: Leite FPA, Ribeiro LLG, Costa Filho WM (eds) Comentários ao estatuto da pessoa com deficiência. Saraiva, São Paulo, pp 35–64
Marques CL (2005) Contratos no código de defesa do consumidor: o novo regime das relações contratuais, 5rd edn. Revista dos Tribunais, São Paulo
Marques CL, Miragem B (2012) O novo direito privado e a proteção dos vulneráveis. Revista dos Tribunais, São Paulo
Ministério Público Federal (2015) Procuradoria-Geral da República. Parecer na ação direta de inconstitucionalidade 5.357/DF. http://portal.stf.jus.br/processos/detalhe.asp?incidente=4818214. Accessed 13 mayo 2018
Nishiyama AM (2016) Proteção jurídica das pessoas com deficiência nas relações de consume. Juruá, Curitiba
Nishiyama AM, Araújo LAD (2016) O estatuto da pessoa com deficiência e a tutela do consumidor: novos direitos? RDC 105:103–121
Oliveira AJG, Fassbinder N (2016) O estatuto da pessoa com deficiência e a hipervulnerabilidade do consumidor: diálogos e desafios. In: Ehrhardt M Jr (ed) Impactos do novo CPC e do EPD no direito civil brasileiro. Fórum, Belo Horizonte, pp 397–414
Rocha MH (2016) Do direito fundamental à educação inclusiva e o estatuto da pessoa com deficiência. RT 963:129–151
Sassaki RK (1997) Inclusão: construindo uma sociedade para todos. WVA, Rio de Janeiro
Solomon A (2013) Longe da árvore: pais, filhos e a busca da identidade (trans: Donaldson MG, Luiz AA, Pedro MS). Companhia das Letras, São Paulo

The Freedom to Contract and the Contract in the Constitution of Peru of 1993

Gunther Hernán Gonzales Barrón

Abstract The contract fulfils the objective of channelling the exchange and allocation of goods or services in society, thus it is an assumption of the market economy. The Constitution of Peru of 1993 regulates the Fundamental right to freedom to contract, in Articles 2, sections 14 and 62, whose contents include: (i) freedom to contract (strictly), by which every person has the right to conclude the contract, or not, and to choose the co-contractor; (ii) right to contract, as a security instrument for economic investment; (iii) right to contractual regulation, or set of agreements that outline the legal relationship. However, the social function of the contract generates a reappraisal of the principle of "fair exchange" or "fair agreement."

1 Man and His Circumstances

The human being is an overwhelming force that enters the phenomenon world,[1] but goes in search of new dimensions. It is present in ideas, in beauty, in spirituality and also in the physical.[2] Another area of his is morality and juridicity, that is, what is about the valuation of behaviour. An animal could have an altruistic behaviour, and even kindly with its fellows, but not ethical. The difference is in the moral conscience.[3]

Man is to be free, within his great physical and temporal limitations,[4] and this translates into thoughts, desires, decisions and acts. Yet, he does not just think, he also interferes. Life could not develop from pure interiority, from pure Cartesian

---

[1]Heidegger (2011), pp. 33–34.
[2]Wahl (1997), p. 55.
[3]Sobrevilla (1988), p. 352.
[4]Savater (2004), pp. 38–39.

G. H. Gonzales Barrón (✉)
Civil Law at the Universities Antonio Ruiz de Montoya, San Ignacio de Loyola, Lima, Peru

Water Administrative Court, Lima, Peru

National of San Marcos, Lima, Peru
e-mail: ggonzales@pucp.pe

© Springer Nature Switzerland AG 2019
L. Siliquini-Cinelli, A. Hutchison (eds.), *More Constitutional Dimensions of Contract Law*, https://doi.org/10.1007/978-3-030-15107-2_8

thinking, no more, for it is necessary to act on the outside. The freedom of this being leaves a mark on the world; prints with his stroke wherever he goes. He is a subjectivity that acts and decides[5]; and subsequently, he also does the same in the Law.

1.1 Man as an Economic Being

Man is an economic being from the beginning of time, because the need for subsistence requires him to go to his environment to appropriate things and their different utilities. The satisfaction of that interest is transferred from the plane of religion and morals, to the law, so that the concept of property, at that moment, whether individual, family or communal, is identified with the peaceful enjoyment of things.

In primitive societies, the economy is based on self-consumption; therefore, families or small social groups produce all the goods they need, so the social group only cares about protecting the property, which is the only patrimonial right that is required to maintain order in the tribe or political organisation in question.

However, later on, every society begins a slow period of greater complexity, which arises from the birth of the social classes: rulers, religious and producers, which basically serves the purpose of maintaining the order of society, by which a privileged political group surpasses the self-consumption, with the consequent demand of new goods inside or outside its environment, that originates internal or external trade. On the other hand, the technological advances originate surpluses, notwithstanding that the more skilful or strong subjects manage to accumulate wealth, which results in the birth of more complex or sumptuary interests.

The demand for goods always implies the supply of goods, so a new situation arises that modifies the structure of society. Self-consumption ceases to be the only economic formula; on the contrary, the exchange of goods begins to gain increasing importance, commerce, and with this, production is made to compete in the market; that is, aiming at third parties. Again, social changes drag Law, since rules for the exchange of goods arise. In such a context, the concept of property is not sufficient to face the new needs, so that the ideas of "bond", "obligation" and "contract" are born as legal mechanisms that explain the exchange.

Specialised production, in short, the situation whereby each agent produces a specific type of good—and therefore, does it with greater efficiency, productivity and quality—originates trade through commerce, from the economic scope; but it also gives rise to the notions of obligation and contract, from the field of law. It is no coincidence that in Rome, the contract of sale is typified by the law of nations, that is, by the effect of international trade.

---

[5]Jaspers (2003), p. 67.

For its part, the market economy arises properly when economic freedom, the division of labour, the specialisation of each agent in production, and state intervention as a guarantor of these freedoms, are generalised; but not in the productive function, although its intervention, because of various factors, is becoming more relevant today.

The theoretical support of the market economy, as well as the respect for freedom, is found in the general welfare that is achieved through the liberation of productive forces, innovation, creativity and appropriation of effort by the protagonist of the action. In this sense, individuals have the freedom to produce, trade, contract, work, as well as freedom in the use, enjoyment and disposition of property.

The market is the abstract place where supply and demand meet, sellers and buyers, but this requires a technical figure linking both opposing interests: "the contract", as well as the right that is the object of the exchange: "the property." Then, property is based on the primitive idea of "exclusive appropriation", with a pure individualism (the self), without relevance of otherness; while the contract is based on the idea of "cooperation" between two subjects, therefore, both need each other, which, unlike property, presupposes otherness (the other).[6]

1.2 Man as a Legal Being

Man is an acting and social being, so he creates institutions or social frameworks for action. The validity of the rules is based on the originating fact of the institutions, and these, in turn, can only exist when they contain a nucleus of practical information.[7] The theory of social fact is an excellent model justifying legal systems, because it is based on a phenomenological reality, and not on a mere idea or metaphysical speculation.

Law, as a general and institutionalised normative system, is always based on the social will to organise a group of people under an authority that invests power to issue rules with binding effect for others, and determines the validity of the system and of its components. It is also a communicational human act, but of coercive character, sometimes even of force, although it also affirms a will, which is always a fact (phenomenon) that appears or is externalised in the sensible world. However, law also requires, in one way or another, widespread acceptance (sometimes, in fact, submission), which entails assuming the compulsory mandate and, to a large extent, the relative legitimacy of the mandate. In any case, the mere passive obedience of Law constitutes the sufficient assumption to understand, as long as the requirement of the acceptance is fulfilled.

Law is an act of authority, but also an act of acceptance and recognition, therefore, authority is softened with the fresh aroma of social consciousness that

---

[6]Betti (1969), p. 3.
[7]Weinberger (1992), pp. 319–320.

supports it, but all this, in both poles of the relationship, constitutes a complex social fact, not a metaphysical abstraction.[8] While it is true that the idea of the social contract, which supports society and law, is a simple metaphor, nevertheless, it has logical value. In good account, it is a speculative concept that charts a long and slow social phenomenon that has given rise to ethics and the rules of what *ought to be*. The social contract, the will to impose, and the acceptance, as consented act, is the basis of the law. There is no legal phenomenon without sociological fact. The fact bases the law, not the other way around.

2   The Constitution and the New Way of Being of Law

The twentieth century will witness the explicit recognition of Human rights, the normative force of the Constitution, the constitutional jurisdiction, among other distinguishing marks of this new era. This situation has not gone unnoticed: "In my opinion, the great merit of anti-positivism is that it has known how to act as a healthy revulsion of legal knowledge and forensic practice that are excessively formalistic, self-sufficient, anchored in the nineteenth-century liberal state model and, above all, far removed from the other social sciences as well as moral and political philosophy".[9] To reach this point they have needed two world wars, totalitarian states and other political catastrophes, which finally led to the birth of the UN, the internationalisation of Human rights, and the generalisation of Constitutions with legal significance.[10]

The primacy of the human being in the human rights system causes, as a direct consequence in Civil law, the ontological centrality of existential rights (rights of the person), and consequently, the "functionalisation" of patrimonial situations, such as the property, the contract, and the company, which not only look at profit, but also fulfil the more general function of guaranteeing freedom of initiative, against any attempt at state absolutism.[11] Normative Constitutions and Human rights originate a new way of *being* of Law.

The rights of man are situated from two perspectives, not necessarily coincident and difficult to amalgamate: freedom and equality. The coexistence of two opposing values is not peaceful and offers great difficulties, especially when reductionism leads to fanaticism. In this sense, the primacy of freedom easily degenerates into the abuse of economic and political powers, which subjugate freedom; on the contrary, the preponderance of equality ends up drowning freedom, and, with this, conformist attitudes and anti-economic behaviours are fostered.

---

[8]Hart (2012), p. 145.

[9]Prieto (2005), p. 93.

[10]Ferrajoli (2001), pp. 134–135.

[11]Perlingieri (1984), p. 94.

These two conceptions, in principle antagonistic, have their expression in the "liberal state" against the "Social State" (*Welfare State*).[12]

For its part, history shows that freedom, by itself, is not enough to equal the possibilities of men; and an intervening action is needed to provide a minimum material base that allows individuals to exercise their freedom in a real and effective way.[13] Alternatively, "formal equality" is not enough, but "substantial equality or opportunities equality". The effectiveness of freedom depends on the improvement of the material conditions of life for all, that is, it is not intended to eliminate freedom to recognise social rights; on the contrary, the guarantee of these guarantees and generalises freedom.[14] Amartya Sen would say that negative freedom is not enough, because it is necessary to equip the subjects with capabilities.

The social demands, as well as the new ideologies and conceptions, are the powerful driving force that will push the provision of services by the State (health, education, water, among others). It is the origin of the Constitutional and Social State of Law.

2.1   Constitution and Private Law

The classical theory of Private Law, at least in countries inspired by the Roman-Germanic tradition, uses abstraction to formulate definitions and create concepts, almost filigree, along with the classifications to infinity, the "mathematical" systematics and the coherence of the "system",[15] which seeks the impossible "perfection". Therefore, in this perspective, the function of the jurist is almost exclusively dogmatic, by means of which the precise definitions, the adequate concepts and the profile of the institutions are pursued under the canons of coherence, systematic and logic, with that finally there will be an alphabet of voices and terms essential for legal communication,[16] but from a formal perspective.

For this reason, it is not surprising that the German Civil Code, an example of dogmatism, begins with a "General Part" that deals precisely with the cross-cutting concepts of the legal-civil system, which are applied in the field of contracts, successions, family and, even, in disciplines far from the private order, because it

---

[12]Ferrajoli (2001), pp. 81–82.

[13]"El Estado social y democrático de derecho, como alternativa política al Estado liberal, asume los fundamentos de este, pero además le imprime funciones de carácter social. Pretende que los principios que lo sustentan y justifican tengan una base y un contenido material. Y es que la libertad reclama condiciones materiales mínimas para hacer factible su ejercicio. . . . La seguridad e igualdad jurídicas requieren de una estructura económica adecuada que haga posible estos principios": Sentence of Peruvian Constitutional Court N° 0008-2003-AI/TC de 11.11.2003, n. 12th.

[14]Canosa (2004), pp. 117–118.

[15]Larenz (1994), p. 39.

[16]Zatti and Colussi (2005), p. 71.

seeks to achieve the coveted coherence of the legal order.[17] In this sense, the BGB breaks with the previous systematics,[18] be it the Roman law or the French codification, based on persons, things and actions; or in persons, things and obligations.[19] It is no longer enough to divide the Code by "regulated topics", but rather to move towards a system headed by basic notions.[20] Therefore, it is said that the "General Part" fulfils a systematic function, of valorative concordance, of saving precepts, of purified legislative technique, as recognised by the German doctrine itself,[21] which would avoid the risk of deviations in the solution of the same problem, or redundancies of a different type, which would hinder the work of the interpreter or the judge.

These are the lights that, theoretically, illuminate the so-called "jurisprudence of concepts",[22] but the shadows that obscure it are so great that they make the cost-benefit analysis clearly negative.

In effect, dogmatic conceptualism generates a conservative, individualistic regulation, without social base, because it is concerned with "chemically" pure concepts,[23] without contamination, with abstractions that go beyond time and space. However, let us not forget that the legislator and legal doctrine are ideological; and behind the rules are hiding ideas about economy and society. Consequently, the aseptic definition of Fundamental legal figures is related to the maintenance of the *status quo*, which no one questions, since these are universal concepts. Thus, for example, the notion of property as "absolute power over a thing" allows deducing an entire liberal ideological conception favourable to individualistic forces, which is clearly opposed to social visions. There is, then, a clear conservative tinge.

On the other hand, postmodern philosophy rejects metaphysics, ontological truths, the "nature of things", essences, absolutes, nevertheless, the traditional legal dogmatics became aware that its base ideas are outdated some time ago, while Law is not ontological, nor does it exist in heaven as a revealed truth that we must discover by means of logical operations, because, in reality, it is a technique created by men to fulfil practical purposes of coexistence, which is continually being made, recreated, by the societies themselves, and not dictated by a supreme being, by reason or by dogmas that go beyond time. Law does not belong to nature, it is not "natural"; on the contrary, it is a practical-formal apparatus, created by men, but susceptible to endless adjustments for social, economic and valuation needs, always changing.[24] There are no unique truths, not even in the field of Human rights, where

---

[17]Morales (2012), p. 109.

[18]The German Civil Code has five books: general part, law of obligations, law of property, law of family and law of inheritances.

[19]Guzmán (2014), pp. 25–58.

[20]García (1983), p. 37.

[21]Oertmann (1933), p. 30.

[22]Larenz (1994), p. 41.

[23]Merryman (2012), p. 275.

[24]Fernández (2015), p. 13.

there is talk of practical "justification," and not of metaphysical "foundation".[25] Let alone, there can be no ontological truth or "supernatural reality" in the definitions of Civil law, patrimonial or not.

The legal conceptions that are based on truths that go beyond history, borders, societies, national laws, and that are imposed as ontological realities that jurists discover through a series of logical, deductive operations, inspired by coherence and systematic, are excluded from current philosophical thinking. It is not possible to construct the new way of being of the juridical phenomenon, when the theoretical bases continue being the absolute or ontological truths, the eternal classifications, the ethical neutrality or the overvaluation of the formalist coherence. It is necessary that our discipline revises its concepts and definitions to achieve the adequacy with the Constitution, and to overcome its antinomies with the ordinary legislation, but under the premise that law has a cultural, changing and particular character; which is not based in fundamentalist foundations, but in practical justifications, so as not to return to metaphysics, not even to the rather naive type of stony or immovable Constitutions, with what is intended to put "an end to history".

The program of action of the Civil Law, with mantle in the Constitution, covers the most diverse subjects, among others, the protection of the honest and reasonable ends in the legal transaction; the protection of the weak contracting party through contractual justice mechanisms that overcome the subjection to a pact; the consumer's defence against a monopolistic, abusive market that is not free; the nullity of abusive general clauses even without express regulation that sanctions them, and by effect of the constitutional norms of consumer protection or of prohibition of the abuse of right; the reform of the law of contracts to examine whether contractual freedom is really operating or whether it is a simple label; the re-evaluation of arbitration as private justice that in many cases results in a fraud against judicial protection, or an abuse against the weak party and that suffers the same defects of state justice; the weighting of the different interests in the conflicts of rights in rem without the registration being the only adjudication criterion since it has the advantages and disadvantages of all formalism; and so many other issues on which progress must be made to achieve legal relations with substantial equality and material justice in the solutions. That is, a Civil law that seeks the progress of society, while respecting the dignity of man.

2.2   Constitution and Codes

The codification is a legislative technique that is characterised by regulating a certain plot of social life with the pretension of integrity, clarity, order, systematic and security; whose purpose is that all legal conflicts can be resolved by simply consulting that legal text. In good account, it is like a book in which you will find easily and

---

[25]Rorty and Habermas (2012), pp. 12–13.

simply all the answers that are sought. The Codes are based on the ideas of universality (medium) and security (purpose); but its philosophical background is none other than formalism.

Nevertheless, the constitutional influx, Human rights and modern philosophical conceptions of law have produced the outbreak of codification, since the phenomenon known as "indetermination of law" occurs, especially in "hard cases", as it does not only enter at stake a norm of the Code, but also one or more elastic principles contained in the Constitution, or an international norm of Human rights, or the jurisprudence of a High Court, or even the report of a thematic rapporteur of the universal human rights system that it has an impact on the case. To this is added that the judge is no longer the mouth of the law, but the centre of the legal system as the ultimate guarantor of the Fundamental rights of man.

The lack of certainty is a direct consequence of the application of Fundamental rights in the solution of civil conflicts.[26] The sources of law have expanded vertically (more rules and more decisions, sometimes overlapping each other), but also horizontally (the content of each legal rule, which must be adapted to the Constitution or a Human rights treaty interpreted by an International Court, it has become indeterminate). The Law acted by means of open principles and of difficult concretion, and not by exact rules and of unconditioned application, is the very negation of the spirit that animated in its moment the phenomenon of the codification. Therefore, it is not that Codes are in trouble or outdated in relation to modern technology or the new society, but that the very idea of code is that which is in a deep crisis of justification, even in decline, and perhaps surpassed.

Law has become more complex, and that does not fit with the conception of clear and simple rules that animates codes. Moreover, today it is said that all principles, or almost all, are defeasible, that is, they themselves come into conflict, precisely because of their natural indeterminacy, and consequently, in the specific case, it must be elucidated which principle prevails; however, this preference cannot be generalised nor can an abstract rule be established, since it only serves to resolve a certain factual circumstance. In short, legal decisions by principles have the advantage of adapting to the true nature of Law, not only reduced to standards, with entry of morality and importance of argumentation, but have the disadvantage of greater uncertainty regarding the solution of the case. In these circumstances, codification can be considered, today, a legislative technique that is not so compatible with the current way of being of Law. For this reason, general clauses of Codes, such as good faith, abuse of right or the prohibition of going against one's own actions, are becoming more and more important to overcome the unacceptable solutions of strict rules.

But, notice that there is talk of a crisis of legislative technique, but not of a crisis of the rights of the person. Codes lose importance, but not Private Law, only that this is resized through Constitution. The new legal system based on Human rights is

---

[26]Hesse (2001), pp. 59–60.

simply not on the same frequency as Codes with simple rules, which, by definition, sought to achieve certainty and security.

2.3   Constitution and Enjoyment of Goods

Property, according to civil law, is a direct, exclusive, absolute and inherent attribution that falls on goods, and whose interest is the enjoyment and advantage, always within the limits established by the common good and social interest (Article 923 Peruvian Civil Code). However, property has changed radically in terms of its definition, content and function. This is because of the social, political and economic changes that have taken place in the last century, which includes phenomena as important as the progressive universalisation of Human rights, technological advances, among others.

At present, there is not the same notion of property as that prevailing during the liberal state of the nineteenth century, and that still remains by inertia in Civil codes, anchored in the individualism and in the sacrosanct right of the owner even to abuse the thing, since only the holder's voluntarism is protected.

The definition of property has evolved from the individualist-liberal perspective to a social one. For its part, the current property, of constitutional and social profile, is subject from its own interior to a series of limitations and restrictions aimed at the common good. The owner does not live alone, nor does his wealth originate from his own efforts. For this reason, it is not surprising that from the philosophy of law it is said that property not only protects an individual interest (of the owner), but also different collective goods that are materialised in guidelines. A property based or justified only in the autonomy of the owner would jeopardise its own purpose, because in reality what is sought is that all individuals have the *quantum* of property necessary to carry out an autonomous existence. Consequently, the owner's autonomy cannot ignore the demand for other collective goods, such as a more equitable distribution of income, access to work, the modernisation of all economic sectors, the right environment, the conservation of cultural heritage, the right to adequate housing, the protection of consumers, the protection of health, etc.[27]

The civil definition, founded on the absolutism of the owner and on the protection of his free will, has been outdated for some time. Property is neither protected by purely individualistic or selfish causes, nor by the will of the owner. Today, property is recognised in man for the purpose of fulfilling a social mission in accordance with his dignity in the world; with his rights to be free and equal but with a substantial character, and to achieve a just society with minimal possibilities for all. In such a context, property only makes sense as a "function" that allows meeting the needs of the human being within an environment of solidarity, peace, tranquillity, security and well-being.

---

[27]Atienza and Ruiz (2006), p. 52.

The definition of property, within the scope of Human rights, has re-dimensioned the civil, liberal and proper notion of codifications, therefore, from a "right-will", has been passed to a "right-function". From this we have that property has ceased to be absolute or unlimited; or a simple right of liberty over things, or where limitations on domain are exceptions. On the contrary, property becomes a prerogative recognised by the legal system, but conditioned to the fulfilment of social duties, to the function of promoting general wealth, to protect general interests. Therefore, there is recognition of individual prerogative, although mediated by the common good.

The definition of property, voluntarist in Codes, becomes a function for the general interest, which is seen in constitutions and in Human rights treaties. This new conception of property not only affects its definition, but also radiates throughout the institution; and this is seen in the regulation that begins to be dictated. Therefore, the extinction of property is now recognised, without compensation, when there are grounds for equity (abandonment), and this right also begins to be protected as long as the owner complies with the socio-economic functions imposed on him, such as permanent work, economic exploitation for the purpose of general welfare. Work is the justification of property, which is why the importance of possession and usucapion is revitalised.[28] It is a right rooted in the social phenomenon.

The postmodern notion of property right-sizes that notion embodied in Codes, while moving away from the absolutist, individualist and liberal conception. Today, the social function goes through the content of property itself, while Law fulfils the objective of procuring the common good. In this sense, Civil codes require a rereading, and this is noted in the influence and importance that the social function gains in the new understanding of the freedoms and powers of the owner, but that will then expand to other individual rights. This configuration, before exceptional and anomalous, happens to become, not only in natural, but in the justifying end of dominion and rights that are recognised on things or objects of the nature. In short, there is no property without a social function, since individual utility and solidarity clearly shape the new concept of property.[29]

2.4 Constitution and Freedom to Contract

Pure individualism (the "Self") is based on the arbitrariness of one will imposed on the other, whether by force, tradition or resources. On the contrary, the idea of a contract implies an overcoming of that coarse individualism, insofar as it entails the recognition of the other, the existence of an intersubjective relationship of the type

---

[28]Caicedo (1988), p. 231.

[29]SSTC de España 37/1987, of March 26th; 227/1988, of November 29th; 170/1989, of October 19th: Martínez-Pereda et al. (2002), pp. 363–364. See too: European Court of Human Rights, S 1979, June 13th, Case *Marckx/Bélgica*): Álvarez-Osorio (n.d.), p. 5.

"I-you", therefore, in such case is required the concurrent will of two people, in which neither imposes itself on the other, but is conjugated in an area of freedom and equality, for what is materialised in the agreement, or in the consent, which etymologically means "to feel together", which is quite graphic and expressive.

Agreement is the very essence of contracting, which led to support the doctrine of legal liberalism that: "to say contract is to say fair", while its bases are based on equal relationships, and not on imposition or discrimination, so that a concordant, stable result is achieved, typical of a social peace system, even from a theoretical or philosophical perspective. Well then, the influence of the Constitution on Civil law means that the general and abstract rules of codification have to be revised when faced with concrete material conditions. This is the origin of labour law, agrarian law and consumer law, which are sectors, now, broken off from the common core of Private law Codes.

3   Social Market Economy

3.1   Definition

Article 58 of the Constitution of Peru, of 1993 (hereinafter: CP), states that: "*private initiative is free. It is exercised in a social market economy*", which means that economic relations are shaped by the free competition between supply (sellers) and demand (buyers), for the direct achievement of individual benefit, under the premise that each person is the one who "better" knows his own interests, which, multiplying in all cases, will allow achieving general welfare.

This free market presupposes "*respect for property, private initiative and free competition governed, prima facie, by supply and demand, and, on the other hand, the fight against oligopolies or monopolies*" (Judgment of the Constitutional Court of Peru , hereinafter, STC No. 00008-2003-AI/TC, 13th f.j.); likewise: "*social market economy is representative of the constitutional values of freedom and justice, therefore, it is compatible with the axiological and teleological foundations that inspire a social and democratic rule of law. In this, the principles of freedom and promotion of material equality within a democratic order guaranteed by State prevail*" (16th f.j.).

For the rest, social market economy has the important function of safeguarding patrimonial freedom, granting the individual a scope of free action ahead of exaggerated interferences of public and private powers. Thus, "(guarantees) freedom of the private and their autonomy in the exercise of economic power with respect to political power, that is, the denial of authoritarian directed economy, but with the simultaneous affirmation of the state prerogative where it is imposed by needs of protection that transcend market".[30]

---

[30]Mazzamuto (2012), pp. 192–193.

The act of circulation of wealth, in market economy, is based, fundamentally, on private initiative, free and autonomous, so it is necessary the willingness of economic agents to sell or transfer ownership, and not for state heteronomous decisions.[31] In good account, "to say that private initiative is free is to affirm that market belongs to individuals and not to the State. It means that it is not the State's task to create wealth; this function is reserved to individuals".[32] In effect, material well-being is achieved through work and individual or social effort, which allows production of goods and productivity of resources, therefore, wealth is originated by the activity of man, and not by the activity of the State, which is finally a fiction that brings together human beings. In this sense, social market economy recognises the practical justification of wealth, based on freedom and individual initiative, but corrected by excesses or shortcomings of the system.

In social market economy, the individual is a leading actor, while the State is a supervisor or arbitrator, so according to our legal system, planned or centralised economy is rejected,[33] but not strategic planning, which is the set of plans that guide state action.

3.2 Assumptions

Social market economy, based on voluntary exchanges of goods, constitutes the most efficient mechanism for the best allocation of resources to create wealth and economic development. It is a historical observation that in the last hundred and fifty years, capitalism in its superior phase managed to lift many nations out of poverty, especially since the industrial revolution,[34] which placed on the agenda a relevant issue: wealth is created through the increase in productivity, through scientific and technological progress, so that the same resources serve to achieve greater production; however, this technical development requires capitalist legal institutions, such as respect for property, protection of inventions and patents, freedom of trade, freedom of the productive forces to seek better products at lower prices.[35]

However, market cannot develop on its own; it needs supports that allow the game of supply and demand, such as fundamental economic freedoms, provided by a Constitution: freedom of enterprise, freedom of trade and industry, free competition, freedom of contracting and property rights. All of them "are part of the hard core of the Economic constitution[36]".

---

[31]Rey (1994), p. 321.

[32]Gutiérrez (2013), p. 21.

[33]Ariño (2004), p. 295.

[34]Cortázar (2011), pp. 13–14.

[35]Pipes (1999), p. 364.

[36]Gutiérrez (2013), p. 38.

At this point, it is necessary to emphasise that social market economy supports are not mere abstract concepts, but concepts in operation, that is, institutions that make them effective are required.

3.2.1 Freedom of Enterprise

Freedom of enterprise means that individuals can freely engage in economic activities of production of goods or provision of services, for profit, which is an essential part of a market economy, because if the foundation, organisation and management of private companies were not possible, then, who would be responsible for the production, distribution and trade actions? The State as business manager has demonstrated its inefficiency, not forgetting that public resources are risked in this adventure, so failure would have to be assumed by taxpayers.

Article 58 CP clearly links freedom of enterprise with creation of wealth, which is correct, because freedom is the means to achieve wealth, which is the purpose.

3.2.2 Freedom of Commerce and Industry

Freedom of trade and industry means that individuals have in their hands the decision to undertake the specific economic activity that represents the greatest utility, so protections of certain professions or activities are repealed, which would configure a monopoly or inconvenient oligopoly, in as much beneficiaries would be a group of privileged, excluded of the free competition regime, in which they would obtain a monopolistic rent, which is not justified, with the consequent damage to consumers and, with this, to the whole society.

Freedom of trade represents the extinction of trade unions, with their patents, limited number and protectionism; therefore, from liberal constitutionalism, any person may engage in the exchange of goods or services, without the need for prior permits or authorisations, except legal exceptions. On the other hand, freedom of industry put an end to production quotas and to legal privileges of producers, typical of pre-capitalism; therefore, from the first constitutionalism, people will have the possibility of carrying out any continuous and permanent action of transforming material reality for economic purposes.

3.2.3 Free Competition

Free competition means that economic agents, such as companies, can go to the market without restrictions, to trade or produce goods and services of their choice, in conditions of equality, without privileges, freely and honestly, which allows that goods reach consumers in better conditions and at lower prices. The consequence is that the production of wealth and productivity of resources are encouraged.

Free competition constitutes an economic system that rejects the previous order, based on privileges, prohibitions and authorisations,[37] which prevented liberation of productive forces for the achievement of greater production at lower cost.

3.2.4 Freedom to Contract

Freedom of contracting is also a fundamental assumption of a market economy, in that it allows exchange of goods and services through voluntary acts, which, in this way, ensures that patrimonial resources are voluntarily assigned to their most valuable uses. Without contract, there would be no supply or demand; therefore, goods of the economy would be stagnant in the same people, so that from a market economy there would be a transition to one of individual consumption, because the subject could only subsist with its own production, intended for consumption. In such conditions it is difficult to suppose that one could advance towards an advanced capitalist economy, in that resources would be stagnant and immobilised in the same person.

3.2.5 Right of Private Property

Property rights ensure that the owner can freely use and enjoy the good, according to the form that is more in line with his interests; therefore, owners are allowed to constantly improve productivity, that is, increase production with the least amount of resources invested. The consequence is that property serves to take care of assets, internalises the external and allows production.

Market economy requires constant and continuous exchange of goods, but this can only happen if legal order recognises, in a preliminary way, private property, that is, the individual right of man over realities of the external world (things), among which is the one of disposition, by which, the owner, without giving account to anyone, can transfer those same goods to third person, freely and by act of his will. Without private property, with free disposal, a market economy simply would not be possible. However, at present, the concept of property is not reduced to the individual enjoyment of the owner, always relevant, but also to the fulfilment of the social function consisting in the achievement of common good.

4 Freedom to Contract and Contract in the Constitution of 1993

Article 2, subsection 14) CP establishes that every person has the right "*to contract for lawful purposes, provided they do not contravene laws of public order*"; while Article 62 CP points out that:

---

[37]Cortázar (2011), p. 14.

The freedom to contract guarantees that the parties can agree validly according to the regulations in force at the time of the contract. The contractual terms cannot be modified by laws or other provisions of any kind. Conflicts arising from the contractual relationship are solved only in the arbitral or judicial way, according to the protection mechanisms provided in the contract or contemplated in the law. Through contracts-law, the State can establish guarantees and grant securities. They cannot be modified legislatively, without prejudice to the protection referred to in the preceding paragraph.

4.1 Definition

The constitutional right to "contract for lawful purposes", provided in Article 2, subsection 14 CP, constitutes a legal freedom, which operates in the economic field, so the subject-holder has the alternative to exercise its prerogative in a positive way (to contract), under a certain set of agreements, or decline from it, through its negative performance (refusing to contract). The STC No. 0008-2003-AI/TC, dated 11.11.2003, states: "This right guarantees, prima facie: i. Self-determination to decide the execution of a contract, as well as the power to choose the co-contractor. ii. Self-determination to decide, by mutual agreement, the subject matter of contractual regulation".

4.2 Content

The "freedom to contract", in its positive face, originates the "contract", as a voluntary "act" of the parties, as well as the "legal relationship", which constitutes the effects that one produces in the world of law, be it prerogatives, obligations or duties of all kinds, which are acted on in social reality. That is, the freedom to contract not only includes its own definition, as freedom, but also the result of its exercise, in its manifestation of "contract-act" and "contract-relationship".

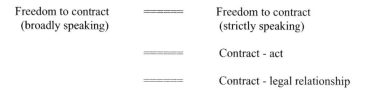

Therefore, freedom to contract, as a constitutional right of broad content, includes the following manifestations:

(a) Freedom to contract or not (strictly speaking): The human being develops his abilities by exercising his freedom, but in the economic sphere, this is expressed mainly through the figure of the contract, then, through this, man can obtain economic goods through voluntary agreements that allow him to act in the market. Capitalist economy is based on work specialisation, so each one requires the other, in an exchange system by contracts. The life of man, in individual perspective, and the socioeconomic system, in a general sense, cannot renounce voluntary agreements, which is the best formula for ordering a society, through consensus, mutual and reciprocal advantages, responsibility for own actions, etc., so it is not surprising that the freedom to contract, almost in a natural way, is recognised, albeit timidly, in the catalogue of constitutional rights.

This freedom to contract (strictly speaking) is manifested in various areas, whether in the conclusion of contract, or not, which is expressed at the decisive moment of the voluntary decision (premise) that gives rise to the contract (result), or, in the choice of the co-contractor, that is, freedom would not be complete if it only refers to the act, but not to the subject, since the lack of one of them would eliminate freedom. A forced contract, with a specific counterpart, can only be justified when a constitutional value, from equivalent rank, justifies the restriction of the will, as occurs, for example, in case of concessionaires, who must provide the service in a compulsory manner to all the users, because it is about benefits of general interest, in which discriminatory treatment is not accepted, but the universality of coverage; therefore, in this case, the usual regime is that of the contract imposed, whereby the concessionaire is not free to choose the counterpart, since, in such case, it has the legal obligation to accept anyone who meets the assumptions and requirements provided by law.

(b) Right to the contract (or "contract-act"): Individuals not only have freedom on the premise ("to contract"), but also on the consequence ("contract"); therefore, once it was decided to exercise freedom, then there is the right to "contract-act", which implies having a shell, or feature of immunity against ordinary laws that could not sanction its nullity for superfluous causes; or establish its lack of enforceability; or point out ridiculous deadlines to improperly validate it. The "contract-act" is the result of the freedom to contract, and by itself determines a sphere of individual guardianship against attempts to ignore it by the authorities of the administration, by judges or by factual powers.

(c) Right to own contractual regulation (or "contract-relationship"): The exercise of economic freedom, manifested through the contract, requires the recognition to individuals of a regulatory power to establish and regulate their own legal relationships. The system considers that the best way to promote economic development is to admit a set of postulates that make market economy possible, among which is the freedom to contract in its regulatory modality. Therefore, this sphere is reserved for the individuals themselves, in the exercise of their "private autonomy", to dictate the most convenient rules -according to themselves, and who are the main stakeholders-, to satisfy their own needs, or to obtain reciprocal advantages, or to tend to social improvement, with greater efficiency, production and/or productivity. In short, freedom to contract, broadly speaking, also includes the so-called right to "contract-relationship", that is, the possibility of delineating the legal effects, both rights and obligations that are manifested in the legal link. Indeed, very little would be achieved if autonomy served to celebrate the act, but not to delineate its effects within it, through specific clauses and pacts that respond to the needs of the specific agreement, under the premise that individuals know better than anyone, including the State, the formulas that allow arriving at the individual and collective welfare.

Therefore, freedom to contract guarantees the recognition of contracts entered into by individuals, in the exercise of their private autonomy,[38] which is materialised with the conclusion of the contract for lawful purposes.[39]

4.3 Limits

In the scope of the contract, there is an old philosophical dispute about the basis of the contract and its enforceability, which can be summarised with the following questions: Is the voluntary agreement (premise) sufficient to be fair? Or is the recognition of the agreement justified by the effect of fair exchange (conclusion)? "The distinction between these two types of questions suggests that we can conceive the morality of a contract as consisting of two related but separable ideals. One is the ideal of autonomy, which perceives the contract as an agreement of wills, whose morality consists in the voluntary nature of transaction. The other is the ideal of reciprocity, which sees the contract as an instrument of mutual benefit, whose morality depends on the underlying justice of exchange".[40] In short, what is at stake are two opposing conceptions of life: the individual ethics of the will and freedom, or the social ethics of responsibility. This means that not only the public power, but also society and its unique members respond for each of the members of society. Civil Law no longer only addresses the individual autonomy of each one, but also social justice, so that, in addition to the defence of one's own interests, the defence of the weak is pursued.

Private autonomy, at present, is not mere form, but the consequence of a real freedom, by virtue of which, the interested parties find themselves in a situation, factual and juridical, of approximate equality of opportunities.[41]

The philosophical debate has legal relevance of the first order. In effect, two free and equal persons who reach an agreement, not only exercise their individual rights, but also presuppose that the economic operation is mutually advantageous, for example, in theory, the exchange improves the initial position of each of the participants. "The attractiveness of the agreement, then, is not only related to the welfare of the parties, but also, with the justice of the exchange".[42] This liberal perspective is compatible with negotiated contracts in which the parties are in a situation of approximate parity. On the contrary, this conclusion does not seem valid when there is an imbalance between the contracting parties, since inequality compresses or annuls the freedom of the decision, therefore, in these material conditions, the agreement is purely formal, to the extent that, in these cases, the agreement

---

[38]Mazzamuto (2012), p. 175.

[39]Gutiérrez (2013), p. 257.

[40]Sandel (2000), p. 138.

[41]Hesse (2001), pp. 73–79.

[42]De La Maza (2018), p. 1.

(subjectivism) is not enough to ensure a fair act, but the balance of exchange (objectivism). "The lack of freedom and equality of the parties tends to produce a domino effect with respect to the liberal conception of the contract. In the following terms: if the parties should not be considered free and equal (1) then there is no reason to assume that the content of the contract represents what was convenient for both, (2) therefore, it is no longer possible to consider contracts as fair, (3) nor is it convenient (in fact, as will be seen, it is not possible) to interpret the contract seeking the agreement of the parties".[43]

4.4 Social Function of the Contract

Nowadays, it is not only spoken of the social function of property, but the same concept has been transferred to the scope of contract, which means to recognise the overcoming of the liberal concept of contract, based on the justice of the agreement that arises from free and equal people, by one of social scope, as it is also considered, increasingly to a greater extent, the justice that is born from the economic operation with balanced exchange. For this reason, the new trends in the law of contracts are the following, by way of example[44]: (a) recourse to subjective good faith in the pursuit of contractual justice *in the* relationship, and not *of the* relationship, since the latter would involve seeking external parameters to the same contract, or what is the same: "a general model of exchange"; (b) the mechanism of objective good faith to fill the gaps or correct, without nullifying it, the inequities of the contractual regulation through the integrative function; (c) the call to general clauses that prevent the abusive exercise of discretional freedoms of one of the contracting parties, such as the prohibition of the abuse of right, of fraud to the law or of acting against one's actions; (d) respect to Fundamental rights, for example, the principle of equality before the law, and the prohibition of discriminatory acts, which would entail the nullity of the contractual regulation by contrasting public order; (e) restriction of the contractual regulation itself when the freedom is mediated by effect of the factual power of one of the parties.

For a long time, law has been understood as a simple instrument that postulates the legal security of investors and financiers, because, in this way, efficiency in the use of scarce resources can be achieved and, consequently, the assets will be assigned little by little to the most valuable ends. Under this perspective, economic development is built from the "top to bottom", that is, the greater production and the increase in income of the powerful will end up having an impact sooner or later on the weakest and most vulnerable layers of society. In this context, the increase in productivity leads to better wages, and working conditions, with the consequent increase in demand, after production, and so on in a virtuous circuit of growth.

[43]Ibíd.
[44]Mazzamuto (2012), pp. 200–201.

However, economic power is also a form of power, and perhaps, more violent, insofar as it is not channelled through institutional mechanisms, since in the sphere of private relations, solutions are imposed through agreements of subjects that are formally equal only. For this reason, the abuses committed against the workers, consumers or inexperienced contractors are recurrent. In the absence of legal limits or strict controls, the law of the jungle is imposed, because of the arrogance of one and the fear of the other,[45] without the so-called "self-regulation" that implies a withdrawal from the State to favour the "goodwill" of a group or category, which only fuels social inequalities and economic inequities. Market cannot function without an impartial regulatory context, but also, in many cases, with corrective measures in the face of its inexorable undesirable consequences.

5 Principles of Private Contracting

The contract fulfils the objective of channelling the exchange and allocation of goods or services in society, through the recognition of certain principles that allow its functionality: (a) freedom, since it is an act of autonomy; (b) equality, insofar as this guarantees the protection of the operation; (c) patrimoniality, since it is an economic operation that serves the satisfaction of individual and social interests; (d) regulations, while the agreement is binding, so it creates private norms, which generates legal security, pillar of any economic system that encourages the creation of wealth.

The basic principles are those that underlie the very notion of contract, among which is the "normative", because the contract has the function of creating rules to ensure economic relations. The famous "*pacta sunt servanda*" is a phrase that summarises the normative purpose of contract, related to legal security.

6 The Contract as a General Category

Contracts, from the structural perspective, are bilateral human acts, of a patrimonial nature; but, from the functional aspect, it consists of the mechanism that allows the exchange of goods and services for the achievement of valuable purposes, such as the satisfaction of immediate or complex needs, but under the principles of economic efficiency, social development, greater productivity and life quality, without prejudice to the growing problems of abuse in the exercise of freedoms.

In this sense, people buy, sell, lease or take loans, so that at each moment they enter into particular contracts (sales, lease, mutual, etc.) that aim to obtain practical economic results, but with full, express or presumed conviction, that the relationship has an impact on the legal world.

---

[45]Ferrajoli (2001), pp. 128–129.

The multiplicity of contracts can make it difficult to solve cases, which requires the use of analogy; therefore, if the system has a rule in the contract of sale, by virtue of which, the expenses are divided between the two parties, but that same rule has not been contemplated in the lease, so the uncertainty arises by a normative gap. On such occasion, the following outlets are available: first, to go to the judge, after the conflict, so that the rule of one sector is transferred in the specific case to another sector; second, to go to the theoretical or practical jurist, to recommend filling the gap, prior to the conflict, with a private rule in the same contractual text; third, to go to the legislator so that he establishes positive norms that solve cases in anticipatory form to the conflict, but with general character.

Let us concentrate on this last possibility.

The legislator can establish the same rule of sales in the legal sector of lease, but then would have to do the same in the construction contract, mandate, loan, etc. The result is the reiteration of norms. The second possibility is to create a more general category, which abstracts all the common elements of sales, lease or mutual, which gives rise to the regulation on "the contract", which in principle applies to all types of contracts, except that there is a special provision to the contrary. The result is the legislative economy, or the *elegantia iuris*, as the Roman jurists would say, as a single rule can cover the multiplicity of contractual agreements.

Codification is characterised by the claim of systematic; therefore, it is not strange that it has chosen to regulate a set of rules on the "contract in general" as an abstract category, and then, different rules for each type of contract.

The Peruvian Civil Code of 1984 (hereinafter, CCP) is not the exception, then: Book VII, Sources of Obligations, includes the First Section, the "contracts in general", which contains one hundred and seventy-seven norms, from the Article 1351 to Article 1528 CCP. After that, follows the Second Section, on sixteen "nominated contracts", namely, sales, exchange, supply, donation, mutual, lease, lodging, loan, service location, construction, mandate, deposit, sequestration, bond, rent for life, gambling and betting (Article 1529 to Article 1949 CCP), having repealed the rules on contracts related to arbitration.

The First Section, of "contracts in general", regulates the following fifteen subjects: (i) General provisions (general norms of a category, which by itself, is already general); (ii) Consent; (iii) Object; (iv) Form; (v) Preparatory contracts; (vi) Contract with reciprocal benefits; (vii) Transfer of contractual position; (viii) Excessive onerousness of the service; (ix) Injury; (x) Contract in favour of third party; (xi) Promise of the obligation or act of a third party; (xii) Contract per person to be appointed; (xiii) Confirmatory deposits; (xiv) Non-refundable security deposits; and, (xv) Sanitation obligations.

7 The Agreement in Contracts

The agreement is a communicative fact by two people, not a psychological or intimate event, so it needs to materialise in the social field. Throughout history, this communication has occurred through different mechanisms, according to the valuations of each society. For example, ancient rights demanded that the will be manifested through public or religious ceremonies, as in the case of the Roman testament that was to be pronounced in a public assembly, or with the act of transfer of property, or mancipation, that required a complicated ceremonial with a scale, seven witnesses, seller and buyer, in which the metal representative of the price was weighed. In any case, the naked will, the only external manifestation of wanting, was not enough to produce legal linkage. The informal agreement, in this context, does not generate obligations. For the rest, a prescription of this type is natural in systems that still do not completely abandon the religious origin, because sacredness is usually linked to rites, formulas or magical acts, which, for this reason, are necessary for a simple will, without any transcendence, which differs from the will translated into rites, which only in this way produce legal agreements.[46] Roman law is a good example of these ideas, but, in general, the same has happened in all the rights or legal systems of antiquity.[47]

However, sacrality and exaggerated formalism is inconvenient when commercial relationships begin to flourish, then, the professional exchange requires speed and simplicity of operations. Trade is the decisive cause in the elimination of contractual formalism. It is no coincidence that one of the consensual contracts of classical Roman law is the sales contract, typical mercantile business, which needed simple rules for its making. Many centuries later, with the advent of capitalism, and, consequently, of its legal instrument, commercial law, once again the formal rules of contracting were repealed according to trade rules, which were finally transferred to Civil codes.

In summary, Modern civil law embraces the consensual principle in contracting, that is, for the formation of contract, and its binding effect, the consent expressed by the parties is sufficient, either verbally, in written form or by actions (Articles 141, 1352 CCP). That is to say, private norms born of contract can be originated, even, and in the most extreme case, by a will manifested by words. The rule is the consensus declared by any valid form of communication (Article 141 CCP), on the other hand, the exception is strict formality. The main cause of such change is the economy: traffic of goods needs agile and simplified means.[48]

8   The Obligatory Nature of Contracts

The binding (normative) force of legal transactions, and especially of contract, is based on the Constitution, which establishes contractual freedom as a Fundamental right (Article 2, paragraph 14 of the Peruvian Constitution), but, from a pragmatic perspective, is based in the needs of the traffic, since the economy is developed,

---

[46]Guzmán (2013), T. I, p. 789.
[47]Olivecrona (2004), p. 27.
[48]De La Puente (2001), T. I, p. 131.

fundamentally, by the work of private initiative, which among other things requires market economy, property and contractual freedom. In this context, contracts are the main means by which men use to knit together the warp of their legal relationships, which is why it is the essential instrument for economic life and the promotion of wealth.[49] It is worth remembering that private autonomy, before a legal phenomenon, is a social phenomenon. Therefore, "the recognition of private autonomy is a requirement that involves the same human person, so it is inadmissible to consider it as a simple opportunity for the State machine to act (normativist conception). It is also inaccurate to say that it is something that, as of their own matters, only the interested parties care about".[50] This statement is true at the sociological level, but not at the legal level, because, effectively, contract creates legal norms.

Article 1361, 1st CCP establishes in strict form: "Contracts are obligatory as insofar as it has been expressed in them", which gives rise to a series of considerations.

First, contract is a legal act that creates specific rules, but binding for their authors: "they are mandatory", therefore, there is no possibility to desist or retract the commitments already made.

Secondly, contract is a legal act of social, non-intimist or psychological scope, therefore, the obligation of its rules derives from what: "has been expressed in them", that is, contract is an expressive, communicative phenomenon, of manifestation in front of the world, and it is not reduced to the narrow limit of thought or internal will, which nothing expresses to others.

Third, if contract is an expressive fact ("as insofar as it has been expressed in them"), then the validity of the act is related to the coincidence of the communicative manifestations between the two parties, therefore, while the statement by both contracting parties are concordant in the same expression, then the contract will be perfected by "the consent of the parties" (Article 1352 CCP).

References

Álvarez-Osorio F (n.d.) La construcción del derecho de propiedad por el Tribunal Europeo de Derechos Humanos. Paper

Ariño G (2004) Principios de derecho público económico. Ara, Lima

Atienza M, Ruiz J (2006) Ilícitos atípicos. Trotta, Madrid

Betti E (1969) Teoría general de las obligaciones (trans: De Los Mozos J). Edersa, Madrid

Borda G (1978) Manual de Contratos. Abeledo Perrot, Buenos Aires

Caicedo E (1988) Función social y derechos humanos económico-sociales. In VV.AA. Derecho Agrario y Derechos Humanos. Cultural Cuzco, Lima

Canosa R (2004) Constitución y Medio Ambiente. Jurista Editores, Lima

Cortázar J (2011) Curso de derecho de la competencia (antimonopolios). Javeriana- Temis, Bogotá

De Castro F (1985) El negocio jurídico. Civitas, Madrid

---

[49]Borda (1978), p. 114.

[50]De Castro (1985), p. 12.

De La Maza I (2018) Acuerdo y equilibrio contractual. In http://www.elmercurio.com/Legal/Noticias/Analisis-Juridico/2018/05/16/Acuerdo-y-equilibrio-contractual.aspx   (consulted: 10.06.2018)

De La Puente M (2001) El contrato en general. Palestra, Lima

Fernández C (2015) Derecho y Persona. 5° edición. Astrea, Buenos Aires

Ferrajoli L (2001) El garantismo y la filosofía del derecho (trans: Pisarello G et al). Externado. Bogotá

García G (1983) Parte General del Derecho Civil Español. Civitas, Madrid

Gutiérrez W (2013) "Comentario al artículo 58". In: Íd. (ed) La Constitución Comentada. Gaceta Jurídica, Lima

Guzmán A (2013) Derecho privado romano. 2° edición. Thomson Reuters, Santiago

Guzmán A (2014) Estudios Varios de Derecho Civil. Jurista Editores, Lima

Hart H (2012) El concepto de derecho. 3° edición (trans: Carrió G). Abeledo Perrot, Buenos Aires

Heidegger M (2011) Tiempo y Ser (trans: Garrido M et al). Tecnos, Madrid

Hesse K (2001) Derecho Constitucional y Derecho Privado (trans: Gutiérrez I). Civitas, Madrid

Jaspers K (2003) La Filosofía desde el punto de vista de la existencia (trans: Gaos J). FCE, México

Larenz K (1994) Metodología de la Ciencia del Derecho (trans: Rodríguez M). Ariel, Barcelona

Martínez-Pereda J et al (2002) Constitución Española. Colex, Madrid

Mazzamuto S (2012) Libertà contrattuale e utilità sociale. In: Salvi C (Dir) Diritto civile e principi costituzionali europei e italiani. Giappichelli, Turín

Merryman J (2012) La tradición jurídica romano-canónica (trans: Sierra C). FCE, México

Morales R (2012) La propiedad en las situaciones jurídicas subjetivas. In: Priori G (ed) Estudios sobre la propiedad. PUCP, Lima

Oertmann P (1933) Introducción al Derecho Civil (trans: Sancho L). Labor, Barcelona

Olivecrona K (2004) Lenguaje jurídico y realidad (trans: Garzón E). Fontamara, México

Perlingieri P (1984) Il diritto civile nella legalità costituzionale. ESI, Naples

Pipes R (1999) Propiedad y libertad (trans: De Diego J). FCE, México

Prieto L (2005) Constitucionalismo y Positivismo. Fontamara, México

Rey F (1994) La propiedad privada en la Constitución Española. CEC, Madrid

Rorty R, Habermas J (2012) Sobre la verdad: ¿validez universal o justificación? (trans: Wilson P). Amorrortu, Buenos Aires

Sandel M (2000) El liberalismo y los límites de la justicia. Trad. Melón M. Gedisa, Barcelona

Savater F (2004) El valor de elegir. Ariel, Barcelona

Sobrevilla D (1988) "Biología y Ética". In VV.AA Estudios Jurídicos en Honor de los profesores Carlos Fernández Sessarego y Max Arias Schreiber Pezet, Cultural Cuzco, Lima

Wahl J (1997) Introducción a la Filosofía. w/trans. FCE, Bogotá

Weinberger O (1992) Entrevista de Eugenio Bulygin. In DOXA. Cuadernos de Filosofía del Derecho. N° 11, Alicante

Zatti P, Colussi V (2005) Lineamenti di diritto privato, 10th edn. CEDAM, Padua

Printed by Printforce, the Netherlands